Encyclopedia of Title IX and Sports

NICOLE MITCHELL AND LISA A. ENNIS

Greenwood Press
Westport, Connecticut • London

Library of Congress Cataloging-in-Publication Data

Mitchell, Nicole.
   Encyclopedia of Title IX and sports / Nicole Mitchell and Lisa A. Ennis.
     p. cm.
   Includes bibliographical references and index.
   ISBN 978–0–313–33587–7 (alk. paper)
  1. Women athletes—Government policy—United States—Encyclopedias 2. Sex
discrimination in sports—Law and legislation—United States—Encyclopedias 3. College
sports—United States—Encyclopedias 4. United States. Education Amendments of 1972.
Title IX I. Ennis, Lisa A., 1969– II. Title. III. Title: Encyclopedia of Title nine and sports.
  GV709.18.U6M58   2007
  306.4'83—dc22   2007027957

British Library Cataloguing in Publication Data is available.

Library of Congress Catalog Card Number: 2007027957
ISBN-13: 978–0–313–33587–7

First published in 2007

Greenwood Press, 88 Post Road West, Westport, CT 06881
An imprint of Greenwood Publishing Group, Inc.
www.greenwood.com

Printed in the United States of America

∞

The paper used in this book complies with the
Permanent Paper Standard issued by the National
Information Standards Organization (Z39.48–1984).

10 9 8 7 6 5 4 3 2 1

Dedicated to everyone who has laughed in the face of ignorance and adversity and done what they were told they could not do.

"Without Title IX, I'd be nowhere."
—Cheryl Miller

Contents

List of Entries

List of Entries

List of Entries by Topic

Preface

Both Title IX and the subsequent enforcement of Title IX are controversial and divisive issues, and the emotions and passions run especially deep in the athletic arena. Supporters of Title IX claim that the legislation prevents discrimination and ensures that female athletes have the same opportunities and benefits as their male counterparts. Critics, on the other hand, claim that Title IX only enforces a quota system that hurts male athletes and even athletics overall. Indeed there are some heart-wrenching stories of girls having to use the school's old gym with no heat and hand-me-down equipment as well as stories of men's wrestling and swimming teams being cut so that schools can meet the proportionality requirement of Title IX. The *Encyclopedia of Title IX and Sports* is not intended to be an argument for or against Title IX; rather, it attempts to bring together a cohesive collection of information in an objective and dispassionate manner.

Encyclopedia of Title IX and Sports is intended to provide an overview of Title IX and its impact on sports to a broad range of readers, while serving as a starting point for further research and exploration. The work includes an Introduction to Title IX that explains what the law is, how it came to be, what it covers, and its application to high school and college athletics; the Introduction also contains a discussion of both proponents and critics of the law. It is intended to provide readers with enough background to give the individual entries added meaning and context. Also included are a list of the most frequently used abbreviations, a chronology of Title IX and sports from 1921 to the present day, and an alphabetical listing of the entries. The entries are also broken down into three lists—Court Cases, Organizations, and People—to give readers quick access to the material thematically as well as alphabetically.

Choosing which entries to include, however, proved to be a challenging undertaking. Since this work covers Title IX *and* sports, the authors attempted to choose a variety of entries to demonstrate the impact of Title IX on athletics as well as topics directly related to Title IX and athletics. For instance, court cases were chosen either because they were important Title IX cases, such as *North Haven Board of Education v. Bell*, or because they deal specifically with athletics. Also included is a list of related court cases, many of which can be found online through free services such as findlaw.com or through commercial databases such as Lexis/Nexis. It is important to note that neither of the authors is a lawyer and they are not licensed to practice law. The summaries of court cases within this work are not intended to serve as legal advice. Legal advice should be obtained only from a licensed attorney.

The people chosen for inclusion in this encyclopedia come from a variety of places: some were involved in creating the Title IX legislation; some advocated for Title IX or equity in sports, and some serve as examples of what women can and have achieved in sports both before and after Title IX. For instance, President Gerald Ford, who signed the Title IX legislation, is included, as are Roberta Gibb, the first woman to run the Boston Marathon (1966) by disguising herself as a man, and Pat Summitt, the architect of the University of Tennessee's Lady Vols basketball dynasty and the winningest college basketball coach in history, male or female. The people presented here were chosen to provide a well-rounded look at Title IX and sports. Likewise, the organizations and other entries were chosen for their role in Title IX and sports. The origin of the National Girls and Women in Sports Day (NGWSD) is covered, as is the Tower Amendment, which sought to exclude revenue-producing sports from having to comply with Title IX.

The encyclopedia includes a few other reference tools for students and general readers, including five appendices and a resource guide. The appendices include Title IX Regulations, A Policy Interpretation, Clarification of Intercollegiate Athletics Policy Guidance, Further Clarification of Intercollegiate Athletics Policy Guidance Regarding Title IX Compliance, and Additional Clarification of Intercollegiate Athletics Policy. These may save the reader time and be convenient resources. The authors have also compiled a Resource Guide that includes a selected bibliography, addresses and URLs for relevant organizations, a list of related films and videos, selected related court cases, and pertinent Web sites.

In addition to the alphabetical list of entries, readers can access information in a variety of ways. Within each entry, related entries in the encyclopedia appear in **boldface type** so readers can quickly navigate to them. Each entry also has at least one resource listed for further reading. The authors have also included a detailed subject index that allows readers to find a topic mentioned in the text even if it does not have its own entry.

The authors hope that, taken together, the breadth of the *Encyclopedia of Title IX and Sports* will provide readers with a valuable reference source for beginning their exploration of Title IX and sports. The authors would love to hear from their readers! Please send suggestions and comments to Lisa Ennis (hslibrn@gmail.com) and Nicole Mitchell (nmitchell79@gmail.com). For more information about anything in this book, visit a local library and talk with a librarian.

Acknowledgments

A host of people played support roles in helping us get this project completed; we thank them all, but we would like to mention a few standouts. We thank Wanda "Flash" Hubbard, for setting us up with a wireless router so we could do research and share files from anywhere in the house; Mary Moore Jones, for a daily demonstration of strength and dogged determination in the face of adversity; Dr. Frank B. Vinson and William Harris Bragg, for instilling a love of research and writing; Jason Baker, for helping us stay nourished with venison burgers and roasted vegetables; and the entire staff of the Lister Hill Library of the Health Sciences, whose patience and support has meant the world.

Introduction

No person in the United States shall, on the basis of sex, be excluded from participation in, be denied the benefits of, or be subjected to discrimination under any education program or activity receiving Federal financial assistance.

These thirty-seven words, signed into law by President Richard M. Nixon on June 23, 1972, constitute the entire Title IX legislation. As the women's movement gained momentum in the late 1960s and early 1970s, widespread sex discrimination in America's schools became apparent. Citing gender inequalities, a number of civil rights groups and advocacy organizations began filing lawsuits against colleges, universities, and the federal government. The foundations of Title IX began with President Lyndon B. Johnson's 1968 Executive Order 11246, which prohibits federal contractors from discriminating in employing workers on the basis of sex, race, color, religion, or national origin. Johnson himself had felt the sting and unfairness of gender discrimination when his daughter Luci was denied readmission to Georgetown University's nursing school after her marriage in 1966, because the school did not accept married women in its program. Medical fields were not alone in holding biased policies; women, for instance, were not admitted to the College of Arts and Sciences at the University of Virginia until 1970. Gender inequities and sex discrimination in education finally caught the attention of Congress during the summer of 1970. Chaired by Representative Edith Green of Oregon, the House Subcommittee on Education held a series of hearings to discuss discrimination against women and girls. Green, known as Mrs. Education, introduced an amendment to Titles VI and VII of the 1964 Civil Rights Act, which provided for sex equity in higher education. Though she was unable get the bill added to the Education Amendments of 1971, Green did not give up her fight to achieve gender equity. She and Representative Patsy Mink of Hawaii teamed up to draft the bill that eventually became Title IX.

In 1972 Senator Birch Bayh of Indiana introduced Green's higher-education bill to the Senate as a way to fight "the continuation of corrosive and unjustified discrimination against women in the American educational system" (118 *Congressional Record* 5803). Bayh's wife Marvella had encountered sex discrimination when she applied to law school at the University of Virginia, which had a strict "women need not apply" policy. During Senate discussions, Bayh pointed out that many economic opportunities are denied to women because of educational bias in favor of males. Bayh believed that "the field of education is just one of many areas where differential treatment has been documented but because education provides access to jobs and financial security, discrimination here is doubly destructive for women. Therefore, a strong and comprehensive measure is needed to provide women with solid legal protection from the persistent, pernicious discrimination which is serving to perpetuate second-class citizenship for American women" (118 *Congressional Record* 5806-07). He went on to affirm that the sexual discrimination women and girls face impacts all areas of education, including admissions, scholarships, employment, and salaries. Senator Bayh simply wanted women to be "judged on [their] merit, without regard to [their] sex" (117 *Congressional Record* 30, 409).

Over the entire course of the Senate and House debates on educational equity for women, sports were mentioned only twice. Senator Peter H. Dominick of Colorado questioned whether Bayh's proposed bill to make all programs and activities free of gender discrimination included sports programs, or just those programs that directly received federal monies. Bayh responded that his proposal would indeed encompass sports and extracurricular activities, in addition to other educational activities. Paradoxically, while Title IX of the Education Amendment of 1972 makes no specific reference to athletics or sports, one of its greatest and most publicized impacts has been on high school and college athletics.

On June 8, 1972, the House and Senate passed the version of the bill that included Title IX. President Nixon signed it into law on June 23, 1972, and it went into effect the following month. Once the bill passed, however, someone had to be granted the power to enforce it. Congress delegated this responsibility to the Department of Health, Education, and Welfare (HEW). Devising regulations for the new law, however, proved a more difficult task, and three years would pass before HEW finally issued its regulations.

The language in Title IX is intentionally vague; nowhere, for instance, are educational activities or programs defined. As with the education equity hearings, people questioned whether the law applied to all programs at an institution or just specific programs, such as scholarships and financial aid, that directly received federal dollars. Further, if Title IX did apply to sports, would college and university athletics directors be forced to create football teams for women, since they had football teams for men? Fearing that HEW would decide that Title IX applied to sports, legislators proposed amendments that would exclude revenue-producing sports, such as football and basketball. In

May 1974 Senator John Tower of Texas proposed an amendment to the impending Elementary and Secondary Education Act. Backed by organizations such as the National Collegiate Athletic Association (NCAA), the Tower Amendment called for revenue-producing sports to be exempt from Title IX, maintaining that "grave concern has been expressed that the HEW rules will undercut revenue-raising sports programs and damage the overall sports program of the institution. Were HEW, in its laudable zeal to guarantee equal athletic opportunities to women, to promulgate rules which damaged the financial base of intercollegiate sports, it will have thrown the baby out with the bath water" (120 *Congressional Record*). Though the amendment passed in the Senate, the House did not approve it.

When HEW released the draft regulations the following month, revenue-producing sports were included. Before issuing its final regulations, however, HEW asked for public comment on the draft regulations for Title IX compliance and received almost 10,000 responses. One response came from Senator Jacob R. Javits of New York, who proposed the Javits Amendment, which requested HEW to issue Title IX regulations that incorporate "with respect to intercollegiate athletic activities reasonable provisions considering the nature of particular sports" (Senate Conference Report No. 1026, 93rd Congress, 1974). Essentially, the Javits Amendment did not require that the same amount of money be spent on each sport. Proponents of the Javits amendment, for example, wanted recognition that football teams required more money to run and equip than a soccer team. HEW published its final Title IX regulations regarding athletics in May 1975.

President Gerald R. Ford signed the regulations on May 27, 1975, and they went into effect the following July. HEW allowed one year for elementary school sports programs to be compliant while high school and college programs were given three years to comply. Under the regulations, colleges were required to "allocate the same proportion of their athletic-scholarship budget to women as there were women on varsity teams" (Suggs, *A Place on the Team*, 74). The regulations also required programs that receive federal funds to provide equal sports opportunities for both sexes. In determining compliance, HEW indicated that it would look specifically at equal opportunity rather than equal expenditure. At the time the regulations were released, Congress had the authority to review any regulations within forty-five days. A number of senators and representatives found things they disliked and proposed bills to limit Title IX's authority over athletics. Senator Jesse Helms of North Carolina even went so far as to propose that Title IX be eliminated entirely. Though several bills were introduced in committee, none were successful and the HEW regulations went into effect on July 21, 1975, as planned. The following September, HEW also released its "Elimination of Sex Discrimination in Athletics Programs."

Still unhappy with the regulations, the NCAA filed a lawsuit against HEW in 1976. No other institutions joined in the NCAA's case, however, and in 1980 the U.S. Court of Appeals ruled that the organization did not have the ability to sue HEW since it was an independent association. Previously, the NCAA's executive director Walter Byers had said that Title IX signaled the "possible doom of intercollegiate sports" (*Washington Post*, May 12, 1974, p. A14).

After the regulations were released, Title IX continued to make national headlines. People all over the country predicted the demise of sports if women were allowed the same athletic opportunities as men. One Connecticut judge stated that "athletic competition builds character in our boys. We do not need that kind of character in our girls, the women of tomorrow" (*Washington Post*, May 12, 1974, p. A14). A New Jersey man claimed Little League baseball was "going right down the sewer" since girls would be allowed to play alongside the boys (*Washington Post*, May 12, 1974, p. A14). The sports editor for the *Atlanta Journal* warned male readers of the consequences if female athletes were afforded the same opportunities as males. "Do you want to bring home a companion or a broad that chews tobacco? What do you want for the darling daughter, a boudoir or a locker room full of cussing and bruises?" (*Washington Post*, May 12, 1974, p. A14).

According to HEW regulations, high school and college athletics departments were supposed to be compliant with Title IX by 1978. By July of that year, HEW had received almost 100 complaints against high school and college sports departments for noncompliance. In response, HEW in December 1978 published the draft policy interpretation on "Title IX and Intercollegiate Athletics" in the *Federal Register* for public comment. More than 700 comments were received. HEW released the final policy interpretation on "Title IX and Intercollegiate Athletics" in December 1979. This time the policy detailed specific factors that must be taken into account when assessing a high school or college sports program for compliance with Title IX. HEW and the Office of Civil Rights (OCR) also hoped that the policy interpretation would "provide a framework within which the complaints can be resolved . . . and provide institutions of higher education with additional guidance on the requirements for compliance with Title IX in intercollegiate athletics programs" (44 *Federal Register* 1979).

The 1979 policy is considered by some to be "from a legal standpoint, the most influential document issued to explain how gender equity should work in college sports" (Suggs 78). The 1979 policy is very different from the previous policy interpretations, dividing Title IX compliance into three areas and establishing the *Three-Part Test*. The Three-Part Test consists of three options that schools can employ when determining "the athletic interests and abilities of their students" (*Federal Register* 44). The first choice is to have the same proportion of female athletes as there are female students. The second option is to demonstrate a "history and continuing practice of program expansion" for women's sports. The third option is to demonstrate "that the interests and abilities of the members of that sex [which have been and are underrepresented among intercollegiate athletes] have been fully and effectively accommodated by the present program" (*Federal Register* 44). An institution or program will be found in compliance if it meets any part of the Three-Part Test.

After the legislation passed in June 1972, reports on Title IX and women's sports inundated the news media. Everyone was talking about the new legislation and women's and girls' sports. An examination of Waco's athletics department found that while the school was spending more than $250,000 on boys' sports, only $950 went toward girls' sports (*Washington Post*, May 12, 1974, p. A14). In 1973 *Sports Illustrated* magazine published a three-part series on sexism in sports. Two years after Title IX was enacted, tennis player Billie Jean King established the Women's Sports Foundation as a way to champion women's sports activities and to increase the number of females involved in sports. King had also led a 1970 boycott to protest salary inequities in professional tennis and had organized the Women's Tennis Association to represent female players. The situation for women's sports continued to change and evolve. In 1972 just one out of twenty-seven high school girls played sports; by 1998 that number had increased to one in three. In college sports the number of female athletes in 1972 was 32,000 compared to 172,000 male athletes (Lopiano 2000). Today the number of female college athletes has risen to more than 100,000 (U.S. Dept. Ed., *Title IX: 25 Years*).

In June 1978, the year that high school and college athletics programs were supposed to be compliant with Title IX, women's sports made the front cover of *Time* magazine, signifying the "com[ing of] the revolution" and how "women [were] transforming American athletics" (June 26, 1978). With the advent of Title IX, girls and women everywhere were participating in sports more than ever before. The secretary for the Association for Intercollegiate Athletics for Women (AIAW) asserted that it is because "women no longer feel that taking part in athletics is a privilege. They believe it is a right." For Liz Murphey, the University of Georgia's women's athletics director, the rise in women's and girls' sports was because "the stigma is nearly erased. Sweating girls are becoming socially acceptable" (*Time*, p. 2). Donna Lopiano, executive director of the Women's Sports Foundation, thinks that while the media coverage of women's sports has improved since Title IX, it could still be better: "men's sports receives 90% of all sport section column inches and hours of television sports coverage, women's sports receive 5%, and horses and dogs get 3%." It was not until 1992 that women's sports coverage surpassed that of horses and dogs (Lopiano 2000).

Almost immediately after the Title IX regulations went into effect, a number of complaints and lawsuits were filed that detailed widespread discrimination and gender inequities in education. Several cases that involved other aspects of Title IX also had an impact on case law regarding Title IX and sports. Though female athletes initially made great strides forward, this all came to a screeching halt in 1984. The case *Grove City College v. Bell* (1984), for instance, dealt a major blow to the strength and authority of Title IX. Because Pennsylvania's Grove City College was a private institution that did not receive federal funding, it did not file a letter of compliance with the OCR.

The OCR, however, asked the school to submit a letter of compliance because the school did receive federal funds in the form of Better Education Opportunity Grants (BEOGs). When the OCR initiated the process to terminate Grove City's BEOGs, the school filed a lawsuit against the OCR. In its decision of February 1984, the Supreme Court ruled that Title IX's reach applied only to the individual unit or department that received federal funding and not to the entire institution. This meant that only those athletic scholarships funded through federal financial aid came under the purview of Title IX. The *Grove City* ruling set a precedent that impacted other Title IX case decisions for the next four years, until the Civil Rights Restoration Act of 1988.

Franklin v. Gwinnett County Public Schools also had a direct impact on sports cases, although the case itself was not specifically about athletics. Claiming that she was sexually harassed by a male coach, student Christine Franklin filed a lawsuit under Title IX in February 1992. The coach resigned his position after Franklin filed her complaint with the OCR, but she also sought compensatory and punitive damages. In 1992 the *Franklin* case went before the Supreme Court, which ruled that Franklin was entitled to damages. *Franklin* greatly impacted other Title IX cases over the years, as institutions were held liable for damages to plaintiffs if they were noncompliant. *Franklin* also made it more appealing for others to sue under Title IX, since victims of sexual discrimination were allowed to receive monetary as well as punitive damages. The threat of lawsuits under Title IX had a much greater effect once institutions realized they might have to pay a plaintiff's legal fees, as well as compensatory damages.

Initially filed in 1980, the ruling in *Haffer et al. v. Temple University* was directly affected by the Civil Rights Restoration Act. Haffer and other female athletes filed suit against the university, alleging inadequate equipment and a meager budget. Female athletes made up more than 40 percent of the university's varsity players but received less than 15 percent of the university's athletic budget. Unable to claim Title IX violations because of the 1984 *Grove City* ruling, Haffer et al. claimed that Temple violated the athletes' Fourteenth Amendment rights. It took eight years for a decision to be reached in the *Haffer* case, but eventually the university settled with the athletes and distributed more funds to women's athletics.

In March 1988 Congress passed the Civil Rights Restoration Act over President Ronald Reagan's veto. This act expanded the definition of a program that receives federal funding and essentially overturned the decision in *Grove City College v. Bell*. Following the Civil Rights Restoration Act, Title IX became applicable to the institution as a whole, instead of just the individual program or unit that receives federal monies. In 1992 a group of women's ice hockey players filed a lawsuit against Colgate University in an effort to elevate the women's ice hockey club to varsity status. The district court agreed that varsity status had better benefits (such as a larger budget and better equipment) than club status, and Colgate was ordered to raise the women's ice hockey team to varsity status. The university appealed the court's decision on the grounds that the plaintiffs would all graduate before the next hockey season started. The university further claimed that compliance with Title IX should be measured by their overall athletics program, rather than by a comparison of similar sports. The following year, female athletes at Indiana University of Pennsylvania filed suit against the university after the women's gymnastics and field hockey programs were cut. Finding that the university failed to comply with any part of the Three-Part Test, the court ruled that the two women's teams be reinstated.

Over the course of the 1990s and early 2000s, a number of cases alleging violation of Title IX were filed against universities and athletics associations. Several cases, including *Kelley v. Board of Trustees, University of Illinois, Chalenor v. University of North Dakota,* and *Gonyo v. Drake University,* were filed by male athletes. In all three cases the plaintiffs claimed that the institution violated both Title IX and the Fourteenth Amendment. Unfortunately, some schools had opted to cut "less popular" men's teams, such as swimming and wrestling, in an effort to meet the proportionality part of the Three-Part Test. The lawsuits brought by the male athletes were largely unsuccessful, since men are not seen as a historically underrepresented group. Although the practice of cutting men's teams is usually described as not within the spirit of Title IX, it is legal.

Several other pieces of legislation have been passed that support Title IX. In 1974 Congress passed the Women's Educational Equity Act (WEEA). WEEA provides support, training, and research programs that "support local efforts to remove barriers for females in all areas of education" (*Title IX: 25 Years*). In 1976 Congress made amendments to the Vocational Education Act of 1963, "requiring states to act affirmatively to eliminate sex bias, stereotyping, and discrimination in vocational education" (*Title IX: 25 Years*). In 1978 Congress also passed the Amateur Sports Act, which prohibits gender discrimination in nonschool, amateur sports. In October 1994 the Equity in Athletics Disclosure Act (EADA) was passed. The EADA requires all coeducational institutions that receive any federal funding to submit certain information about its intercollegiate athletics programs to the U.S. Department of Education each year. After being separated into men's and women's teams, data are gathered on athletic participation, staffing, expenses, and revenue. The Department of Education submits a report to Congress each year in October, detailing both statistical and financial information on gender equity and intercollegiate athletics.

In July 2002, the thirtieth anniversary of Title IX, Secretary of Education Rod Paige established a Commission on Opportunity in Athletics to examine the effectiveness of the OCR's current policies for enforcing Title IX. Consisting of fifteen members, the commission was led by former Women's National Basketball Association (WNBA) player Cynthia Cooper and Stanford University athletics director Ted Leland. After holding six town hall meetings to gather public comment on the various issues relating to Title IX and sports, the commission submitted its final report, "Open to All: Title IX at Thirty," to Secretary Paige in February 2003. As a result of the Commission's findings, the

Department of Education issued its "Further Clarification of Intercollegiate Athletics Policy Guidance Regarding Title IX Compliance."

President Nixon signed Title IX into effect thirty-five years ago, and since that time there has been tremendous growth and increased opportunities in women's sports. In 1971, the year before Title IX, fewer than 300,000 girls were active in sports. This number had risen to more than 2.6 million by 1999 (Gender Equity in Sports). Over the years there have also been several leagues and organizations, such as the Women's National Basketball Association, created solely for female athletes. Despite such strides in gender equity, the *Chronicle of Higher Education* found that just thirty-six of the nation's leading programs are compliant with Title IX (*Chronicle* Facts and Figures 2000). In an attempt to combat this disparity and to "help track gender-equity issues at the collegiate level," the NCAA has produced a gender equity report on the status of its member institutions each year since 1991 (2003–2004 NCAA Gender Equity Report). Several women's organizations, including the National Women's Law Center and the Women's Sports Foundation, have worked to promote increased awareness of Title IX and to increase sports opportunities for women and girls.

In its thirty-five years Title IX has promoted significant improvements in women's and girls' athletics. Females are now playing sports and reaping the rewards: more opportunities to participate, better facilities and equipment, more scholarships, and other benefits. There are still, however, a number of obstacles that must be addressed before female athletes enjoy the same equality as their male counterparts. Donna Lopiano, executive director of the Women's Sports Foundation, best sums up the issue when she says, "it's ok to have sympathy for that walk-on. It's ok to have sympathy for every male who loses his opportunity to play, but you must have unbiased sympathy. You have to feel just as sorry for every woman who didn't have the chance to play, for women who still, at the institutional level, are not getting chances to play, who are not getting benefits, and you simply can't discriminate on the basis of sex in your empathy" (*Open to All: Title IX at Thirty*, 11).

List of Abbreviations

AAGPBL	All-American Girls Professional Baseball League
AAU	Amateur Athletic Union
AAUW	American Association of University Women
AAHPER	American Association for Health, Physical Education, and Recreation
AAHPERD	American Alliance for Health, Physical Education, Recreation, and Dance
ABL	American Basketball League
AIAW	Association of Intercollegiate Athletics for Women
APEA	American Physical Education Association
ASA	American Softball Association
AWSM	Association for Women in Sports Media
BWSF	Black Women in Sport Foundation
HEW	U.S. Department of Health, Education, and Welfare
IOC	International Olympic Committee
LPGA	Ladies Professional Golf Association
NACWAA	National Association of Collegiate Women Athletic Administrators
NAGWS	National Association for Girls and Women in Sport
NAIA	National Association for Intercollegiate Athletics
NAPBL	National Association of Professional Baseball Leagues
NASCAR	National Association for Stock Car Auto Racing
NBA	National Basketball League
NCAA	National Collegiate Athletics Association
NCWGE	National Coalition for Women and Girls in Education
NEA	National Education Association
NFL	National Football League
NGWSD	National Girls and Women in Sports Day
NHRA	National Hot Rod Association
NWLC	National Women's Law Center
OCR	Office of Civil Rights
WABA	Women's American Basketball Association

List of Abbreviations

WBCA	Women's Basketball Coaches Association
WBL	Women's Professional Basketball League
WISE	Women in Sports and Events
WNBA	Women's National Basketball Association
WSF	Women's Sports Foundation

Chronology

1921	The American Association of University Women (AAUW) is established.
1943	All-American Girls Professional Baseball League (AAGPBL) is created.
1961	President John F. Kennedy establishes the President's Commission on the Status of Women.
1967	Commission on Intercollegiate Athletics for Women is established to sponsor national tournaments for women's college athletics.
1968	Women's Equity Action League (WEAL) is founded; focuses on women's issues in research, education, and legislation.
1971	Association for Intercollegiate Athletics for Women (AIAW) is established to govern women's collegiate athletics. Evolving from the Commission on Intercollegiate Athletics for Women, the AIAW becomes official on July 1, 1972.
1972	*Clinton v. Nagy*; federal court allows girl to play on all boys football team.
	Women's Educational Equity Act (WEAA) is passed to "promote educational equity for girls and women, including those who suffer multiple discrimination based on gender and on race, ethnicity, national origin, disability, or age, and to provide funds to help education agencies and institutions meet the requirements of Title IX."
	Critics propose the "Tower Amendment" to exclude revenue-producing sports from Title IX; amendment passes through the Senate but not the House.
May	Women's Sports Foundation is established by tennis player Billie Jean King and swimmer Donna de Varona.
June 23	President Richard M. Nixon signs Title IX of the Education Amendments which bans sex discrimination in schools.

| July | Congress passes the "Javits Amendment" an alternative to the "Tower Amendment"; Congress requires the Dept. of Health, Education, and Welfare (HEW) to issue Title IX regulations that allow for "reasonable provisions considering the nature of particular sports." |

1975

| May | President Gerald R. Ford signs the Title IX athletics regulations issued by HEW. |

| July | Senator Jesse Helms proposes bill to restrict Title IX to athletic programs where participation is not a required part of curriculum. |

| July 21 | Title IX regulations become effective; elementary school athletics programs are given one year to comply and high schools and colleges are given three years to comply with Title IX regulations on athletics. |

| September | HEW issues "Elimination of Sex Discrimination in Athletics Programs." |

1976 — National Collegiate Athletic Association (NCAA) files law suit against HEW, challenging Title IX's authority in athletics regulations.

1978 — Amateur Sports Act is passed; prohibits gender discrimination in amateur sports.

| December 11 | HEW's draft policy interpretation on "Title IX and Intercollegiate Athletics" is published in the *Federal Register* for public comment; HEW receives more than 700 comments to the draft. |

1979 — *Cannon v. University of Chicago*; U.S. Supreme Court rules than an implied private right of action exists to enforce Title IX.

| December 11 | HEW issues final Three-Part Test and policy interpretation on "Title IX and Intercollegiate Athletics," which details factors to include when assessing Title IX compliance. |

1980

| May | U.S. Department of Education replaces HEW and reissues Title IX policies. Through the Office of Civil Rights (OCR), the Department of Education now oversees the enforcement of Title IX. |

| July | OCR develops an interim Title IX Intercollegiate Athletics Investigator's Manual for internal use. |

1982 — *North Haven Board of Education v. Bell*; U.S. Supreme Court rules that Title IX regulations prohibit sex discrimination in employment.

| March | OCR publishes "Guidance for Writing Title IX Intercollegiate Athletics Letters of Findings," detailing specific procedures for OCR regional offices to follow when issuing letters of findings. |

1984 — *Association for Intercollegiate Athletics for Women v. NCAA*; AIAW sues the NCAA claiming that the latter was violating antitrust laws and was trying to monopolize women's intercollegiate athletics.

| February 28 | *Grove City College v. Bell*; the Supreme Court rules that only the specific program receiving federal funding is required to comply with Title IX; essentially determines that Title IX does not apply to athletics programs. |

1987   OCR publishes "Title IX Grievance Procedures: An Introductory Manual" to aid schools in the requirement to establish both a Title IX complaint procedure and a Title IX officer to receive complaints.

Association for Women in Sports Media (AWSM) is established.

1988
March   Congress passes Civil Rights Restoration Act (20 USC 1687) over President Reagan's veto; overturns the decision in *Grove City College v. Bell*, expanding the definition of a program which receives federal funding. Title IX now applies to institutions as a whole not just the individual programs receiving federal funds.

September   *Haffer v. Temple University*; female athletes sue university, claiming violations of the Fourteenth Amendment.

1989   NCAA establishes Committee on Women's Athletics to "provide leadership and assistance [to the NCAA] . . . and to expand and promote opportunities for female student-athletes, administrators, and coaches."

1990
April   OCR issues "Title IX Investigation Manual" to help institutions comply with Title IX; provides guidelines and specific interview questions.

1991   NCAA establishes Gender-Equity Task Force to explore conditions of member institutions.

1992   NCAA issues landmark Gender Equity study of member institutions, detailing widespread gender discrimination.

Cook v. Colgate University; women's ice hockey players sue under Title IX to gain varsity team status.

February 26   *Franklin v. Gwinnett County Public Schools*; Supreme Court rules that monetary damages can be awarded under Title IX.

1993   *Favia v. Indiana University of Pennsylvania*; court rules in favor of female athletes who sued university for cutting two women's teams.

NCAA issues final report of Gender-Equity Task Force; identifies nine emerging sports and recommends standards and regulations to help achieve gender equity.

1994
October   Equity in Athletics Disclosure Act (20 USC 1092); requires institutions that receive any federal funding to disclose information about intercollegiate athletics programs to the U.S. Department of Education.

1996

January 16   Dept. of Education and OCR issue "Clarification of Intercollegiate Athletics Policy Guidance: The Three-Part Test" to clarify the 1979 policy interpretation.

November   *Cohen v. Brown University*; court rules that Brown University illegally discriminated against female athletes and the university is ordered to reinstate two women's teams.

1997   Women's National Basketball Association (WNBA) is established.

              U.S. Equal Employment Opportunity Commission issues guidelines for hiring, paying, and promoting high school and college coaches; determines that inequalities between male and female coaches of similar sports violate federal law.

June   Twenty-fifth anniversary of Title IX.

1998   *NCAA v. Smith*; Supreme Court determines that NCAA is subject to Title IX and must address gender equity issues.

July   OCR issues new compliance procedures while investigating the National Women's Law Center's twenty-five complaints about athletic scholarships.

1999   *Mercer v. Duke University*; woman makes football team and says school discriminated against her because of her gender.

              Boucher v. Syracuse University; female athletes sued in effort to gain varsity status; court ruled in favor of university.

2001   U.S. Department of Justice issues "Title IX Legal Manual."

February   *Brentwood v. Tennessee Secondary School Athletic Association*; Supreme Court rules that high school athletic association is state actor and is subject to Constitution.

December   *Communities for Equity v. Michigan High School Athletic Association*; holds state athletic association liable under Title IX as well as the Equal Protection Clause and Michigan state law for discriminating against females by scheduling six of the girls' sports in nontraditional seasons.

2002   *Chalenor v. University of North Dakota*; male wrestling team sues university for cutting wrestling program as a method of complying with Title IX's Three-Part Test.

February   *National Wrestling Coaches Association v. U.S. Dept. of Education*; association claims that Title IX regulations are unconstitutional after college men's wrestling programs were dropped.

June 27   U.S. Secretary of Education Rod Paige announces the establishment of the Commission on Opportunities in Athletics to issue a report on Title IX by February 2003. Report is to make recommendations on the

application of the three-part test. Commission members include former WNBA player and coach Cynthia Cooper and the Women's
Sports Foundation's Donna de Varona.

2003   U.S. Department of Education issues "Further Clarification of Intercollegiate Athletics Policy Guidance Regarding Title IX Compliance"
in response to report of U.S. Secretary of Education's Commission on
Opportunities in Athletics.

2004
December   *Jackson v. Birmingham Board of Education*; girls' basketball coach sues
board of education, claiming that the latter fired him because he com-
plained of Title IX violations.

2005
March   U.S. Department of Education issues "Additional Clarification of
Intercollegiate Athletics Policy: Three-Part Test—Part Three"; allows
institutions to use email surveys to document their compliance with
Title IX.

A

Abbott, Senda Berenson (March 19, 1868–February 16, 1954)

Women's physical education innovator and developer of women's basketball, Berenson was born Senda Valrojenski in Biturmansk, Lithuania. Her father, Albert Valrojenski, immigrated to Boston in 1874 where he sold pots and pans. The rest of the family—Senda, her mother Julia, and two brothers—arrived a year later, at which time the surname Valrojenski was changed to Berenson. Two more girls were born after the move to America.

Although they struggled financially, Albert encouraged his children to get an education. Senda's brother, Bernard, graduated from Harvard and became a noted art historian and critic. Frail health, however, kept Senda from completing a full year at the Boston Girls' Latin School, and a weak back prevented her from playing the piano with any regularity. In 1890, despite her reluctance, Senda was enrolled at the Boston Normal School of Gymnastics and in just a few months she felt healthier and stronger. After two years, convinced that physical exercise was beneficial for everyone, Senda accepted the position of physical education director at Smith College, a women's school in Massachusetts.

While at Smith, Berenson assisted in organizing the college's Gymnastics and Field Association, became the second woman to attend the Royal Central Institute of Gymnastics in Stockholm, and introduced fencing, folk dance, and (along with Lady **Constance Applebee**) field hockey to Smith. Berenson's most significant contribution, however, was her development of women's basketball. After reading a YMCA publication about a new game called "basket ball" that had been created by James Naismith, Berenson quickly adapted the game for women and introduced it to the students. An 1893 game between Smith College freshmen and sophomores is considered the first women's basketball game in history.

Berenson's version of basketball, however, had to adapt to Victorian ideals for proper women's behavior. For instance, to keep women from overexerting themselves by playing full court, the court was divided into three zones and players were required to stay within their zone. Dribbling was limited to three bounces, and players could only hold the ball for three seconds. In 1899 Berenson, who advocated intramural rather than intercollegiate competition, compiled her rules into a book of regulations called *Basketball Guide for Women*, which she then edited for the next eighteen years. Her modifications during this time, however, were relatively insignificant, and her rules remained the standard for women's basketball until the 1960s. Berenson also chaired the Basketball Committee for Women from 1905 to 1917, which was the forerunner of the **National Association for Girls and Women in Sport** (NAGWS).

In 1911 Berenson married Smith College English professor Herbert Abbott and resigned from her position as physical education director. Over the next ten years she taught physical education at the Mary A. Burnham School, a private school in Northampton, Massachusetts. She also continued to write articles and give lectures on basketball and physical education. When her husband died in 1929, she moved to Santa Barbara, California, to live with one of her sisters. It was there that she died in 1954 at age eighty-five. In recognition of her contributions to women's sports, Berenson has been inducted into the Naismith Hall of Fame (1985), the International Jewish Sports Hall of Fame (1987), and the Women's Basketball Hall of Fame (1991). *Sports Illustrated* recognized her as one of the twentieth century's greatest sports figures.

Further Reading

Hult, Joan, and Marianna Trekell, eds. *A Century of Women's Basketball: From Frailty to Final Four*. Reston, VA: National Association for Girls and Women in Sport, 1991.

Seelye, L. Clark. *The Early History of Smith College, 1871–1910*. Boston: Houghton Mifflin, 1923.

Stillman, Agnes C. "Senda Berenson Abbott: Her Life and Contributions to Smith College and to the Physical Education Profession." MA thesis, Smith College, 1971.

Ackerman, Valerie B. "Val" (November 7, 1959–)

Former basketball player and **Women's National Basketball Association** (WNBA) president from 1996 to 2005, Val Ackerman was born in Pennington, New Jersey. Both her grandfather and father were athletic directors and coaches. In high school Ackerman participated in swimming, track and field, and field hockey, but she excelled in basketball. After high school she enrolled at the University of Virginia (UVA), where she started all four years (1978–1981), earned All-American honors twice, and was the first UVA player to be a three-time team captain. With little money provided for women's athletic programs, Ackerman shared the one basketball scholarship with her roommate. She graduated from UVA with a bachelor's degree in political and social thought and with the Jettie Hill Award, given to the senior female athlete with the highest grade point average. After graduation Ackerman traveled to France to play professional basketball for one season.

During the years 1983–85 Ackerman attended the University of California in Los Angeles School of Law. After graduation she worked for two years as a staff attorney for a New York City firm before accepting a position with the National Basketball Association (NBA) in 1988. By 1990 she was appointed NBA Commissioner David Stern's special assistant and in 1994 was named the NBA's vice president of business affairs. Ackerman was also pivotal in the creation of the USA Basketball Women's Team that went undefeated and won the gold medal at the 1996 Atlanta Olympic Games. In 1996 she was chosen to be the president of the newly formed Women's National Basketball Association (WNBA). She resigned from this position in 2005.

Speaking on the success of the WNBA, Ackerman credits Title IX, saying that the WNBA "has been a direct beneficiary of Title IX because of what the women's college and high school game has done to develop the players, to create a baseline of interest and support."

In February 2005 Ackerman became the first woman to serve as president of USA Basketball (her term runs until 2008). In 1998 she received one of the Women in Sports and Events (WISE) Women of the Year awards. She has also served on the Naismith Memorial Basketball Hall of Fame executive committee, the March of Dimes National Board of Trustees, and the National Board of Directors of Girls Incorporated.

Further Reading

Sherman, Casey. "Through the Hoops, Up the Ladder" (http://www.womenssports foundation.org/cgi-bin/iowa/career/article.html?record=21).

Whiteside, Kelly. *WNBA: A Celebration, Commemorating the Birth of a League.* New York: Harper Horizon, 1998.

Acosta, Ruth Vivian

Former college basketball player and professor emerita in physical education and exercise science at the City University of New York's Brooklyn College, R. Vivian Acosta is one of the leading researchers and scholars of Title IX.

Graduating from Brigham Young University (BYU) in 1965, Acosta obtained her master's degree two years later and in 1974 received a PhD in sport administration from the University of Southern California. From 1965 to 1967 she coached women's field hockey and women's volleyball at BYU. In 1967 she began teaching at Brooklyn College and coached women's basketball and softball, as well as men's and women's badminton. She also served as the director for the **Association of Intercollegiate Athletics for Women** (AIAW) regional tournament held at Brooklyn College. From 1969 to 1974, she served as Brooklyn College's women's athletic director.

In 1977 Acosta teamed up with fellow faculty member Linda Jean Carpenter to conduct research into women's intercollegiate sport and gender equity issues. She and Carpenter have continued this research for more than thirty years. In 2006 they published their research study "Women in Intercollegiate Sport: A Longitudinal, National Study Twenty Nine Year Update, 1977–2006."

Acosta has served as president of the **National Association for Girls and Women in Sport** (NAGWS) and as a member of the **Women's Sports Foundation** Advisory Board. In 1991 the Women's Sports Foundation honored her and Carpenter with the Billie Jean King Contribution Award for their part in the advancement of women in sport. Acosta and Carpenter have authored several works on Title IX and women's intercollegiate athletics, including *Title IX*, published in 2005.

Further Reading

Encyclopedia of Women and Sports in America. Phoenix, AZ: Oryx Press, 1998.

Skaine, Rosemarie. *Women College Basketball Coaches*. Jefferson, NC: McFarland & Co., 2001.

Akers, Michelle Anne (February 1, 1966–)

All-American and Olympic soccer player Michelle Akers is one of the highest-scoring women soccer players in history. Born in Santa Clara, California, to Robert Akers, a family counselor, and Anne Falaschi, a firefighter, she began playing soccer at eight years old. In 1975 the family moved to Seattle, where she was a three-time All-American at Shorecrest High School. During her senior year her team won the state championship. Akers received a scholarship to attend the University of Central Florida (UCF), where she continued to excel, being named an All-American each of her four years in college (1985–88). In 1985 she joined the first U.S. national women's soccer team and was the first player on the team to score a goal. She was also the 1988 recipient of the Hermann Trophy (awarded to the best female college player), and was UCF's 1988–89 athlete of the year. When she graduated in 1989 with a bachelor's degree in liberal studies and health, UCF retired her jersey.

After graduation Akers played semiprofessional soccer in Sweden, coached at UCF, and continued to play for the U.S. team. Between 1985 and 1990 she scored fifteen goals in twenty-four games for the United States; in 1991 she scored a record thirty-nine goals in twenty-six games. In the inaugural Women's World Championship (1991), Akers scored ten goals in six games, including the championship-winning goal against Norway, and was awarded the tournament's Gold Boot award.

In 1977 soccer was the nation's twentieth most popular sport. Today soccer has become America's third most popular sport for women and girls. Photo from authors' private collection.

Akers began to promote women's soccer as a representative of the International Federation of Association Football (FIFA), and became a regular contributor to *Soccer Junior* magazine. In 1993, however, her health started to fail and she was eventually diagnosed with Epstein-Barr virus.

Akers returned to soccer during the 1996 Summer Olympics in Atlanta, Georgia, but injuries limited her play. That same year she founded Soccer Outreach International, a Christian ministry that teaches people how to blend faith and sport into daily life. In 1998 FIFA bestowed its highest honor on Akers with their Order of Merit, in appreciation for her contributions to soccer. In 1999, at age thirty-three, she decided to play in one more World Cup; she retired with a career record of 105 goals and thirty-seven assists, second only to Mia Hamm. In 2002 FIFA honored her as the Woman Player of the Century (along with Sun Wen of China). In 2004 Akers and Hamm were selected by Brazilian soccer player Pele to the FIFA list of 100 greatest living soccer players; they were the only two women named.

Akers continues to promote women's soccer worldwide and is the author of several books.

Further Reading

Akers, Michelle, and Gregg Lewis. *The Game and the Glory: An Autobiography.* Grand Rapids, MI: Zondervan Publishing, 2000.

Alcott, Amy (February 22, 1956–)

Amy Alcott, the 1975 Ladies Professional Golf Association's (LPGA) Rookie of the Year, winner of over thirty tournaments, and golf course designer, was born in Kansas City, Missouri, in February 1956. She began playing golf at an early age and left the amateur ranks after winning the United States Junior Girls championship in 1973. With her "go for the pin" style, Alcott has won a number of awards, including Player of the Year for *Golf Magazine* in 1980, the Mickey Wright Award, and the LPGA Founders Cup Award.

In 1987 she was named Female Golfer of the Year by the California Golf Writers Association. Alcott has over thirty LPGA tour wins that include five major titles, such as the 1980 U.S. Women's Open. In 2001 she founded Amy Alcott/GOLF, a consulting company that designs and manages women's golf academies. She is a member of the LPGA Hall of Fame and was inducted into the World Golf Hall of Fame in 1999. Author of *A Woman's Guide to Golf*, Alcott is currently working on a second book entitled *Spiked Shoes: Golf Lessons, Life Lessons*. In 1997 she made an appearance in the film *Tin Cup*, starring Kevin Costner and Rene Russo.

Further Reading

Alcott, Amy, and Don Wade. *Amy Alcott's Guide to Women's Golf*. New York: Dutton, 1991.

Chambers, Marcia. *The Unplayable Lie: The Untold Story of Women and Discrimination in Women's Golf*. New York: Pocket Books, 1995.

All-American Girls Professional Baseball League

In 1943 the All-American Girls Professional Baseball League began as a substitute for men's professional baseball during World War II. With men being drafted into service and several minor league teams folding, Chicago Cubs' owner and chewing-gum mogul Philip K. Wrigley sought a way to continue the game. He and other team owners feared that game attendance would falter because of the war and that they would ultimately lose money. Acknowledging the success of women's softball teams around the country, and hoping to attract fans back to the parks, Wrigley created a special baseball league for women. To stir interest, the teams were managed by well-known, former players and coaches in men's professional baseball.

Originally known as the All-American Girls Softball League, the league recruited women throughout the United States and Canada, and play began in the spring of 1943. Halfway through the first season, the league's name was changed to the All-American Girls Baseball League in an attempt to distinguish it from other softball leagues around the country. At the end of the first season, the league's name was changed to the All-American Girls Professional Ball League, before reverting back two years later to the All-American Girls Baseball League. The league kept this name until 1950, when it became known as the American Girls Baseball League. Despite its many name changes, the league is still popularly known as the All-American Girls Professional Baseball League (AAGPBL).

Because it was formed as a women's softball league, teams initially played with a softball and underhand pitching. The pitching distance and distance between bases was lengthened, however, and players were allowed to steal bases. Eventually, the league began using a baseball and overhand pitching. Women selected to play in the league were chosen for their athletic ability and femininity. In addition to practicing baseball, players were required to attend charm school classes. The uniforms consisted of a short skirt and satin shorts. Each team was assigned a female chaperone to ensure that the players maintained modest conduct befitting the "girl next door." To this end, league officials established rules of conduct that players had to obey. Besides regulations regarding social activities and behavior on the field, players were also expected to have long hair and wear lipstick at all times.

In its first season the league consisted of only four teams. The new league was so successful, however, that two more teams were added the following year. During the war teams often played exhibition games, and on nongame days the players visited injured soldiers in military hospitals. By 1948 more teams had been added and attendance was soaring. But with men's major league baseball back in full swing, attendance at AAGPBL games began to decline; by 1954 only five teams remained in the league. The league disbanded at the end of the 1954 season because of financial difficulties. Lasting for twelve seasons, the AAGPBL provided the opportunity for more than 600 women to play professional baseball.

The movie *A League of Their Own*, released in 1992 and filled with an all-star cast, was based on the founding of the AAGPBL and its first season of play. In 1986 former players banded together to form the Players' Association in an attempt to achieve recognition from the National Baseball Hall of Fame. This move was successful, and in 1988 the AAGPBL was recognized by the opening of a women's section at the National Baseball Hall of Fame.

Further Reading

Berlage, Gai Ingham. *Women in Baseball: The Forgotten History*. Westport, CT: Praeger Publishers, 1994.

Fidler, Merrie A. *The Origins and History of the All-American Girls Professional Baseball League*. Jefferson, NC: McFarland, 2006.

Amateur Athletic Union

One of the country's largest sports organizations, the Amateur Athletic Union (AAU)—composed of national and regional associations, amateur sports clubs, and educational institutions—was founded in 1888 as a way to advance the development of a variety of amateur sports and physical fitness programs and to establish standards for various sports.

With the motto "Sports for All, Forever," the AAU's mission is "to offer amateur sports programs through a volunteer base for all people to have the physical, mental, and moral development of amateur athletes and to promote good sportsmanship and good citizenship." When it was first founded, the AAU took charge of America's participation in international sports, including the Olympics, and sought to train amateur athletes for participation in the Olympic Games. With the Amateur Sports Act of 1978, however, the U.S. Olympic Committee became the governing body for amateur sports.

Although it initially focused on sports for young males, the AAU now encompasses all amateur athletes in more than thirty sports, including swimming, track and field, golf, gymnastics, dance, karate, table tennis, and aerobics. The AAU held its first women's swimming competition in 1916 and continued to add other women's sports over the years: women's track and field in 1924, women's basketball in 1926, and women's gymnastics in 1931. It was not until 1972, however, the same year that Title IX was enacted, that the AAU established a girls' basketball program as part of the organization's Junior Olympic program. By 2003 more than 700 teams would compete in the AAU girls' basketball national championship.

Since 1930 the AAU has presented the Sullivan Award to the nation's top amateur athlete in recognition of the individual's athletic accomplishments and strong moral character. The award is named in honor of James E. Sullivan, a founder and former president of the AAU. Past recipients of the award include marathon runner **Joan Benoit Samuelson** (1985), speed skater **Bonnie Blair** (1992), and basketball player Chamique Holdsclaw (1998).

Today the AAU offers a number of national programs, such as the AAU Sports Program and the AAU Junior Olympic Games. Partnering with the **National Association for Girls and Women in Sport** (NAGWS), AAU girls' basketball offers the Complete Athlete program, an educational program "designed for athletes, coaches, and family members with content focused on NCAA academic rules and regulations, life skills, and sportsmanship." The AAU also administers the President's Challenge program established by the President's Council on Physical Fitness and Sports. In 1996 the AAU teamed with Disney's Wide World of Sports and relocated its headquarters to Orlando, Florida. More than forty national AAU competitions are now held at Disney's sports complexes.

Further Reading

Amateur Athletic Union Web site (http://aausports.org/).

Ikard, Robert W. *Just for Fun: The Story of AAU Women's Basketball*. Fayetteville, AR: University of Arkansas Press, 2005.

Lucas, John. *The Amateur Athletic Union of the United States 1888-1988: A Century of Progress*. S.l.: s.n., 1988.

American Basketball League (1996–1998)

Founded in October 1996, the American Basketball League (ABL), the fifth women's basketball league, folded two years later in December 1998.

In September 1995 cofounders Gary Cavalli (former sports information director at Stanford University), Anne Cribbs, and Steve Hams met to discuss forming a women's professional basketball league. Taking advantage of the popularity of the women's Olympic basketball team, the ABL debuted a year later in October 1996, with eight franchise teams in Atlanta, Seattle, Denver, and San Jose, among other cities. With the slogans "It's a Whole New Ballgame" and "Real Basketball," the league enjoyed great success its first season, due in part to corporate sponsors such as Reebok and Lady Foot Locker. A number of star players, including Teresa Edwards, Kate Starbird, Dawn Staley, and thirteen former Olympians, signed with the new league. In addition to attractive salaries, players in the ABL also had stock options, which made them part owners of the league.

The ABL's second season, however, was not as successful as the first, primarily because the National Basketball Association (NBA) created the **Women's National Basketball Association** (WNBA), which premiered in June 1997. Though Nike had originally agreed to sponsor the ABL, the company soon began sponsoring the new WNBA. ABL officials also had trouble getting major networks to air their games, while WNBA games were being shown live on networks such as NBC, Lifetime, and ESPN; ABL games were often tape delayed and shown later on SportsChannel, Fox Sports Net, or Black Entertainment Television. The ABL was simply unable to compete with the NBA-backed league. In 1998 the ABL filed for bankruptcy and announced its termination just after the beginning of its third season. After the league's demise, many of the ABL's former players signed with the WNBA.

Further Reading

Gogol, Sara. *Playing in a New League: The Women of the American Basketball League's First Season*. Indianapolis: Masters Press, 1998.

Staffo, Donald F. "The History of Women's Professional Basketball in the United States with an Emphasis on the Old WBL and the New ABL and WNBA." *Physical Educator* 55.4 (Winter 1998): 187–199.

Applebee, Constance Mary Katherine (June 4, 1873–January 26, 1981)

Field hockey pioneer, cofounder of the United States Field Hockey Association (USFHA), and publisher and editor of *Sportswoman* magazine, Constance Applebee, affectionately known as "The Apple," was born in Essex, England, in June 1873. After graduating from the British College of Physical Education, in 1901 Applebee journeyed to the United States to participate in a summer class at Harvard. While she was there, she introduced the sport of field hockey to women's colleges such as Vassar, Wellesley, Radcliffe, Smith, Mt. Holyoke, and Bryn Mawr. The sport quickly gained popularity and became a regular sport in many high schools and colleges.

Three years after coming to America, Applebee became the director of outdoor sports at Bryn Mawr College in Pennsylvania. In 1906 she became the college's physical education director; two years later she formed the school's health department. While at Bryn Mawr, Applebee founded and edited *The Sportswoman*, the first women's sports magazine in America. In addition to articles on field hockey, she included pieces on other women's sports such as fencing, swimming, and bowling.

In 1922 Applebee teamed up with fellow educators **Senda Berenson Abbott** and Lucile E. Hill to establish the USFHA. This organization formulated the official rules for field hockey and in just ten years boasted more than 400 clubs. With the USFHA in place, Applebee began her own field hockey camp the next year at Camp Tegawitha in Mt. Pocono, Pennsylvania.

For her contributions to women's sports, Applebee received the Distinguished Service Award from the American Association for Health, Physical Education, and Recreation (AAHPER) and an Award of Merit from the **Association of Intercollegiate Athletics for Women** (AIAW). Applebee was inducted into the International Women's Sports Hall of Fame in 1991. Continuing to coach field hockey until her mid-nineties, she died in 1981.

Further Reading

Smith, Hilda W., and Helen Kirk Welsh. *Constance M. K. Applebee and the Story of Hockey.* S.l.: s.n., 1975.

Woolum, Janet. *Outstanding Women Athletes: Who They Are and How They Influenced Sports in America.* Phoenix, AZ: Oryx Press, 1992.

Association for Intercollegiate Athletics for Women

Officially established in October 1971, the Association for Intercollegiate Athletics for Women (AIAW) was the first organization to govern women's college sports (including regional and national championships) until its demise in 1983. The AIAW grew out of the Commission on Intercollegiate Athletics for Women, which was founded four years earlier to oversee national championships for college women and to organize more women's college sports opportunities.

The AIAW began actual operation in 1972, the same year that Title IX was passed, with almost 300 member institutions. It organized and managed annual tournaments for a variety of sports, including basketball, softball, volleyball, tennis, badminton, and fencing. At its height, the organization numbered more than 900 member schools and hosted almost 800 state, regional, and national championships. AIAW presidents included **Christine H. B. Grant**, Laurie Mabry, and **Donna Lopiano**.

When the AIAW was created, the **National Collegiate Athletic Association** (NCAA) only offered championships for men's sports. But by the late 1970s the NCAA had begun sponsoring tournaments for women's sports in Divisions II and III. The early 1980s saw the emergence of NCAA Division I women's championships (the first NCAA women's basketball tournament was held in 1982). In 1975, when Title IX regulations were enacted, the AIAW and NCAA formed a joint committee in an attempt to merge. The NCAA, however, believed it was only natural that it govern men *and* women's collegiate athletics. During the time the AIAW was discussing control of women's athletics with the NCAA, it was experiencing various internal struggles. By 1980 some of its member institutions had left to form the Council of Collegiate Women Athletic Administrators, which was but a prelude to their joining the NCAA.

During the 1981–82 academic year, women's collegiate teams were permitted to compete in either AIAW or NCAA championships. In some instances, schools participated in both tournaments during the same year. Increasingly, AIAW schools (such as the University of Tennessee and Old Dominion University) began to enroll their women's teams with the NCAA in the belief that the NCAA could provide better leadership for women's intercollegiate athletics. In just one year the AIAW lost more than 200 members to the NCAA.

In 1982 the remaining members of the AIAW filed a lawsuit against the NCAA, claiming that the NCAA sought to monopolize women's sports and was thus in violation of antitrust laws. When the AIAW lost this lawsuit, it officially came to an end in June 1983, but not before it had successfully created more than forty national championships for college women's athletics.

Female participation in intercollegiate athletics has increased since Title IX was enacted. In just four years, more than 800 women's teams were added to intercollegiate sports. Library of Congress, Prints & Photographs Division.

UAB Archives, University of Alabama at Birmingham.

Further Reading

National Association for Girls & Women in Sport. Sport Governance. *AIAW: A Retrospective on a Brief Existence*. Crofton, MD: Recorded Resources Corp., 1985.

Willey, Suzanne. "The Governance of Women's Intercollegiate Athletics: Association for Intercollegiate Athletics for Women (AIAW), 1976–1982." P.E.D. dissertation, Indiana University, 1996.

Wushanley, Ying. *Playing Nice and Losing: The Struggle for Control of Women's Intercollegiate Athletics, 1960–2000*. Syracuse, NY: Syracuse University Press, 2004.

Association for Women in Sports Media

The Association for Women in Sports Media (AWSM) was founded in 1987 as a way to bring together men and women who work in sports media careers, such as sports writing, editing, broadcasting; production, public relations, and sports information. **Christine Brennan** served as the organization's first president.

One of AWSM's aims has been to help women overcome various obstacles that bar them from the same opportunities male sports journalists have, including access to locker rooms and equitable salaries. AWSM serves as an advocate for women currently involved in sports media and for those seeking a career in sports media. The organization has established an internship and scholarship program for individuals interested in pursuing jobs in sports media. All interns and scholarship recipients must be full-time female college students. Organizations that have employed AWSM interns include ESPN, Nike, *Sports Illustrated* magazine, and a number of newspapers across the country, such as the *Miami Herald* and *Newsday*. AWSM has teamed up with Associated Press Sports Editors to offer a program to students particularly interested in sports editing careers and has also partnered with Women's Sports Services to provide an online career center for members.

In 1999 AWSM established its Pioneer Award, bestowed annually to honor pioneers (male or female) in the field of sports media who have "paved the way for women in sports media and who serve as a role model" for AWSM members. Honorees are chosen for their ability to "inspire others to achieve and continue to open doors for young women who follow." Sportscaster **Lesley Visser** was the first recipient; other winners have included Claire Smith, the assistant sports editor for the *Philadelphia Inquirer*; former *Sports Illustrated* writer **Melissa Ludtke**; and *USA Today* columnist Christine Brennan. In 2006 the AWSM board of directors voted to rename the award the Mary Garber Pioneer Award, in honor of former sportswriter **Mary Garber**.

Since 1988 the AWSM has held an annual convention, which includes a job fair and provides a forum for female sports reporters and others involved in sports media to discuss various issues. The organization also publishes a quarterly newsletter, which includes articles about members, news of the industry, profiles of pioneers, and upcoming events.

Today, the AWSM is a worldwide organization boasting more than 600 members.

Further Reading

Association for Women in Sports Media Web site (http://www.awsmonline.org).

B

Bancroft, Ann (September 29, 1955–)

The first woman to reach the North Pole on foot and by sled, Ann Bancroft was born in Mendota Heights, Minnesota, in September 1955. After high school and college, she began teaching wilderness classes and gymnastics. In 1986 she resigned her teaching position so that she could go on the Will Steger International North Pole Expedition. The journey took fifty-six days, but the six-member team eventually made it to the North Pole using dogsleds.

In 1992–93 Bancroft teamed up with Liv Arnesen in an attempt to reach the South Pole on skis and subsequently became the first women to accomplish this feat. Bancroft was named *Ms. Magazine*'s Woman of the Year in 1987, and she was one of *Glamour* magazine's Women of the Year in 2001. She was inducted into the National Women's Hall of Fame in 1995.

Bancroft and Arnesen founded yourexpedition, a company that provides resources for organizations and individuals to succeed in life's journeys. Bancroft also established the Ann Bancroft Foundation, a nonprofit organization in Minnesota that develops programs especially for adolescent girls.

Further Reading

Bancroft, Ann, and Liv Arnesen. *No Horizon Is So Far: Two Women and Their Extraordinary Journey across Antarctica*. Cambridge, MA: Da Capo Press, 2003.

Wenzel, Dorothy. *Ann Bancroft: On Top of the World*. Minneapolis: Dillon Press, 1990.

Baugh, Laura Zonetta (May 31, 1955–)

Golfer Laura Baugh was born in Gainesville, Florida, in May 1955. A five-time winner of the National PeeWee Championship, she won her first tournament at age three. Moving to Long Beach, California, after her parents' divorce, Baugh continued to participate in golf championships, winning two consecutive Los Angeles Women's City Golf Championships. In 1971, while just sixteen years old, she won the U.S. Women's Amateur Golf Championship in Atlanta, Georgia. At that time she was the youngest winner in the history of the tournament. After winning this significant event, Baugh was named Woman of the Year by the *Los Angeles Times*. The following year *Golf Digest* named her 1972's Most Beautiful Golfer.

Following her win in Atlanta, Baugh became a member of the U.S. national team and competed in the Curtis Cup and World Amateur Gold Team championships. Soon after, she decided to play professionally in the Ladies Professional Golf Association (LPGA) and was named Rookie of the Year in 1973. Though she never won an LPGA tournament, she did place in the top ten more than sixty times.

During her time as a professional golfer, Baugh developed a problem with alcohol. She eventually overcame her dependence on alcohol and was awarded the 1999 Ethos Award in recognition of her efforts to raise awareness about substance abuse. Baugh has now created the Laura Baugh Golf Workshops for Women Only, which is a program designed to teach women the basics of the game.

Further Reading

Altman, Linda Jacobs. *Laura Baugh: Golf's Golden Girl*. St. Paul, MN: EMC, 1975.

Baugh, Laura, and Steve Eubanks. *Out of the Rough: An Intimate Portrait of Laura Baugh and Her Sobering Journey*. Nashville: Rutledge Hill Press, 1999.

Bayh, Senator Birch Evans (January 22, 1928–)

Lawyer, senator from Indiana, and "Father of Title IX," Birch Evans Bayh II was born in Terre Haute, Indiana, in January 1928 to Birch Bayh, a physical education teacher and athletics director, and his wife, Leah. After a two-year stint in the army, Bayh attended Purdue University and Indiana University's School of Law. He served in the Indiana House of Representatives from 1954 to 1962, before being elected to the U.S. Senate, where he served from 1963 to 1981.

As a senator Bayh helped draft the 1964 Civil Rights Act and supported the Equal Rights Amendment (ERA). Though the ERA did not become law, Bayh was instrumental in the passage of the Title IX legislation, which he coauthored with Representatives **Edith Green** and **Patsy T. Mink**. While working on the draft, he was reminded of the "women need not apply" policy that his wife, Marvella, faced when she applied to the University of Virginia law school. Bayh credits Marvella, who was rejected solely because of her gender, with introducing him to the discrimination women encounter.

In October 2003 President George W. Bush signed Public Law 108-35, which designated an Indianapolis courthouse as the Birch Bayh Federal Building &

United States Courthouse. Housed in this building is a museum that highlights Bayh's career.

In recognition of his work with Title IX, Bayh was awarded the **National Collegiate Athletic Association's** Gerald R. Ford Award in February 2006. This award is given to those who have continuously advocated for intercollegiate athletics through their careers.

Bayh continues to practice law, while serving on the Citizens' Commission on Civil Rights—a bipartisan organization that monitors the federal government's civil rights policies and practices and promotes equal opportunity in education. In discussing the legendary Title IX legislation, Bayh notes that "the word quota does not appear. . . . What we were really looking for was equal opportunity for young women and for girls in the educational system in the United States of America. Equality of opportunity." In 1997 Bayh received the Honors Award from the **National Association of Collegiate Women Athletic Administrators** (NACWAA) in recognition of his "outstanding support of women in athletics and their success." In March 2007 he was a keynote speaker at the Girls & Women Rock: Celebrating 35 Years of Sport & Title IX, which was part of the Title IX Academic & Legal Conference held prior to the NCAA Women's Final Four.

Further Reading

Bayh, Birch. *One Heartbeat Away: Presidential Disability and Succession.* Indianapolis: Bobbs Merrill, 1968.

Bayh, Evan. *From Father to Son: A Private Life in the Public Eye.* Indianapolis: Guild Press/Emmis Books, 2003.

Senator Birch Bayh: The Man and His Record. S.l.: s.n., 1978.

Benoit Samuelson, Joan (May 16, 1957–)

Olympic marathon runner Joan Benoit Samuelson was born in Cape Elizabeth, Maine, in May 1957 to Andre and Nancy Benoit. An athletic child, Benoit participated in a variety of sports, including skiing. When she was fifteen, she broke her leg while skiing and turned to running to help her get back in shape. Benoit soon fell in love with running. Enrolling in 1976 in Bowdoin College in Brunswick, Maine, she continued to run and qualified to participate in the Olympic trials being held that year.

Though she did not make the Olympic team, Benoit became determined to win the Boston Marathon. After training for three years, she entered the 1979 Marathon and set a new United States record for the event with a time of two hours, thirty-five minutes, and fifteen seconds.

For the next few years Benoit was unable to run, as she underwent surgery on her Achilles tendon and an appendectomy. Between 1981 and 1983 she coached track and field at Boston University. While working with her students, she also worked on getting into shape to run another marathon. In 1983 Benoit won her second Boston Marathon in the world record time of two hours, twenty-two minutes, and forty-three seconds.

Following this victory, she began training for the Olympics and won a spot on the 1984 U.S. Olympic team. Three months before the games, however, she underwent arthroscopic surgery on her right knee. Immediately after the surgery she resumed training, determined to compete in the Olympics. Although she had not fully recovered from her surgery, Benoit won the gold medal in the 1984 in the first-ever women's Olympics marathon. That same year she was awarded the Sullivan Memorial Trophy as the best amateur athlete in the country.

In 1984 Benoit married Scott Samuelson and retired from running to have children. She attempted a comeback for the 1996 Olympics but finished thirteenth at the trials. She now lives with her family in her hometown of Cape Elizabeth.

Further Reading
Benoit, Joan, and Sally Baker. *Running Tide*. New York: Alfred A. Knopf, 1987.
Wickham, Martha. *Superstars of Women's Track and Field*. New York: Chelsea House Publishers, 1997.

Black Women in Sport Foundation

Established in 1992, the Black Women in Sport Foundation (BWSF) is a grassroots organization "dedicated to increasing the involvement of Black women and girls in health, sports [and] fitness activities and career opportunities." The BWSF was cofounded by Dr. Tina Sloan Green, professor emeritus at Pennsylvania's Temple University, and Dr. Alpha Alexander, an associate professor at Lane College in Tennessee.

Serving as BWSF's president and vice president, respectively, Sloan Green and Alexander started the organization to introduce young black girls to nontraditional sports such as golf, lacrosse, fencing, tennis, and gymnastics. Officers and advisory board members for BWSF include Dr. Nikki Franke, head women's fencing coach at Temple University; Linda Greene, associate vice chancellor for academic affairs and professor of law at the University of Wisconsin-Madison; Rochelle M. Taylor, president of the National Youth Sports Corporation; and Lucille Hester, project director for the **National Collegiate Athletic Association**'s Youth Sports Program.

Since 1992 the BWSF has established several community sports programs in efforts to reach out to young black women and sports educators. In the BWSF Sports Mentoring Programs, adolescents between the ages of eight and sixteen participate in sports clinics in combination with mentoring activities. The Project Challenge Program provides opportunities for mentoring and scholarships to girls interested in tennis. Individuals in this program also participate in community service events to maintain local tennis facilities. The BWSF conducts the Reading through Sport Program and the BWSF Internship Program. Aimed at elementary- and middle-school-age children, the Reading through Sport Program provides sports-related books to inner-city schools to create a BWSF Sports Library. The BWSF Internship Program provides internship opportunities for young women wishing to pursue a career in sports management, sports administration, or sports marketing. The BWSF also maintains an online career resource center for women and girls interested in sports-related careers.

The BWSF is dedicated to raising awareness and promoting opportunities for black women and girls in sport. To this end the organization has produced two videos that highlight the accomplishments of black female athletes and professionals, along with student workbooks and teacher manuals that supplement the videos. The BWSF also funds scholarships for college students involved in athletics. Membership in the BWSF is open to anyone interested in "increasing the involvement of Black women and girls in health, sports & fitness activities and career opportunities."

Further Reading
Black Women in Sport Foundation Web site (http://www.blackwomeninsport.org/).

Blair, Bonnie Kathleen (March 18, 1964–)

Olympic speedskater Bonnie Blair was born in March 1964 in Cornwall, New York. After moving to Champaign, Illinois, as a child, Blair relocated to Milwaukee, Wisconsin, after high school to train for the U.S. speedskating team. When she was just nineteen years old, Blair participated in the 1984 Olympic Games in Sarajevo and placed eighth in the 500-meter race. At the 1988 Winter Olympics in Calgary, she won her first gold medal for the 500 meters and won a bronze medal in the 1,000-meter skate. Blair also competed in the next two Olympics, winning a total of five gold medals. She is the first U.S. woman to win five gold medals and the first American to win gold medals in three consecutive Winter Olympics.

In 1992 Blair was presented with the James E. Sullivan Award and became the first woman to win the Oscar Mathisen Award. She was also selected as the 1994 *Sports Illustrated's* Sportsman of the Year. That same year the Associated Press named her its Female Athlete of the Year. Inducted into the United States Olympic Hall of Fame in 2004, Blair has won the most medals in the history of U.S. Winter Olympics. ESPN named Blair the sixty-ninth greatest athlete of the twentieth century.

Further Reading
Burby, Liza N. *Bonnie Blair, Top Speed Skater*. New York: Rosen Publishing Group, 1997.
Daly, Wendy. *Bonnie Blair: Power on Ice*. New York: Random House, 1996.

Blair v. Washington State University (1987)

Even though the **Tower Amendment**, which proposed to exempt revenue-producing sports from Title IX, was defeated in 1974, the issue of excluding revenue-producing teams, such as football, from Title IX compliance continued to surface. In the case of *Blair v. Washington State University*, a state law was used in an attempt to exempt the Washington State University (WSU) football team from Title IX jurisdiction.

In October 1979 female coaches and athletes at WSU filed suit, claiming that the university had violated the state's equal rights amendment and a law prohibiting discrimination. The court found WSU in violation of Title IX and ordered the school to increase funding for women's athletics and sports scholarships by more than 37 percent in the 1982–83 academic year. Each year thereafter, funding was to increase by 2 percent until it matched the ratio of undergraduate women enrolled in the university. The funding increases, however, were not required to include the participation and funding rates for football. In 1987 the case reached the state appellate court, which determined that the trial court had "abused its discretion" by excluding football from the extent of the equal rights amendment. The higher court did, however, uphold the lower court's decision that "revenue generated by a specific sport or program be excluded from the University funding that was to be divided proportionate to enrollment."

The *Blair* case is important because it was a resounding affirmation that all sports were to be considered equal under Title IX, in terms of scholarships and participation. The Washington appellate court was firm and clear in its opinion that football not be excluded from Title IX, and that participation, scholarships, and funds be calculated equally for all sports.

Further Reading

Blair v. Washington State University, 740 P.2d 1379 (Wash. 1987); 108 Wash.2d 558.

Reynvaan, Juli Anne. "Sex Discrimination in Washington State University's Intercollegiate Athletics Program: An Examination of Washington State University's Administrative Response to *Blair v. WSU* from an Organizational Cultural Perspective." M.A. thesis, Washington State University, 1992.

Blazejowski, Carol Ann (September 29, 1956–)

Born in Elizabeth, New Jersey, to Leon and Grace Blazejowski, Carol "The Blaze" Blazejowski was one of the nation's foremost women's basketball players. Blazejowski attended Montclair State College in Montclair, New Jersey, where she became one of the top scorers in women's basketball. With a total of 3,199 points in her college career, she is second in scoring only to Pete Maravich. When Montclair State participated in the **Association for Intercollegiate**

Athletics for Women (AIAW) tournament during her sophomore year, Blazejowski set a single-game scoring record with forty-four points. Her performance in this game helped place her on the All-Tournament team. She was named an All-American from 1976 to 1978 and received the first Wade Trophy in 1978.

After college, Blazejowski played for the Crestettes of Allentown, Pennsylvania, in the **Amateur Athletic Union** (AAU) league. While playing in the eighth women's World Basketball Championships, she became the only American selected for that year's All-Tournament team. At the 1977 and 1979 World University Games she was the leading scorer, and she was chosen to play on the 1980 Olympic team.

When the U.S. boycott of the 1980 Olympics prevented her from playing in the games, Blazejowski signed a three-year, $150,000 contract with the New Jersey Gems of the newly formed **Women's Professional Basketball League** (WBL). She was the highest-paid player in the league, which disbanded after just one season. Following a ten-year stint as a promotional representative for Adidas, Blazejowski spent several years working for the National Basketball Association, before becoming vice president and general manager of the **Women's National Basketball Association's** New York Liberty in 1997.

Entering college just two years after the passage of Title IX, Blazejowski was truly one of the best players in women's basketball history. She was inducted into the Women's Basketball Hall of Fame in 1999.

Further Reading

Porter, Karra. *Mad Seasons: The Story of the First Women's Professional Basketball League, 1978–1981.* Lincoln, NE: University of Nebraska Press, 2006.

Bolin, Molly "Machine Gun" (November 13, 1957–)

"Machine Gun" Molly Bolin, the first player to sign with the **Women's Professional Basketball League** (WBL), was born Monna Lea Van Venthuysen in Canada in November 1957. Raised in Moravia, Iowa, she began playing basketball with the Moravia Mohawkettes in her junior year of high school. She attended Grand View College in Des Moines, Iowa, where she met and married Dennis Bolin. She graduated with an associate degree in telecommunications in 1978.

After college Bolin signed with the Iowa Cornets and became the first player to sign with the WBL. As a high scorer (she once scored fifty-three points in a game), she quickly gained the nickname "Machine Gun" Molly. During her second season she was named the league's Most Valuable Player, along with **Ann Meyers** of the New Jersey Gems. In 1980, after just two seasons, the Iowa Cornets folded, leaving Bolin available to play for another team. She initially signed with the Southern California Breeze of the Ladies Professional Basketball League (LPBL) but returned to the WBL when she signed with the San Francisco Pioneers.

In 1984 Bolin began playing with the Columbus Minks in the newly formed **Women's American Basketball Association** (WABA). Unfortunately for her, the WABA lasted only one season. Despite the unsettled nature of her professional career, Bolin was chosen to play on the 1984 women's Olympic team coached by **Sue Gunter** and **Jody Conradt**.

Bolin was inducted into the Iowa Basketball Hall of Fame in 1986. That same year she was appointed assistant commissioner of the National Women's Basketball Association, but the league never became operational. Her chance finally came, however, in 1995, when she was hired by Liberty Sports (now Fox Sports) to promote women's professional basketball.

Bolin married John Kazmer in 1989, and they currently live in La Quinta, California.

Further Reading

Iowa Women's Archives, University of Iowa Libraries. "Molly Bolin Papers Finding Aid" (http://sdrc.lib.uiowa.edu/iwa/findingaids/html/BolinMolly.htm).

Porter, Karra. *Mad Seasons: The Story of the First Women's Professional Basketball League, 1978–1981*. Lincoln: University of Nebraska Press, 2006.

Borders, Ila (February 18, 1975–)

Ila Borders, the first woman to pitch in a professional baseball game, was born in La Mirada, California, in February 1975. Since attending her first major league baseball game at the age of ten, she wanted to play baseball. She played Little League baseball and became the most valuable player on her high school team. Her passion for the game paid off when she was awarded a baseball scholarship to Southern California College (SCC) in Costa Mesa, California. As the first woman to receive a baseball scholarship, Borders met with a wealth of publicity.

During her freshman year Borders was a regular pitcher for the SCC team, becoming the first woman to pitch and win a complete college game. In 1994 she became the first woman to pitch in a men's **National Collegiate Athletics Association** (NCAA) or National Association of Intercollegiate Athletics (NAIA) baseball game. In her senior year she transferred to Whittier College, where she continued to play baseball. After college Borders played in 1997 for the St. Paul Saints of the independent Northern League, becoming the first woman to pitch in a regular season game. After just a few games with the Saints she was traded to the Duluth-Superior Dukes. Borders played in the Northern League for three years, finishing with the Madison Black Wolf. In 2000 she played for the Zion Pioneerzz in the Western League.

After becoming the first woman to pitch in a men's professional baseball game, Borders retired after the 2000 season at just twenty-six years old. Though she retired, she did not leave the game completely; she signed a contract with

ESPN to work as a commentator for college baseball games. Borders's glove, ball, and uniform are on display at the Baseball Hall of Fame in an exhibit honoring women's contributions to the game.

Further Reading

Ardell, Jean Hastings. *Breaking Into Baseball: Women and the National Pastime.* Carbondale, IL: Southern Illinois University Press, 2005.

Boucher v. Syracuse University (1999)

In May 1995 eight female athletes (seven lacrosse players and one softball player) filed a lawsuit against Syracuse University in an effort to gain varsity status for the women's lacrosse and softball teams. Since these teams only held club status, they also sued for the scholarship money that would have been awarded had the teams held varsity status. At the time of the lawsuit Syracuse had eleven varsity men's teams and nine varsity women's teams. Although women made up 50 percent of the school's enrollment, only 32 percent of the female students participated in a sport. Both the district and circuit courts ruled that, because the plaintiffs were not varsity athletes, they could not sue for scholarship money, but could pursue the issue of varsity status for their teams.

Although Syracuse University had a strong history of adding women's sports teams and upgrading club teams to varsity status, the school had not added a women's team since 1982. For the 1996–97 academic year, however, the university added a women's soccer team. A women's lacrosse team was added the following year. The school also had plans to add a women's softball team for the 1999–2000 academic year. In addition, the school had increased the number of scholarships for women athletes and had made other improvements to their women's programs, including better facilities and more coaches. Further, the percentage of female athletes had increased 47 percent since 1982, while the number of male athletes had increased only 3 percent.

The Second Circuit Court ruled that the university met the second part of the Three-Part Test (see Introduction), since it could show efforts to expand the women's athletics program. The court further stated that, because lacrosse had been upgraded to varsity status since the lawsuit began, the lacrosse players' case was no longer valid. And because the university had plans to upgrade the women's softball team to varsity status, the softball players' case was also dismissed.

Further Reading

Bonnette, Valerie McMurtrie. *Title IX and Intercollegiate Athletics: How It All Works— In Plain English.* San Diego, CA: Good Sports, 2004.

Boucher v. Syracuse University, 164 F.3d 113 (2nd Cir. 1999).

Brennan, Christine (May 1958–)

USA Today sports journalist Christine Brennan, the first woman to cover the Washington Redskins as a staff writer for *The Washington Post* and the first president of the **Association for Women in Sports Media** (AWSM), is one of America's leading sports commentators. She grew up in Toledo, Ohio, and attended college at Northwestern University. After graduating in 1981 with a master's degree in journalism she went to work for *The Miami Herald* and became the newspaper's first full-time woman sports writer.

After leaving *The Miami Herald* in 1984 Brennan moved to *The Washington Post*. In 1988 she became the first president of the Association for Women in Sports Media. During her term in office she established a scholarship and internship program for college women.

Brennan has authored five books, including *Inside Edge* and *Best Seat in the House*. She has won the **Women's Sports Foundation's** journalism award four times. In 2001 she was named one of the top ten sports columnists by the Associated Press sports editors. *Sports Illustrated* named her 1996 book *Inside Edge* one of the top 100 sports books of all time.

In addition to her work at *USA Today*, Brennan is a sports analyst for ABC and ESPN. She received the **Association of Women in Sports Media's** Pioneer Award in 2004 and has been inducted into Northwestern University's Medill School of Journalism's Hall of Achievement, as well as the Ohio Women's Hall of Fame. In 2005 she was one of the recipients of the Women in Sports and Events Women of the Year Award, in recognition for her work as a sports columnist for *USA Today*.

Further Reading

Brennan, Christine. *Best Seat in the House: A Father, a Daughter, a Journey through Sports*. New York: Scribner, 2006.

Butcher, Susan (December 26, 1954–August 5, 2006)

Dogsled racer Susan Butcher was born in December 1954 in Boston, Massachusetts, to Charlie and Agnes Butcher. As a child she learned to sail and build boats. When she was sixteen years old, Butcher applied to a boat-building school in Maine but was turned down because she was a woman. After graduating from high school she attended Colorado State University and became a veterinary technician. While in Colorado she discovered that she wanted to breed and race sled dogs, and in 1975 she moved to Alaska to train her first dogs. Along the way she dreamed of racing in the Iditarod, an eleven-day dogsled race across Alaska.

Butcher entered her first Iditarod in 1978 and finished in nineteenth place. She did much better the next year and continued to train. Eventually, she teamed up with Iditarod organizer Joe Redington and was the first to race sled dogs to the top of Mount McKinley. After finishing second in the 1984 Iditarod, Butcher's team was leading in the 1985 race when a moose killed two of her dogs, which forced her to drop out of the race.

Butcher then won the next three Iditarods. In 1987 and 1988 she was named Professional Sportswoman of the Year for the Women's Sports Foundation. In 1989 she was also named Sled Dog Racer of the Decade. Also in 1989 the International Academy of Sports chose her as its Outstanding Female Athlete of the World.

In 2005 Butcher was diagnosed with leukemia. She died in August 2006.

Further Reading

Butcher, Susan, and Kerby Smith. "A Woman's Icy Struggle: Thousand-Mile Race to Nome." *National Geographic*, 163.3 (March 1983): 410–422.

Dolan, Ellen M. *Susan Butcher and the Iditarod Trail.* New York: Walker and Co., 1993.

C

Cannon v. University of Chicago (1979)

After being denied admission to the University of Chicago Medical School because of the school's age limit policy, Geraldine G. Cannon claimed that she had cause for a lawsuit under Title IX because the school was part of a university that received federal funding, and its refusal to admit students over the age of thirty was disproportionately harmful to women. The language of Title IX was unclear, however, regarding whether it provided individuals with private right of action, or the right to take a case to court without first going through an administrative office, such as the Office for Civil Rights. If Title IX did imply private right of action, then a complainant could decide to have his or her case addressed directly in court, thus saving the time it would take the case to filter through an administrative agency. Importantly, only through a lawsuit can compensatory and punitive damages be sought.

After having been dismissed by lower courts on the grounds that issues of private right of action were the sole responsibility of Congress, Cannon's case was argued in the Supreme Court on January 9, 1979. In the appeal, Cannon's attorneys argued that Congress had already approved private actions, based on similar language in both Title VI and the Civil Rights Act of 1964, and that the Supreme Court had previously ruled that those pieces of legislation implied a private remedy. In the opinion written by Justice John Paul Stevens, the Supreme Court applied the four-part test outlined in *Cort v. Ash*, 422 U.S. 66 (1975), which is used to determine whether Congress intended for a given law to grant private right of action. First, the Court had to determine whether the plaintiff was a member of the group that the statute was intended to benefit; in Cannon's instance, this was clearly the case. Second, the court had to determine whether the history of the legislation demonstrated intent to grant private right of action. Since the language in Title IX mirrored that of Title VI, and it had already been ruled that Title VI implied private right of action, Cannon met this requirement. Third, the court had to decide whether granting private right of action would advance or hinder the legislative goal behind the law. Allowing private right of action was determined to be consistent with Title IX's goal of protecting individuals from discrimination by denying federal aid to institutions with discriminatory policies. Finally, the court had to determine whether the law in question involved an area of concern generally left up to individual states. Since Cannon's case involved discrimination, and since it is the federal government's responsibility to protect citizens against discrimination, Title IX was deemed not to be an issue of individual state discretion. Thus, all four criteria having been met, the court ruled in favor of Cannon, ultimately setting a precedent for others to bring Title IX complaints directly to court.

With its argument that the University of Chicago Medical School's policy of denying admission to persons over thirty had a greater negative impact on women than on men, Canon's case also laid the groundwork for another lawsuit. In 2001 the issue of policies that create a disparate impact on minorities was fought out in the Title VI case of *Alexander v. Sandoval*, which involved a complaint of discrimination caused by English-only policies. Unlike in Cannon's case, the court determined that Sandoval's complaint did not meet the four criteria for granting a private right of action.

Further Reading

Cannon v. University of Chicago, 441 U.S. 677 (1979).

Zirkel, Perry A., Sharon Nalbone Richardson, and Steven S. Goldberg. *A Digest of Supreme Court Decisions Affecting Education.* Bloomington, IN: Phi Delta Kappa Educational Foundation, 2001.

Chalenor et al. v. University of North Dakota (2002)

Suffering from budget constraints, in 1998 the University of North Dakota decided to attempt to meet Title IX's proportionality requirement by eliminating its men's wrestling program. The male wrestlers responded by filing suit under Title IX, arguing that cutting the men's wrestling team was an act of sex discrimination. The university had already added three women's teams between 1995 and 2000, but men still composed more than 60 percent of the campus's athlete population, even though the university's enrollment was only 51 percent male. Men's athletics also received a larger share of the budget than women's athletics.

With no money to add more women's sports, the university decided to cut men's sports in an effort to address the problem of unequal participation. The district court ruled in favor of the university, stating that Title IX does allow schools to eliminate men's athletics programs, rather than adding more women's sports, in order to meet the proportionality component of the Three-Part Test of compliance. The court also ruled that eliminating a men's team does not violate Title IX, because men are not the historically underrepresented sex and are therefore not a protected class.

The wrestlers appealed to the Eighth Circuit Court, providing the additional information that a private donor had agreed to pay for the wrestling team, in order to attempt to invalidate the university's claim that the decision to cut the team was based on budget shortages. Nevertheless, the Eighth Circuit upheld the lower court's decision. The court ruled that universities are allowed to determine measures for complying with Title IX, even if those measures include cutting men's teams. The court also ruled that support from a private donor would not relieve the university of its Title IX obligations, because, upon receipt by a public university, private donations become public money.

Further Reading

Chalenor et al. v. University of North Dakota, 291 F.3d 1042 (8th Cir. 2002).

Mitten, Matthew J., and Paul M. Anderson, eds. "*Chalenor v. University of North Dakota.*" *You Make the Call: National Sports Law Institute of Marquette University Law School Newsletter* 4.2 (Fall 2002) (available at http://law.marquette.edu/cgi-bin/site.pl?2130&pageID=634).

Chastain, Jane (1943–)

Jane Chastain, the first female sportscaster, made her debut in 1963 as "Coach Friday" for WAGA-TV in Atlanta, Georgia. She soon moved to WTVJ in Miami, Florida, where she was often passed over for assignments in favor of male sportscasters. Frustrated with this gender bias, Chastain worked to create her own syndicated radio show, "Football for Women." This program was such a success that she soon developed "Girls Rules," a series of programs syndicated to more than 200 radio stations across the country.

In 1973 Chastain launched "The Jane Chastain Show—Everything You've Always Wanted to Know about Sports but Were Afraid to Ask." The series was so popular that, in 1974, CBS hired her as the first female sportscaster for a major network. With CBS Chastain traveled the country reporting on sports ranging from football to basketball and covering major events, such as the Cotton Bowl. During this time, she became the first woman allowed on a major league baseball field and the first allowed to enter the National Association for Stock Car Auto Racing (NASCAR) pits.

Since 1978 Chastain has acted as both host and writer for industrial and documentary films. She has maintained her involvement with sports as a commentator for several networks, including National Public Radio. She has also served on the Women's Progress Commission, created by Congress in 1998, and is a columnist for WorldNetDaily.com. She and her husband Roger Chastain currently live in California.

27

Further Reading
Chastain, Jane. *I'd Speak Out on the Issues If I Only Knew What to Say.* Ventura, CA: Regal Books, 1987.

Civil Rights Restoration Act of 1988

In *Grove City College v. Bell* (1984), the Supreme Court interpreted the word "program," in Titles IX and VI, to refer only to a program receiving federal monies, and not to its parent institution as a whole. This meant, for instance, that if the athletic department at a given school did not receive any federal monies, then it was not required to be compliant with Title IX, despite the fact that other departments on the same campus did receive federal monies. This decision greatly limited the scope and power of Title IX. More than 800 Office for Civil Rights (OCR) Title IX investigations were suspended or dropped within one year of the *Grove* decision.

In 1985 Massachusetts Senator Edward Kennedy, a Democrat, introduced a bill stating that if any department of an institution received any federal money, then that whole institution, including all its departments, would be subject to the jurisdiction of Title IX and would thus be required to comply. After the Democrats regained control of the Senate in 1986, the bill passed. President Ronald Reagan, however, vetoed the bill in 1988, arguing that it would "unjustifiably expand the power of the federal government over the decisions and affairs of private organizations." Congress overrode Regan's veto and passed the Civil Rights Restoration Act of 1988 in March of that year.

Further Reading
Bryjak, George J. "The Ongoing Controversy over Title IX." *USA Today.* 129.2662 (July 2000): 62–63.

Cohen et al. v. Brown University (1997)

Perhaps one of the most high-profile of Title IX cases, *Cohen et al. v. Brown University* was the first Title IX case involving the Three-Part Test to be decided at the circuit court level. Facing budget issues in the 1990–91 academic year, Brown University's administration decided to downgrade two women's and two men's teams from varsity status to club status, meaning that women's volleyball and gymnastics and men's golf and water polo would no longer be fully funded by the university. Brown felt cutting the same number of teams without regard to the number of participants on those teams was equitable. Overall, 80 percent of Brown's budget cuts were from women's athletic programs. As the *Favia v. Indiana University of Pennsylvania* (1993) case had demonstrated, however, equity must be measured by the number of athletes, not the number of teams.

In an effort to save their teams, a group of female athletes, led by former gymnastics team captain Amy Cohen, filed a lawsuit, claiming that Brown did not provide enough sports opportunities for its female students, as demonstrated by the discrepancy between the ratios of female to male athletes and female to male students (52 percent of Brown's student body was female, but only 39 percent of the university's athletes were women). Further, female athletes were denied the use of school locker rooms and athletic trainers. Brown University's president was incensed and refused to settle the issue out of court.

On the surface, Brown had a model women's athletic program. The plaintiffs conceded that the women's teams received adequate staff, equipment, coaches, and facilities. Further, since Brown did not offer any athletic aid, Cohen and the others could not argue that the male athletes received more scholarship money. Brown even had more women's varsity teams than men's. Thus, the plaintiffs' argument was based only on the fact that, in proportion to their representation in the student body, women were underrepresented in Brown's athlete population, and on the assertion that Brown did not meet any of the requirements of Title IX's Three-Part Test.

In response, Brown argued that compliance should be judged based on the number of player slots available, not on the actual number of women athletes actually occupying those slots. Thus, if the women's tennis team had ten slots, but only seven players in those slots, Brown wanted to include all ten slots in its calculations. Brown also argued that it should be able to survey the student body to gauge interest before providing athletic opportunities. The university claimed that its female students were simply less interested in sports than its male students. The plaintiffs' lawyers argued that Brown was responsible for much more than just accommodating interested students; the university needed to develop an environment in which interest could be created in the first place. The state court ruled in favor of the student athletes.

Brown appealed the decision, and the U.S. Court of Appeals granted a temporary stay of the state court's ruling. After hearing the arguments, the Court of Appeals upheld the state's ruling and ordered Brown to reinstate the women's teams' varsity status. A long and complicated case, the *Cohen* ruling meant that schools were required to count the number of actual athletes in determining compliance and that using surveys to determine interest in sports was not sufficient for compliance. In 1997 Brown University attempted to appeal the case again, but the U.S. Supreme Court declined to hear the school's appeal.

Further Reading

Cohen et al. v Brown University, 991 F.2d 888 (1st Cir. 1993); 101 F.3d 155 (1st Cir. 1996), *cert. denied*, 520 U.S. 1186 (1997).

Gavora, Jessica. *Tilting the Playing Field: Schools, Sports, Sex, and Title IX*. San Francisco: Encounter Books, 2002.

Milloy, Marilyn. "Amy Cohen." *Ms.* 8.4 (Jan./Feb. 1998): 52–55.

Suggs, Welch. *A Place on the Team: The Triumph and Tragedy of Title IX*. Princeton, NJ: Princeton University Press, 2005.

Cohn, Linda (November 10, 1959–)

ESPN sportscaster Linda Cohn was born and raised on Long Island, New York. Interested in sports as a child, Cohn joined her high school's boys' ice hockey team, playing goalie in eight games during her senior year at Newfield High School. After high school, she attended the State University of New York at Oswego, where she spent four years playing on the women's ice hockey team as a starting goalie. She completed a degree in arts and communication in 1981 and, upon graduating, began her career as a sports anchor for several New York radio stations, including WALK-AM. In 1987 ABC hired Cohn as a sports anchor for its sports news radio show, making her the first full-time female sports anchor to be featured on a national radio network. The following year, Cohn was hired as a sports anchor for cable television's SportsChannel America Network.

In 1988 Cohn moved to Seattle, Washington, where she was hired as a weekend sports anchor for KIRO-TV. After holding several other jobs throughout the country, Cohn was eventually hired by ESPN's SportsCenter in 1992, where she continues to work today. One of only a few women to work for ESPN, Cohn stars in the network's "This is SportsCenter" commercials. In 1998 Cohn also became alternating host of ESPN Radio's Sunday coverage of NFL games. With a contract extension in 2005, Cohn now conducts play-by-play for **Women's National Basketball Association** (WNBA) games, in addition to hosting ESPNews' NFL Blitz and weekly NASCAR segments, among other projects. Cohn is also a 1995 recipient of the **Women's Sports Foundation's** (WSF) Women's Sports Journalism Award.

Further Reading

JournalismJobs.com. "Interview with Linda Cohn" (http://www.journalismjobs.com/interview_cohn.cfm).

McElroy, Tamara. *From Then to Now: The Evolving Role of Women Sports Reporters*. Frederick, MD: Hood College, 2005.

Commission on Opportunity in Athletics

In July 2002, on the eve of Title IX's thirtieth anniversary, Secretary of Education Rod Paige established the Commission on Opportunity in Athletics, in order to investigate the effectiveness of the federal government's current policies for enforcing Title IX. The commission was directed "to collect information, analyze issues, and obtain broad public input directed at improving the application of current federal standards for measuring equal opportunity for men, women, boys, and girls to participate in athletics" (Commission Web site). Its goal was to produce a written report for Secretary Paige, which would offer suggestions for revising current procedures, in order to ensure more effective implementation of Title IX.

The fifteen-member commission was composed of individuals (primarily athletic directors and coaches) from colleges, universities, and public school districts, as well as "persons with special expertise in intercollegiate and secondary school athletics or issues of equal educational opportunity," such as researchers and local officials. Three *ex officio* members from the Department of Education were also appointed to serve on the commission. The commission was cochaired by former **Women's National Basketball Association** player **Cynthia Cooper** and Stanford University athletic director Ted Leland. Other notable members included former Olympic swimmer and cofounder of the **Women's Sports Foundation Donna de Varona** and women's soccer player and current president of the Women's Sports Foundation Julie Foudy.

The commission was instructed to hold at least three town hall meetings to achieve "a public discussion of the issues" (www.ed.gov/about/bdscomm/list/athletics/charter.html). Ultimately, six such meetings were held, over a period of eight months, at various locations throughout the country. The meetings included presentations from key figures involved in Title IX, such as former U.S. Senator **Birch Bayh** and representatives from various sports organizations including the Women's Sports Foundation and the **National Collegiate Athletic Association** (NCAA).

On February 28, 2003, the commission issued its final report to Secretary Paige. The seventy-page *Open to All: Title IX at Thirty* contains background information on the commission and Title IX, the body's findings, and twenty-three recommendations for improving the legislation's implementation. The commission found that, although much had been accomplished in the past thirty years, more needed to be done to increase opportunities for girls, while also maintaining opportunities for boys. Specifically, the commission noted that "escalating operational costs in intercollegiate athletics threaten the effort to end discrimination in athletics and preserve athletic opportunities" (*Open to All*, 25). Among other recommendations, the commission suggested that the Department of Education should provide clear and concise written guidelines for implementing Title IX, and that its Office for Civil Rights should clarify to institutions that "cutting teams in order to demonstrate compliance with Title IX is a disfavored practice" (*Open to All*, 34). Upon issuing its final report in February 2003, the commission disbanded.

Further Reading

U.S. Department of Education. Secretary's Commission on Opportunity in Athletics. *Open to All: Title IX at Thirty*. Washington, DC: U.S. Department of Education, 2003 (available at http://www.ed.gov/about/bdscomm/list/athletics/title9report.pdf).

U.S. Secretary of Education's Commission on Opportunity in Athletics Web site (http://www.ed.gov/about/bdscomm/list/athletics/index.html).

Communities for Equity v. Michigan High School Athletic Association (2006)

In June 1998 Communities for Equity, a Michigan-based advocacy group for female athletes, sued the Michigan High School Athletic Association (MHSAA), which regulates interscholastic athletics in the state, under the umbrella of Title IX. Its complaint was that six girls' sports were scheduled only during nontraditional seasons, whereas no boys' sports were scheduled in this manner. For example, the girls' volleyball team was scheduled to play in the winter, rather than during volleyball's traditional season of fall. Other girls' sports scheduled outside their normal seasons were basketball, tennis, soccer, golf, and swimming and diving. Communities for Equity contended that the scheduling issue caused female athletes to be denied opportunities, such as the chance to be seen by recruiters, to compete for scholarships and awards, and to play on club teams during traditional off-seasons. The group also alleged that female students were only allowed to use older facilities and that the MHSAA supported and promoted the boys' teams more than the girls'. These matters were settled quickly, but the scheduling issue remained problematic.

In responding to the complaint, the MHSAA argued that its scheduling practices provided opportunities for more students to participate, given limited facilities and personnel, and that, when surveyed, female students preferred the nontraditional schedule. MHSAA also argued that the practice was advantageous because it rendered the girls' schedule independent of the boys', so that the girls' teams did not have to compete with the boys for spectators, officials, or space.

In December 2001, the district court ruled in favor of Communities for Equity. First, it deemed the MHSAA to be a state actor, pursuant to *Brentwood Academy v. Tennessee Secondary School Athletic Association*, 531 U.S. 288 (2001), and pronounced it liable under Title IX, based on its "controlling authority" over the sports schedules. Second, the court denied MHSAA's arguments, stating that there was insufficient evidence that the schedule provided the opportunity for more students to participate in sports and that MHSAA's survey design was flawed in numerous ways, particularly with respect to sample size and choice (only one-third of the girls in MHSAA schools were surveyed, and most of them did not participate in any of the affected sports). It also stated that separate seasons did not, in fact, give girls a separate identity, but rather, denied them such independence and made their season appear less important than the boys'. Finally, the court determined that "the girls' sports, unlike the boys' sports, are played in seasons that disadvantage the student-athlete with respect to, inter alia, college recruiting opportunities, skills development, and overall playing experience."

The MHSAA was ordered to submit a compliance plan by May 24, 2002. In reviewing the submitted plan, the court found that MHSAA's proposed schedule changes would still leave a greater total percentage of female athletes playing their sports in nontraditional seasons. It thus ordered the MHSAA either to combine seasons, such that boys and girls would both play at traditional times of year, or to create a schedule that was more equitable, with respect to percentages of male and female athletes playing in nontraditional seasons.

In 2004 this decision was upheld by the Sixth Circuit Court, which ruled that the MSHAA was violating the female athlete's rights under Title IX, the Equal Protection Clause of the Fourteenth Amendment, and Michigan's Elliot-Larsen Civil Rights Act. The MSHAA then appealed to the Supreme Court, which ordered the Sixth Circuit Court to reconsider the case, questioning whether the female athletes could sue under the Constitution, as well as under Title IX. The circuit court upheld the district court's decision, ruling that the plaintiffs could sue under a violation of constitutional rights and that the MHSAA was in violation of both state and federal statutes, as well as the Constitution.

Further Reading

Communities for Equity v. Michigan High School Athletic Association, 80 F. Supp.2d 729, 742 (W.D. Mich. 2000); 178 F. Supp.2d 805, 807–846 (W.D. Mich. 2001); 377 F.3d 504 (6th Cir. 2004).

Mitten, Matthew J., and Paul Anderson, eds. "Court Approves MSHAA Title IX Compliance Plan." *You Make the Call: National Sports Law Institute of Marquette University Law School Newsletter* 5.1–2 (Spring/Fall 2003) (available at http://law.marquette.edu/cgi-bin/site.pl?2130&pageID=1119).

Conradt, Jody (May 13, 1941–)

Basketball player and coach Jody Conradt was born in Goldthwaite, Texas, in May 1941. Conradt played basketball both in high school and in college, at Baylor University, where she received a degree in physical education in 1963. After initially accepting a teaching job upon graduation, Conradt soon discovered that she really enjoyed coaching. In 1969 she became the women's coach for basketball, volleyball, and track and field at Sam Houston University. Just four years later, Conradt was hired to coordinate women's athletics at the University of Texas at Arlington. While there, she developed a strong women's basketball program. In 1976 Conradt left Arlington and accepted the position of head coach of the Lady Longhorns at the University of Texas at Austin, working with athletic director **Donna Lopiano**. With Conradt as coach, the team soon came to lead women's college basketball, and in 1993 Conradt became the first women's coach to achieve 600 wins. Conradt has been voted National Coach of the Year and four times has been named Southwest Coach of the Year; in 1987 she received the Carol Eckman Award from the **Women's Basketball Coaches Association**. She was also inducted into the International Women's Sports Hall of Fame and the Naismith Memorial Basketball Hall of Fame, in 1995 and 1998, respectively. In her spare time, Conradt coaches thirty-five- to sixty-five-year-old women at her "If I Only Had a Chance" basketball camp.

Further Reading

Hawkes, Nena, and John F. A. Seggar. *Celebrating Women Coaches: A Biographical Dictionary*. Westport, CT: Greenwood, 2000.

Skaine, Rosemarie. *Women College Basketball Coaches*. Jefferson, NC: McFarland, 2001.

Cook et al. v. Colgate University (1993)

After numerous attempts in 1979, 1983, 1986, and 1988 to convince Colgate University, a private institution, to raise women's ice hockey from club to varsity status, a group of players led by Jennifer B. Cook decided in 1989 to file suit under Title IX. The female athletes contended that, since Colgate had a male varsity ice hockey team, the school should offer a comparable team for women. They claimed that the university's lack of a women's varsity ice hockey team violated Title IX. Ruling prior to the First Circuit Court's decision in **Cohen et al. v. Brown University** (1997), which affirmed the Three-Part Test as the standard for compliance with Title IX, the district court compared the women's club team with the men's varsity team and decided that varsity status conferred greater benefits, including a larger budget and better equipment. The court ordered Colgate to grant the women's ice hockey team varsity status.

Colgate appealed the decision, arguing that since the players had sued as individuals, rather than bringing a class action suit (which would have included future players), and since they would all graduate before the next ice hockey season, the decision was essentially moot. The university also argued that its compliance with Title IX should be measured not by comparing similar sports, but by considering the institution's entire athletics program. The Second Circuit Court agreed with the university and declared the case moot. The case thus demonstrated the importance of filing future Title IX suits as class actions. Despite winning the appeal, Colgate University ultimately awarded varsity status to the women's ice hockey team in January 1997, thus bringing an end to the almost decade-long battle.

Further Reading

Bonnette, Valerie McMurtrie. *Title IX and Intercollegiate Athletics: How It All Works—In Plain English*. San Diego, CA: Good Sports, Inc., 2004.

Carpenter, Linda Jean, and R. Vivian Acosta. *Title IX*. Champaign, IL: Human Kinetics, 2005.
"Colgate and Women's Hockey Settle," *The Colgate Scene On-Line* (March 1997) (available at http://www4.colgate.edu/scene/mar1997/hockey.html).
Cook v. Colgate University, 992 F.2d 17 (2d Cir. 1993); 802 F. Supp. 737 (N.D. N.Y. 1992).

Cooper, Cynthia Lynne "Coop" (April 14, 1963–)

Basketball player and coach Cynthia Cooper was born in April 1963 in Chicago, Illinois, to Kenney Cooper and Mary Cobbs. Cooper grew up in California and was named Los Angeles Player of the Year during her senior year of high school in 1981. After high school, she attended the University of Southern California, where she played for the Lady Trojans. In 1982, as a first-year student, Cooper was named an All-American, and in her four years at USC, her team achieved **National Collegiate Athletic Association** (NCAA) Final Four status three times and won two national titles. In 1986 she was named to the NCAA Final Four All-Tournament team, as well as the All Pac-West Conference First Team.

After college, Cooper pursued a professional basketball career in Europe, playing for ten years in Spain and Italy. She excelled at the sport and was named most valuable player in the 1987 European All-Star game. During this time, Cooper was also a member of the U.S. women's 1988 and 1992 Olympic teams. After ten years in the European leagues, Cooper came back to the United States to play for the **WNBA's** Houston Comets. She was chosen as most valuable player during her first two seasons with the Comets, and she led the team to four consecutive championships.

Cooper played with the Comets until the end of the 2000 season. The following January, she was named head coach of the Phoenix Mercury. Cooper retired from coaching in the WNBA in 2002. She briefly signed with the Comets again in 2003, but was forced to sit out with a shoulder injury. She later became a reporter for the NBA's Houston Rockets. In May 2005 Cooper was appointed head coach of the women's basketball team at Prairie View A&M University.

Further Reading
Cooper, Cynthia. *She Got Game: My Personal Odyssey*. New York: Warner, 1999.
Ponti, James. *WNBA: Stars of Women's Basketball*. New York: Pocket Books, 1999.

D

DeFrantz, Anita Luceete (October 4, 1952–)

Voted one of *Sporting News*'s 100 Most Powerful People in Sports, Anita DeFrantz, an attorney and the first woman to represent America on the International Olympic Committee (IOC), was born in Philadelphia, Pennsylvania, in October 1952. Though the local schools did not offer sports for girls, DeFrantz played on the girls' basketball team at Connecticut College. During her sophomore year, she stumbled upon the sport of rowing and knew that she had found her niche. A few years later, while pursing a law degree at the University of Pennsylvania, DeFrantz became captain of the U.S. rowing team for the 1976 Olympics in Montreal, where she earned a bronze medal.

Determined that she could do better, DeFrantz dreamed of seeking a gold medal at the 1980 Olympics. She never got the chance, however, because the United States boycotted the games that year. DeFrantz filed a lawsuit against the United States Olympic Committee, contending that each athlete reserved the right to make his or her own decision regarding whether or not to participate in the games. Though she lost the suit, DeFrantz gained the attention of the IOC, which awarded her the Medal of the Olympic Order for her efforts.

DeFrantz's relationship with the Olympics continued, with her service as vice president of the Los Angeles Olympic Organizing Committee for the 1984 games. Soon after, she was appointed president of the Amateur Athletic Foundation, which was established to allocate the surplus funds from the Los Angeles games. Then, in 1986, she was appointed to serve on the IOC, making her not only the first woman, but also the first African American, to represent the United States in this capacity. In 1992 the IOC named her as chair of the group's Committee on Women and Sports. In this role, DeFrantz was instrumental in getting both women's softball and women's soccer included in the 1996 Olympic Games in Atlanta, Georgia. The next year, DeFrantz became the first female vice president of the IOC. During her time with the IOC, DeFrantz has worked to promote increased representation of women on this executive body. She originally set a goal that women would compose at least 10 percent of the committee, and later increased this target to at least 20 percent by 2005. She is currently the chair of the IOC's Women and Sport Commission, which aims to promote women's participation in athletics at all levels of play and administration. DeFrantz is also a member of the Board of Stewards and Board of Trustees for the **Women's Sports Foundation** (WSF), where she continues to promote equal opportunity in athletics.

Further Reading

Hasday, Judy L. *Extraordinary Women Athletes*. New York: Children's Press, 2000.
Woolum, Janet. *Outstanding Women Athletes: Who They Are and How They Influenced Sports in America*. Phoenix, AZ: Oryx, 1992.

de Varona, Donna Elizabeth (April 26, 1947–)

Olympic swimmer, sportscaster, and cofounder of the **Women's Sports Foundation**, Donna de Varona was born in San Diego, California, in April 1947, to Dave and Martha de Varona. De Varona was initially drawn to baseball, but the local Little League did not allow girls to play, so she took up swimming instead, entering several **Amateur Athletic Union** (AAU) swimming meets during her childhood. At just thirteen years old, de Varona was the youngest participant in the 1960 Olympic Games in Rome. At the 1964 Olympic Games in Tokyo, she broke eighteen records and won two gold medals. The Associated Press and United Press International named de Varona the most outstanding female athlete in the world in 1964.

Known as the "Queen of Swimming," de Varona retired from the sport in 1965, the same year that she graduated from high school. Only seventeen years old, she became a sports analyst for ABC the same year. The first full-time female sportscaster to be featured on network television, she appeared on the station's *Wide World of Sports* as a swimming commentator. She also enrolled at the University of California at Los Angeles during this time, but left during her senior year to concentrate on her job with ABC. De Varona received acclaim for her work as a sportscaster, earning an Emmy for a television special on the Olympics, as well as two Gracie Allen Awards for her radio program "Donna de Varona on Sports."

De Varona has long been a prominent advocate of women's sports and a staunch promoter of Title IX, an issue on which she testified before Congress in 1972. With fellow athlete **Billie Jean King**, de Varona founded the Women's Sports Foundation (WSF) in 1974; she also served as its first president, holding office from 1976 to 1984. Additionally, she served as a special consultant to the United States Senate at this time, contributing to the Amateur Sports Act of 1978, which provided additional facilities and money for female athletes. She also held a post on the President's Council on Physical Fitness and Sports for four terms (1966–68, 1984–88), as well as serving on President Gerald Ford's Commission on Olympic Sports (1974–76), President Jimmy Carter's Women's Advisory Commission (1976–80), and the U.S. Secretary of Education's Commission on Opportunity in Athletics (2002–03).

De Verona has received many accolades, both for her athletic achievements and for her service. She is a member of several halls of fame, including the International Swimming Hall of Fame and the International Women's Sports Hall of Fame, and in 1996 she was presented with the Women's Sports Foundation's Flo Hyman Award, at the Tenth Annual **National Girls and Women in Sport Day** (NGWSD) festivities.

Further Reading

Thomas, Bob. *Donna de Varona: Gold Medal Swimmer*. Garden City, NY: Doubleday, 1968.

Didrikson Zaharias, Mildred Ella "Babe"
(June 26, 1911–September 27, 1956)

All-around athlete Mildred "Babe" Zaharias was born Mildred Didrikson in June 1911 in Port Arthur, Texas, to Norwegian immigrants. Her nickname "Babe," derived from baseball's Babe Ruth, was bestowed upon her as a result of her having once achieved five home runs in a single game. She excelled at a number of sports, including basketball, baseball, track and field, and golf, and took a job at the Employers Casualty Insurance Company in Dallas, Texas, so that she could play for the Golden Cyclones, the company basketball team. A three-time All-American, she led her team to the **Amateur Athletic Union** (AAU) championships in 1931. At the AAU championships the following year, Didrikson set five world records and qualified to compete in five Olympic events at the 1932 Summer Games in Los Angeles, California. She was not allowed to compete in all of them, however, due to a rule that had been passed after the 1928 games limiting women's participation to only three events in any given year. For the track and field events in which she ultimately did compete in Los Angeles, Didrikson won two gold medals and one silver. After returning from the Olympics, she launched the Babe Didrikson All-American Basketball Team, which traveled around the country competing against local teams.

By 1934 Didrikson had given up her careers in both track and field and basketball and had begun playing golf. As an amateur, she won seventeen consecutive tournaments, including the 1946 U.S. Women's Amateur. In January 1938 Didrikson participated in an all-male Professional Golf Association (PGA) tournament. It was here that she met George Zaharias, a professional wrestler known as "The Crying Greek from Cripple Creek." The two married in December 1938, and Zaharias became Didrikson's manager and promoter.

By 1945 Didrikson had won her second Texas Women's Open and her third Western Open, and had been named the Associated Press's Woman Athlete of the Year. In 1947 she won the British Women's Amateur Championship in 1947, making her the first American woman to hold this title. With her husband's help, Didrikson was one of the leading founders of the Ladies Professional Golf Association (LPGA), established in 1946. She served as the association's president three times.

Diagnosed with colon cancer in 1953, Didrikson underwent a colostomy and began holding Babe Zaharias Golf Tournaments to raise funds for cancer research. Named Female Athlete of the Half Century in 1950, Didrikson died in September 1956, just forty-five years old.

Further Reading

Cayleff, Susan E. *Babe: The Life and Legend of Babe Didrikson Zaharias.* Urbana, IL: University of Illinois Press, 1995.

Zaharias, Babe Didrikson. *This Life I've Led: My Autobiography.* New York: Barnes, 1955.

Donovan, Anne Theresa (November 1, 1961–)

Born in Ridgewood, New Jersey, in November 1961, Anne Donovan is the first female coach in the **Women's National Basketball Association** (WNBA) ever to have won a league title. While attending Paramus Catholic High School, Donovan played basketball and was the most recruited player in the United States upon her graduation. She was also named Dial Soap's National High School Player of the Year in 1979.

After enrolling in Old Dominion University (ODU), where she majored in Leisure Studies, Donovan continued to play basketball. During her first year at the university, she led her team, the Lady Monarchs, to win the **Association of Intercollegiate Athletics for Women's** (AIAW) national championship. Before graduating in 1983, she set twenty-five ODU records.

After college, Donovan earned a place on the U.S. Olympic team for three sets of games. She was unable to play in the 1980 games, due to the U.S. government's boycott, but she competed in both the 1984 and 1988 games, winning gold medals at each. After the 1988 Olympics, Donovan traveled to Shizuoka, Japan, to play in a professional women's league. After playing in both Japan and Italy, she returned to the United States in 1989 and became an assistant coach at her alma mater. Donovan coached the Lady Monarchs until 1995, when she accepted the position of head coach at East Carolina University (ECU).

Donovan spent only two years at ECU before becoming the assistant coach of the USA Basketball Women's World Championship team in 1997. That same year, she was also named head coach of the **American Basketball League's**

(ABL) Philadelphia Rage. When the ABL folded after just one season, Donovan joined the WNBA in October 1999, and has since coached several teams in that league. In 2005, she became the WNBA's first female coach to win 100 games, and in January 2006, she was named head coach of the U.S. women's team for the 2008 Olympics.

Further Reading

Donovan, Anne. *Women's Basketball: The Post-Player's Handbook.* Terre Haute, IN: Wish Publishers, 2001.

E

Ederle, Gertrude Caroline "Trudy" (October 23, 1906–November 30, 2003)

The first woman to swim the English Channel, Gertrude "Trudy" Ederle was born in New York, New York in October 1906 to German immigrants Henry and Gertrude Ederle. Ederle began swimming at an early age and, at thirteen years old, joined the local Women's Swimming Association, where she took lessons and developed her technique. She gained her first victory in 1921, competing in the 100-meter freestyle. By the time she was seventeen, Ederle had already set eighteen world records and won three medals at the 1924 Olympics in Paris.

After achieving Olympic success, Ederle longed for a greater challenge: to be the first woman to swim the English Channel. The publisher of a local newspaper agreed to sponsor Ederle and also sent a reporter to cover the event. Ederle first attempted to swim the twenty-mile-wide channel on August 18, 1925. She made it over halfway before she had to be pulled from the water. A year later, on August 6, 1926, she returned to complete her goal. This time she successfully swam the English Channel in fourteen hours and thirty-one minutes, becoming the first woman to accomplish this feat and besting the fastest male time by more than two hours.

Suffering from both a nervous breakdown and deafness after her famous swim, Ederle injured her spine in a fall in 1933 and spent the next four years in a body cast. After her recovery, Ederle spent the rest of her career teaching deaf children to swim. She was inducted into the International Swimming Hall of Fame in 1965 and the International Women's Sports Hall of Fame in 1980. More than forty years before the passage of Title IX, Ederle proved that female athletes were just as capable as male athletes.

Further Reading

Condon, Robert J. *Great Women Athletes of the Twentieth Century*. Jefferson, NC: McFarland, 1991.

F

Favia v. Indiana University of Pennsylvania (1993)

In response to a call for university-wide budget cuts, the athletic director at Indiana University of Pennsylvania (IUP) decided to cut men's soccer and tennis and women's gymnastics and field hockey, leaving women and men with seven sports each. The sports were claimed to have been chosen based on an overall lack of national popularity. A group of female athletes from the school's gymnastics and field hockey teams, led by gymnast Dawn Favia, filed a class action lawsuit against Indiana University, in the hope of preventing the university from cutting the two women's programs. The athletic director felt the school's solution was equitable, since men's and women's sports would each lose two teams. Additionally, the university had promised to establish a women's soccer team, once the budget crisis passed.

Despite the athletic director's claim that the situation was equitable, however, a number of other disparities were found and presented to the court. Even though the planned addition of a women's soccer team meant that, overall, women were losing fewer programs than men, women composed only 38 percent of IUP's athlete population, while constituting 55 percent of the larger student body. In addition, only 21 percent of the school's athletic scholarship money was given to female athletes, and for every dollar spent on men's sports, less than 38 cents was spent on women's sports. The men's sports also received more promotion and publicity than the women's, and the men's coaches received a number of perks, such as cars and golf club memberships, that were not offered to the coaches of the women's teams.

After hearing the arguments, the court ruled in favor of the women athletes and required that the university reinstate the two women's teams. In every instance, Indiana University of Pennsylvania failed to meet the Three-Part

Test that serves as the metric for determining equal opportunity under Title IX: achieving proportionality, meeting interest and ability, and demonstrating a history of upgrading underrepresented groups' programs. Upon hearing the court's decision, the university petitioned to substitute women's soccer for gymnastics, which it claimed would increase women's sport participation at the school. When the district court refused the university's request, IUP appealed the decision, but the Supreme Court refused to hear the case.

Favia answered a number of important questions. First, it determined that financial difficulties are not an acceptable excuse for failing to provide equal opportunities. Second, it clarified that the promise of future improvements is not sufficient to demonstrate compliance. Third, it established that having an equal number of men's and women's teams is insufficient to meet Title IX regulations; instead, the ratio of male to female athletes must be in proportion with their representation in the student body, and men's and women's teams must receive equal treatment, in terms of facilities, equipment, scholarship money, promotion, and other related benefits. The court also noted that although the university's athletic director was thoughtful, well-intentioned, and under terrible pressure to cut his budget, his lack of intent to discriminate was insufficient to avoid a Title IX violation. Finally, the ruling empowered the courts to use the Office for Civil Rights' policy interpretation of the Three-Part Test for determining compliance in the future.

Further Reading

Carpenter, Linda Jean, and R. Vivian Acosta. *Title IX*. Champaign, IL: Human Kinetics, 2005.

Favia v. Indiana University of Pennsylvania, 812 F. Supp. 578 (W.D. PA. 1993); 7 F.3d 332 (3d Cir. 1993).

Suggs, Welch. *A Place on the Team: The Triumph and Tragedy of Title IX*. Princeton, NJ: Princeton University Press, 2005.

Ford, Gerald Rudolph (July 14, 1913–December 26, 2006)

Thirty-eighth president of the United States Gerald R. Ford, the man who signed portions of the Title IX legislation, was born Leslie Lynch King Jr., in Omaha, Nebraska, in 1913; his name was soon changed, when his mother married Gerald Ford Sr. of Grand Rapids, Michigan. In 1935 Ford graduated from the University of Michigan, where he studied economics and political science and also played football. Upon graduating, Ford refused offers to play for the NFL, instead enrolling at Yale Law School and serving in the Navy during World War II.

In 1948 Ford married Elizabeth "Betty" Warren and ran for Congress. He was elected minority leader for the House of Representatives in 1956 and remained in this position until he was appointed vice president in 1973. When

President Richard Nixon, who signed the educational amendments that included Title IX into law in 1972, resigned in August 1974, Ford assumed the presidency. On May 27, 1975, President Ford signed Title IX's implementation policies into law. These regulations specifically prohibited sex discrimination in athletics and required institutions to comply within three years.

In October 2003 the **National Collegiate Athletic Association** (NCAA) established the NCAA President's Gerald R. Ford Award to honor individuals who have "provided significant leadership as an advocate for intercollegiate athletics on a continuous basis over the course of their career." NCAA President Myles Brand declared that "both as a public servant and as an athlete, President Ford embodies the qualities of integrity, achievement and dedication that we aspire to in intercollegiate athletics."

Further Reading

Ford, Gerald R. *A Time to Heal: The Autobiography of Gerald R. Ford*. New York: Harper & Row, 1979.

Franklin v. Gwinnett County Public Schools (1992)

The unanimous Supreme Court decision in *Franklin v. Gwinnett County Public Schools* (1992) was a turning point in the history of Title IX because this ruling meant that institutions found to be in violation would not only be threatened with the loss of federal money, but also with the possibility of having to pay damages to victims. During her high school career, Christine Franklin alleged that she had been sexually harassed by a male coach. Franklin accused the school employee of initiating conversations about her sex life, calling her at home to ask her to meet him socially, and eventually forcing himself on her at school. When Franklin reported the events to the school, it was revealed that the employee did, in fact, have a history of sexual harassment. Franklin filed an Office for Civil Rights complaint, but was unsatisfied with the outcome: the employee was simply allowed to resign.

Franklin decided to pursue the matter further under Title IX, which prohibits sexual discrimination in educational programs receiving federal funding; however, the legislation does not specify whether a victim of discrimination suing under Title IX can receive monetary damages. Franklin argued that she was entitled to both compensatory and punitive damages from her school district, since it did not take any legal action against the employee who had allegedly harassed her. Two lower courts ruled against Franklin, and she appealed to the U.S. Supreme Court, which heard the case in 1992.

Against public expectations, the Supreme Court disagreed with the verdicts of the lower courts, ruling unanimously in favor of Franklin. The Court reasoned that if a legal right was violated and a federal statute existed that allowed for a suit in response to that violation, then courts could use any means to correct that violation, including awarding damages. The Gwinnett County school system was ordered to pay Franklin damages. This decision vastly strengthened Title IX's ability to be enforced, as it meant that noncompliant institutions—including institutions moving slowly toward compliance, but not yet having achieved it—would be risking potentially expensive lawsuits. *Franklin* also put much more power into the hands of victims of discrimination because, with the prospect of winning damages, lawyers were more willing to take on Title IX cases and to work for lower rates, thus making the process more affordable for plaintiffs.

Further Reading

Carpenter, Linda Jean, and R. Vivian Acosta. *Title IX*. Champaign, IL: Human Kinetics, 2005.

Franklin v. Gwinnett County Public Schools, 503 U.S. 60 (1992); 112 S. Ct. 1028 (1992).

Zirkel, Perry A., Sharon Nalbone Richardson, and Steven S. Goldberg. *A Digest of Supreme Court Decisions Affecting Education*. Bloomington, IN: Phi Delta Kappa Educational Foundation, 2001.

G

Game Face: What Does a Female Athlete Look Like?

Both a book and an exhibit, *Game Face: What Does a Female Athlete Look Like?* offers a unique look at the "contemporary explosion in women and girls athletics." Launched on a five-year national tour in June 2002, the thirtieth anniversary of Title IX, *Game Face* has been on exhibition at a number of venues, including the Smithsonian and the 2002 Salt Lake City Winter Olympics.

Created by former *San Francisco Chronicle* sports writer Jane Gottesman and photographer Geoffrey Biddle, the *Game Face* book begins with a foreword by actress and director Penny Marshall. Included in the book are more than 180 color and black and white photographs and personal stories of female athletes that "depict the many ways a woman can use athletics to describe her sense of self, her physicality, her aspirations and her involvement in the revision of beliefs about womanly and feminine behavior." The book features both well-known and lesser-known women athletes, including football player Tammie Overstreet, basketball player and coach **Lynette Woodard, Women's Sports Foundation** executive director **Donna Lopiano**, soccer player Brandi Chastain, and basketball referee Dee Kantner. In addition to the mainstream women's sports of basketball, soccer, and softball, *Game Face* also highlights women and girls in sports such as snowboarding, rowing, hunting, bodybuilding, surfing, cycling, and boxing.

Further Reading

Game Face Online Exhibit Web site (http://www.gamefaceonline.org/index.htm).

Gottesman, Jane. *Game Face: What Does a Female Athlete Look Like?* New York: Random House, 2001.

Garber, Mary (April 16, 1916–)

Mary Garber, a longtime sports writer for the *Winston-Salem Journal*, was honored in 2006, when the **Association of Women in Sports Media** renamed its annual Pioneer Award the Mary Garber Pioneer Award. Mary Garber was born in New York City in April 1916 to Mason and Grace Garber. Soon after their daughter's birth, the Garber family moved to Wilmington, and then to Winston-Salem, North Carolina, where Garber continues to live today.

Since the age of eight, Garber had known that she wanted to be a newspaper reporter; instead of writing simple letters to her grandparents, she drew newspapers and wrote headlines and stories for them. Garber's love for sports, especially boxing, developed when she began reading sports news articles. As a young child in North Carolina, she was also the only girl on a local tackle football team called the Buena Vista Devils. One of her heroes was Notre Dame football coach Knute Rockne.

As she grew up, Garber continued to participate in sports, playing on her high school softball team. After graduating from high school, she initially hoped to attend Duke University because of the school's "good football team," but instead enrolled at Hollins University, an all-girls school in Virginia, where she majored in philosophy. After graduating from college, Garber began working for the *Winston-Salem Sentinel*, as its society editor, and there she introduced a special column for women, instructing them on how to watch football. In 1944 Garber transitioned to sports reporting, covering both college and high school athletics. For the next thirty years, she was the only female sports writer in her region, reporting on events for black high schools and colleges, as well as for white institutions. Originally banned from men's locker rooms and press boxes, Garber was finally allowed into a locker room in 1974. Known for her coverage of Atlantic Coast Conference (ACC) basketball and football games, Garber was elected president of both the Atlantic Coast Sports Writers Association and the Football Writers Association of America, two organizations that had previously barred her from membership because she was a woman. Though she officially retired in 1986, Garber continued writing part-time until 2002.

For her work as a sports reporter for the *Winston-Salem Sentinel/Journal*, Garber was inducted into the North Carolina Sports Hall of Fame, as well as the Basketball Writers Hall of Fame. In 2005 she was honored with the Associated Press Sports Editors' Red Smith Award, in recognition of her contributions to sports journalism, making her the first woman to receive this distinction. She was also honored with Hollins University's first Distinguished Alumnae Award in May 2006.

Further Reading

Garber, Mary, and Diane Koos Gentry. *Interviews with Mary Garber*. Washington, DC: Washington Press Club Foundation, 1991.

Rapoport, Ron. *A Kind of Grace: A Treasury of Sportswriting by Women.* Berkeley, CA: Zenobia Press, 1994.

Gera, Bernice (June 15, 1931–September 23, 1992)

Born in June 1931 in Ernest, Pennsylvania, Bernice Gera was the first woman to umpire a men's professional baseball game. Initially accepted to the Al Comers Umpire School in 1967, Gera was later dismissed, after school officials realized that she was a woman; the school had misread the name on her application as "Bernie." After leaving Al Comers, Gera applied and was accepted to Jim Finley's Florida Baseball Camp in West Palm Beach. After completing this program, Gera began umpiring various baseball games, including the National Baseball Congress Tournament in Wichita, Kansas, and the Semi-Pro Invitational Tournament in Bridgeton, New Jersey. In 1969 Gera acquired a contract to umpire in the minor leagues. However, the day before her first game, she received a letter from the president of the National Association of Professional Baseball Leagues (NAPBL), notifying her that her contract had been rescinded. The letter did not specify why the contract had been withdrawn.

In October 1969 Gera filed a complaint with the New York State Human Rights Commission, which ruled in her favor. The NAPBL appealed the commission's decision, stating that Gera's contract had been canceled because she did not meet the league's height, weight, and age requirements. The commission again ruled in Gera's favor, and the NAPBL issued her a contract in June 1972.

Gera umpired her first and only professional league baseball game on June 24, 1972—the first game in a doubleheader between the Auburn Phillies and the Geneva Rangers, of the New York–Pennsylvania Class A League—thus becoming the first woman ever to umpire a professional men's game. She resigned before the beginning of the second game, due to disputes with players, fans, and other umpires throughout the first game. Although she umpired only one professional game in her career, Gera paved the way for future female umpires. In 1992 Gera died of kidney cancer, at the age of sixty-one.

Further Reading
"Bernice Gera Obituary." *The New York Times Biographical Service* 23 (Sept. 1992): 1225.
Edelson, Paula. *A to Z of American Women in Sports.* New York: Facts on File, 2002.
"Lady Ump." *Time,* January 24, 1972, p. 8.

Gibb, Roberta (1940?–)

A runner her whole life, Roberta Gibb has chosen not to give details about her age or childhood. It is known that Gibb grew up in Winchester, Massachusetts, and that she ran the sixteen miles, round-trip, between her home and Tufts University, in order to study art there. Gibb's love for running prompted friends of her family to encourage her to watch the 1964 Boston Marathon runners, as they passed Wellesley College. Inspired by what she saw, Gibb began training immediately. She wore nurses' shoes because no one made running shoes for women, and she used a training strategy adapted from a local horse camp: avoid pavement, eat apples, and do what feels good. She involved her boyfriend in the project as well, encouraging him to drive her to destinations on his motorcycle, from which she would then run home. In 1965, with her malamute puppy Moot for a companion, she drove across country in her Volkswagen van, running and camping along the way; through this process, she gradually increased her running distance to over forty miles.

Having moved to California, Gibb wrote to the Boston Athletic Association in 1966, to request a marathon entry form. She received a curt reply from race director Will Cloney, stating that women were physically unable to run twenty-six miles and hence were ineligible to compete in the Boston Marathon under international sports rules. More determined than ever, Gibb continued to train. Four days before the 1966 race, she boarded a bus and made the trip home to Massachusetts, eating apples and bus station chili the whole way. When she arrived, she announced her plans to run in the race, despite having been told that she was ineligible. The following day, her mother dropped her off near the starting line, with enough money for a cab-ride home.

Wearing a hooded sweatshirt, her brother's Bermuda shorts, and boys' running shoes, Gibb found a secluded wooded area near the starting line. When the gun sounded to start the race, she jumped into the pack of runners. At first she was afraid to remove her hood and reveal her identity, but Gibb soon found the other runners to be supportive, even going so far as to tell her that they wished their girlfriends and wives would run. When she finally discarded the thick sweatshirt, the watching crowds cheered her onward.

Gibb ran conservatively for the first two-thirds of the race, but the last third was a struggle. She was wearing new shoes, which had caused blisters, and following conventional wisdom of the period, she had eaten a heavy meal the night before the race and refrained from drinking any water during the run. In pain and dehydrated, Gibb knew she had to finish to prove that women could indeed run a marathon. The last three miles took her almost an hour to finish, but she ultimately completed them, finishing the race in a total of three hours and twenty minutes.

Although the Boston Marathon did not officially allow women to run until 1972, Gibb's run inspired women to participate unofficially, in the years before they were granted eligibility. Gibb's experience with gender discrimination did not end with her boundary-breaking run; in 1969 she was denied admission to medical school because the admissions committee determined that her physical attractiveness would distract the male students. She later went to law school and continued her work as an artist. A successful lawyer and sculptor,

Considered to have smaller hearts and lungs than men and unable to bear the strain, women were not allowed to compete in many track and field events. Although women's track and field events were added to the Olympics in 1932, women were not allowed to compete in marathons until 1984. Courtesy Library of Congress, Prints & Photographs Division.

she designed the trophies awarded to the female marathon medalists in the 1984 Olympics. Today Gibb continues to run.

Further Reading

Brant, John. "A Woman's Place." *Runner's World* 36.5 (May 2001): 66–68.

Cimons, Marlene. "Four Who Dared: They Changed Marathoning Forever." *Runner's World* 31.4 (April 1996): 72–79.

Gonyo v. Drake University (1993)

Similar to the ***Kelley v. Board of Trustees, University of Illinois*** (1995) case, the plaintiffs in *Gonyo v. Drake University* asserted that the university committed reverse discrimination. Citing budgetary limitations, Drake University chose to discontinue its men's wrestling team, rather than expanding its women's sports program, in an effort to meet the proportionality prong of the Three-Part Test for compliance with Title IX; over 75 percent of Drake's athletes were male, whereas men composed only 42 percent of the overall student enrollment. The Drake wrestlers filed a lawsuit, in the hope of having their team reinstated. In addition to claiming discrimination under both Title IX and the Fourteenth Amendment's Equal Protection Clause, the team members also claimed that the university had committed a breach of contract, since they had been recruited by Drake to wrestle.

Title IX does not protect an individual's right to participate in a particular sport, but instead requires that a school's proportion of athletes be in balance with that of its student body, with respect to gender. In the *Drake* case, the court found that the considerable overrepresentation of men in Drake's athlete population indicated the existence of ample opportunities for male students to participate in athletics. Thus, dropping men's wrestling from the school's athletic program was found not to be a Title IX violation, because the ratio of men to women in the athletic program, as a whole, still favored men. The court also determined the students' claim of discrimination under the Fourteenth Amendment's Equal Protection Clause to be invalid, due to Drake's status as a private university. It also dismissed the students' breach of contract claim, stating that no one at the university had ever guaranteed the athletes that the wrestling team would continue to exist. In the end, the school agreed to continue to honor the wrestlers' scholarships until their anticipated graduation dates, despite the lack of a wrestling team.

Further Reading

Brake, Deborah, and Elizabeth Catlin. "The Path of Most Resistance: The Long Road toward Gender Equity in Intercollegiate Athletics." *Duke Journal of Gender Law & Policy* 3 (Spring 1996) (available at http://www.law.duke.edu/journals/djglp/homepage/djgvol3.htm).

Gonyo v. Drake University, 837 F. Supp. 989 (S.D. Iowa 1993); 879 F. Supp. 1000 (S.D. Iowa 1995).

Grant, Christine H. B. (May 27, 1936–)

University of Iowa women's athletic director, Christine Grant, an expert on Title IX, was born in Scotland in May 1936. She served in her University of Iowa position from 1973 until her retirement in 2000. Through her continuous advocacy for Title IX and gender equity in sports, Grant helped to make the Iowa women's program one of the best in the country.

Grant began her career coaching field hockey and track at two Scotland high schools in 1956. After moving to Canada in 1961, she continued to coach high school field hockey, track, and basketball. In 1965 she helped to establish the first Canadian national field hockey tournament. She was named coach of Canada's Women's Field Hockey Team in 1963, and in 1971 was awarded the Ontario Sports Award for Outstanding Contributions to Canadian Amateur Sport. In 1973 Grant became the athletic director for women at the University of Iowa and, while there, succeeded in building a powerful program.

In addition to her work at the University of Iowa, Grant also served as an expert consultant in a variety of Title IX and sports discrimination cases, testifying before the Health, Education and Welfare Office for Civil Rights' Title IX Task Force. She was called as an expert witness in a number of legal cases against colleges and universities. Serving on the Board of Directors for the **National Association of Collegiate Women Athletic Administrators** (NACWAA), Grant worked to promote awareness of Title IX.

A founding member and former president of the **Association for Intercollegiate Athletics for Women** (AIAW) from 1979 to 1982, Grant has also served on the Advisory Board for the **Women's Sports Foundation** (WSF) since 1988. President of the NACWAA from 1987 to 1989, Grant was named the organization's National Administrator of the Year in 1993. She was also inducted into the Women's Institute on Sport and Education's Hall of Fame in 1994 and received the NCAA Honda Award of Merit for Outstanding Achievement in Women's Collegiate Athletics in 1998. The 2001 recipient of NACWAA's Lifetime Achievement Award, Grant currently teaches three athletic administration courses at the University of Iowa, while also serving as chair of the NACWAA's Gender Equity Committee.

Further Reading

Oglesby, Carole A., and Doreen L. Greenberg. *Encyclopedia of Women and Sport in America.* Phoenix, AZ: Oryx Press, 1998.

Skaine, Rosemarie. *Women College Basketball Coaches.* Jefferson, NC: McFarland, 2001.

Green, Edith Louise Starrett (January 17, 1910–April 21, 1987)

Oregon Congressional Representative Edith Green introduced a higher education bill that ultimately constituted the first legislative step toward the creation of Title IX. Green was born in Trent, South Dakota, but her family moved to Oregon when she was just six years old. Green graduated from the University of Oregon in 1939 and taught school in Salem, Oregon. She became involved in politics in 1952, when she became director of public relations for the Oregon Education Association. She was among the first women to be elected to Congress, serving from 1955 until her retirement in 1975. Quickly earning the nickname "Mrs. Education," Green also served as an advisory board member for the **Women's Equity Action League** (WEAL).

In June and July of 1970, Green served as chair of a subcommittee dealing with higher education, which drafted a bill prohibiting gender discrimination in education and held congressional hearings on the history of women's employment and other issues, with respect to the profession of education. The first version of this bill was part of a larger measure to amend Titles VI and VII of the 1964 Civil Rights Act. Green proposed a change to Title VII, the legislation that prohibits discrimination in employment based on race, color, religion, sex, or national origin, which would extend that guarantee to employees of educational institutions. The subcommittee's proposed amendment to Title VI, which prohibits discrimination based on race, color, or national origin to any programs receiving federal funding, sought to add a prohibition against sex discrimination to this list. As debate over these issues continued, African American leaders began to voice concerns that amending Title VI would weaken enforcement of the law, so Green proposed a new Title, independent of both Titles VI and VII; this legislation became Title IX.

In addition to her work in higher education, Green held a number of important posts, including delegate to the 1959 NATO Conference and the 1964 and 1966 UNESCO General Conferences. She was also a member of the Presidential Commission on the Status of Women and proposed the Equal Pay Act, which was signed into law by President John F. Kennedy in 1963. Green continued an active life of service after her retirement from Congress, serving as professor of government at Warner Pacific College and on the Oregon Board of Higher Education. She died in her home in Portland in 1987.

Further Reading

Rosenberg-Dishman, Marie C. Barovic. "Women in Politics: A Comparative Study of Congresswomen Edith Green and Julia Butler Hansen." PhD dissertation, University of Washington, 1973.

Ross, Naomi V. "Congresswoman Edith Green on Federal Aid to Schools and Colleges." DEd dissertation, Pennsylvania State University, 1980.

Grove City College v. Bell (1984)

By 1978 every postsecondary school receiving federal money was required to comply with Title IX and to demonstrate this compliance by filing a letter with the federal government. The administrators of Grove City College, a private institution in Pennsylvania receiving no direct federal money, determined that their school was not obligated to file a compliance letter because it did not fall under the jurisdiction of Title IX. However, Grove City students did receive Better Education Opportunity Grants (BEOGs), awards supported by federal funds. The Office for Civil Rights contended that receipt of these funds, even indirectly, was sufficient to require the school to comply with Title IX. Unable to convince the college to alter its stance on compliance, the Office for Civil Rights initiated a moratorium on BEOGs to Grove City College students. The college responded with a lawsuit.

Two important questions arose in the *Grove City College* case. First, did the word "program" in Title IX refer to an institution as a whole, or just to the particular part of an institution receiving federal funds? Second, were schools receiving federal monies still required to comply with Title IX, even if they received these funds only indirectly? The case was argued on November 29,

1983, and the Supreme Court delivered its decision almost three months later, on February 28, 1984. The ruling was, in effect, split, and it profoundly affected the strength of Title IX for the next four years. In examining whether indirect federal funds were sufficient to maintain Title IX jurisdiction, the Court upheld the broad scope of the law, answering affirmatively: Indirectly receiving federal funds did indeed mean that an institution would be required to comply with Title IX. Conversely, the Court's decision on the question of whether Title IX applied to entire institutions, or only to the portions of those institutions actually receiving federal money, greatly reduced Title IX's strength and influence. If a department received no federal grants or other forms of funding, then the women studying in it could be discriminated against at will and would have no legal recourse whatsoever.

The Court's decision was devastating for collegiate athletics, because athletics departments rarely, if ever, received federal funds. Furthermore, any financial aid received to fund an athlete only resulted in the financial aid department being placed under Title IX jurisdiction, not the athletics department. Both Civil Rights and women's groups were outraged by the ruling. As a result of the *Grove* decision, female athletes found their scholarships, and even their entire teams, cut. Numerous Office for Civil Rights complaints and lawsuits were also dropped, as a result of the ruling. Four years later, the *Grove* decision was reversed by the 1988 **Civil Rights Restoration Act**, which was passed over the veto of President Ronald Reagan.

Further Reading

Carpenter, Linda Jean, and R. Vivan Acosta. *Title IX.* Champaign, IL: Human Kinetics, 2005.

Grove City College v. Bell, 465 U.S. 555 (1984); 104 S. Ct. 1211 (1984).

Zirkel, Perry A., Sharon Nalbone Richardson, and Steven S. Goldberg. *A Digest of Supreme Court Decisions Affecting Education.* Bloomington, IN: Phi Delta Kappa Educational Foundation, 2001.

Gunter, Sue (May 22, 1939–August 4, 2005)

Women's basketball coach Sue Gunter was born in Walnut Grove, Mississippi, in May 1941. As a guard for her high school team, Gunter went on to play basketball for Nashville Business College from 1958 to 1962 in the **Amateur Athletic Union** (AAU) league. She was awarded All-America honors in 1960 and played on the U.S. National Team against the Soviet Union from 1960 to 1962.

After college, Gunter took her first professional coaching position at Middle Tennessee State University in 1962. During her two years there, she led the Lady Blue Raiders to two undefeated seasons. In 1964 Gunter began coaching at Stephen F. Austin University in Texas. In her sixteen years as head coach of the Ladyjacks, Gunter led the team to a 266–87 record and four top ten national rankings. Under her leadership, the Ladyjacks won four state titles and five **Association of Intercollegiate Athletics for Women** (AIAW) championships. While at Stephen F. Austin, Gunter also coached softball, tennis, and track and field, in addition to basketball. She left her post as head coach in 1980 and served as Director of Women's Athletics for the next two years.

While at Stephen F. Austin, Gunter also participated in Olympic women's basketball. Assistant coach for the 1976 Olympic team in Montreal, Gunter was named head coach for the 1980 team, but the United States eventually boycotted the games. In 1982 Gunter returned to collegiate coaching at Louisiana State University, where she remained until her retirement in 2004. During her twenty-two season career at Louisiana State, Gunter led the Lady Tigers to thirteen **National Collegiate Athletic Association** (NCAA) tournaments and three Elite Eight championships. The team also won a Southeastern Conference (SEC) title and played in the NCAA Final Four. Gunter is the winningest coach in LSU history and the third winningest coach in NCAA women's history.

Named an SEC Coach of the Year for 1997 and 1999, Gunter has received a number of awards, including the 1994 Carol Eckman Award. She was named Louisiana Coach of the Year four times, designated **Women's Basketball Coaches Association** Regional Coach of the Year in 1999 and 2003, and elected to both the Women's Basketball Hall of Fame and the Naismith Memorial Basketball Hall of Fame. Gunter died of respiratory problems in August 2005, at the age of sixty-six.

Further Reading

Douchant, Mike. *Encyclopedia of College Basketball.* New York: Gale Research, 1995.

LSU Women's Basketball Media Guide, 2003–2004. Baton Rouge: Louisiana State University, 2003.

Guthrie, Janet (March 7, 1938–)

Race car driver Janet Guthrie was born in Iowa City, Iowa, in March 1938, to W. Lain and Jean Ruth Guthrie. The family then moved to Miami, Florida, where Guthrie took up flying. Flying her first plane at thirteen years old, she obtained her pilot's license just four years later. After attending the University of Michigan, Guthrie received a physics degree in 1960 and began working as an aerospace engineer for Republic Aviation Corporation in New York. While there, she was one of four women to pass a NASA examination for the astronaut-scientist program. She was later denied entry into the program because she lacked a PhD.

Guthrie started racing after buying her first sports car, a used Jaguar XK 140. She learned much about automobile mechanics and later rebuilt the car. In 1964 Guthrie began entering races, placing first in the Long Island Sports Car

Association's race. Discovering that she loved racing, Guthrie left her job in 1967 to focus on the sport. Though she continuously proved that she could race, she had trouble finding sponsors, because many in the male-dominated sport were not inclined to support a female driver.

Unable to find a sponsor, Guthrie bought a car of her own to race. She began rebuilding her Toyota Celica, so that she could participate in the upcoming Toyota 2.5 Challenge Series. Though the race was canceled before her car was ready, Guthrie continued to race and to look for sponsors. Her break came in 1976, when car designer and owner Rolla Vollstedt invited her to drive one of his cars in the Indianapolis 500. Guthrie was unable to race in the event, however, because she failed to pass the qualifying round.

That same year, Guthrie was invited to race in the National Association for Stock Car Auto Racing (NASCAR) Winston Cup series. Racing in the Charlotte World 600, Guthrie became the first woman to participate in a NASCAR race. She finished fifteenth out of twenty-seven and went on to race in four more NASCAR contests that year. Vollstedt was so impressed with Guthrie that he gave her a newer and faster car to drive in the Indianapolis 500 the following year. In 1977 Guthrie became the first woman to race in the event. She finished in twenty-ninth place, due to engine trouble, but went on to compete in several other Indianapolis 500s over the years. Despite a fractured wrist, Guthrie finished in ninth place in the 1978 race.

The first woman to race in both the Indianapolis 500 and NASCAR events, Guthrie earned the title of Top Rookie at the Daytona 500 race in 1978. She was subsequently inducted into the International Women's Sports Hall of Fame, and her helmet and racing suit are held at the Smithsonian Institution. In 2006 she was inducted into the International Motorsports Hall of Fame.

Further Reading

Guthrie, Janet. *Janet Guthrie: A Life at Full Throttle*. Wilmington, DE: Sport Media Publishers, 2005.

H

In 1980 a group of Temple University female athletes, led by badminton player Rollin Haffer, backed by the **National Women's Law Center** (NWLC) and Trial Lawyers for Public Justice, filed a lawsuit against their school. Women composed 42 percent of Temple's varsity athletes but received only 13 percent of the school's athletic budget. The plaintiffs further claimed that the women's teams' equipment and facilities were inadequate.

Although it carries no legal significance because the parties eventually settled out of court, the eight-year-long *Haffer* case is important for a number of reasons. First, *Haffer* was the first Title IX athletics case to be taken directly to court, bypassing the traditional first step of filing a complaint with the Office for Civil Rights. Second, because during the course of the *Haffer* case the Supreme Court had issued its *Grove City College v. Bell* (1984) decision, which effectively placed athletics programs outside the reach of Title IX by narrowly defining "program" as a department or unit directly receiving federal funds, the *Haffer* legal team changed its strategy and claimed that Temple was violating the female athletes' Fourteenth Amendment rights, as well as the state of Pennsylvania's Equal Rights Amendment. The legal team also worked to have the case designated as a class action suit and began meeting with other female athletes; Temple attempted to halt the class action suit but was unsuccessful and decided to settle with the plaintiffs by diverting more money to women's athletics. Thus, the *Haffer* case demonstrated that a plaintiff could claim discrimination in an athletic program by private right of action. Further, *Haffer* also set the precedent of comparing the benefits received by both male and female athletes as an acceptable method for comparing women's and men's programs to determine discrimination and set forth that lack of funding is no excuse for discrimination. The *Haffer* case therefore helped to lay the foundation for developing techniques for ascertaining equity in the treatment of athletes.

Further Reading

Carpenter, Linda Jean, and R. Vivian Acosta. *Title IX*. Champaign, IL: Human Kinetics, 2005.

Haffer v. Temple University, 678 F. Supp. 517, 527 (E.D. Penn. 1988).

Suggs, Welch. *A Place on the Team: The Triumph and Tragedy of Title IX*. Princeton, NJ: Princeton University Press, 2005.

Harris Stewart, Lusia "Lucy" (February 10, 1955–)

The first woman to be drafted by a men's professional basketball team and the first to score in an Olympic women's basketball game, Lucy Harris Stewart was born on a farm in Minter City, Mississippi, in February 1955. From an early age, Harris played basketball with her siblings, and she went on to become captain of the girls' basketball team at Amanda Elzy High School. She was named the team's most valuable player for three consecutive seasons and was also named a state All-Star.

Enrolling at Delta State University in 1973, Harris began playing on the college's recently reestablished women's basketball team under coach **Margaret Wade**. While at Delta State, Harris scored almost 3,000 points, was named an All-American three times, and was designated the national tournament's most valuable player. In 1975, along with becoming Delta State's first African American homecoming queen, Harris played on both the World University team and the Pan-American team. She played on the first U.S. Olympic women's team the following year. While at the Montreal Olympics, Harris scored the first goal in the history of women's Olympic basketball. In 1977 she received the Broderick Award, an honor given to the most outstanding college basketball player. That same year, she was also presented with the Honda Broderick Cup, given to the best college athlete in any sport.

After her graduation from Delta State in 1977, the New Orleans Jazz, a professional men's team, selected the six-foot three-inch, 185-pound Harris in the seventh round of the National Basketball Association (NBA) draft. Thinking it was a joke, she never played for the team. She was selected as a free agent for the Houston Angels in the **Women's Professional Basketball League** (WBL) the following year. She played briefly for the Houston Angels in 1980, resigning after she became pregnant.

Harris later returned to Delta State University, where she worked as an assistant basketball coach and admissions counselor. After receiving her master's degree in education in 1984, Harris left the university to coach high school basketball in Ruleville, Mississippi. In 1992 she became the first African American woman inducted into the Naismith Memorial Basketball Hall of Fame.

Further Reading

Douchant, Mike. *Encyclopedia of College Basketball.* New York: Gale Research, 1995.

Sherrow, Victoria. *Encyclopedia of Women and Sports.* Santa Barbara, CA: ABC-CLIO, 1996.

Horner v. Kentucky High School Athletic Association (2000)

In 1992 twelve slow-pitch softball players, led by Lorie Ann Horner, sued the Kentucky State Board of Elementary and Secondary Education and the Kentucky High School Athletic Association for violating Title IX and the Fourteenth Amendment's Equal Protection Cause by refusing to create a fast-pitch softball program. Since the **National Collegiate Athletic Association** (NCAA) only extends softball scholarships to fast-pitch players, the plaintiffs claimed that by only being able to play slow-pitch softball, their chances to compete for college fast-pitch softball scholarships were lessened, especially in comparison with the male students' ability to compete for baseball scholarships. The plaintiffs sought the establishment of a fast-pitch softball program, as well as compensatory damages.

The Kentucky school board and the athletic association defended their decision by citing their "25 percent" rule, which stated that new sports would not be sanctioned unless 25 percent of the schools under their jurisdiction were willing to offer the sport. In 1992 only 17 percent of the schools had indicated an interest in fast-pitch softball. The district court held that the defendants had offered equal opportunities and had allowed for students to participate in the sports that were offered without restriction. Thus, they contended that they had violated neither Title IX nor the Equal Protection Clause. The plaintiffs appealed, and the 6th Circuit Court affirmed the district court's ruling that the defendants had not violated the Equal Protection Clause, but reversed the lower court's decision on the Title IX issue, remanding the case back to the district court for reconsideration.

The district court again ruled in favor of the defendants. By the time the case was heard by the district court for the second time, the state of Kentucky had passed an amendment requiring schools having or intending to develop athletic teams similar to those for which the NCAA had scholarships to implement sports that carried the potential of players earning NCAA scholarships. This included women's fast-pitch softball. The amendment made Horner's claim for damages moot. The district court also found that the plaintiffs had not demonstrated intentional discrimination on the part of the school

59

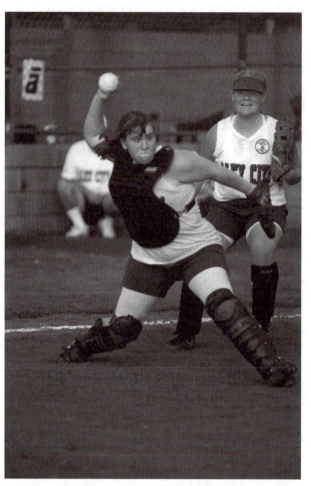

Fast-pitch softball first became an Olympic event in 1996, though today it is in danger of being eliminated from the games. Photo from authors' private collection.

board or of the athletic association. This decision was affirmed by the 6th Circuit Court.

Further Reading

Bonnette, Valerie McMurtrie. *Title IX and Intercollegiate Athletics: How It All Works—In Plain English.* San Diego, CA: Good Sports, Inc., 2004.

Horner v. Kentucky High School Athletic Association, 206 F.3d 685 (6th Cir. 2000).

Mitten, Matthew J., and Paul M. Anderson, eds. "*Horner v. Kentucky High School Athletic Association.*" *You Make the Call: National Sports Law Institute of Marquette University Law School Newsletter* 2.4 (Spring 2000) (available at http://law.marquette.edu/cgi-bin/site.pl?2130&pageID=495).

Hyman, Flora Jean "Flo" (July 29, 1954–January 24, 1986)

Olympic volleyball player Flora "Flo" Hyman was born in Inglewood, California, in July 1954, to George W. and Warrene Hyman. Having played on her high school volleyball team, as well as for the South Bay Spikers, Hyman earned a spot on the U.S. National Volleyball team in 1974. That same year, after graduating from Morningside High School, she enrolled at the University of Houston, where she received a volleyball scholarship—the university's first athletic scholarship ever awarded to a woman. While at the University of Houston, Hyman received the Broderick Sports Award from the **Association of Intercollegiate Athletics for Women** (AIAW), was a three-time All-American, and was named most valuable player on the national team in a 1979 game against Cuba. She graduated in 1980 with a degree in mathematics.

Because of the U.S. boycott of the 1980 Olympics, Hyman had to wait until the 1984 Games to realize her dream of playing in the Olympics. Her team won the silver medal that year in Los Angeles, California. At thirty, she was the oldest member of the team. Hyman left the national team in 1985 and moved to Japan to play in a volleyball league there. During a game the following year, Hyman collapsed and was taken to the hospital, where she was pronounced dead from Marfan's Syndrome, a rare disease that enlarges the heart and ruptures the aorta.

In memory of Hyman's work as a volleyball player and as an advocate of Title IX and increased opportunities for women in sports, the **National Girls and Women in Sport Day** (NGWSD) was established in her honor in 1987. The **Women's Sports Foundation** also created the Flo Hyman Memorial Award, a distinction that is given to the athlete who most demonstrates the volleyball star's "dignity, spirit, and commitment to excellence."

Further Reading

Markel, Robert, and Nancy Brooks. *For the Record: Women in Sports*. New York: World Almanac Publications, 1985.

Woolum, Janet. *Outstanding Women Athletes: Who They Are and How They Influenced Sports in America*. Phoenix, AZ: Oryx Press, 1998.

J

Jackson v. Birmingham Board of Education (2005)

In 1999 Roderick Jackson was hired by Ensley High School, in Birmingham, Alabama, to teach physical education and serve as the girls' basketball coach. Jackson soon noticed a variety of inequities in the treatment of the boys' and girls' teams. For instance, the girls' team was not allowed to practice in the new gym and instead had to use an older gym with outdated equipment and no heating. Furthermore, the boys' team was transported by bus to away games, whereas the girls had to make their own travel arrangements. The girls were also denied a portion of the money donated by the City of Birmingham for school athletics, and unlike the boys' team, they were not allowed to keep any of the money generated by admissions and concessions at their games. Even the simplest of amenities were denied to the girls' team; in one instance, Jackson was forced to use a screwdriver to break into the school's ice machine to make an ice pack for an injured player.

After informing the school's administration of the situation, Jackson soon began to receive negative evaluations and was eventually relieved of his coaching duties in May 2001. He immediately filed suit against the Birmingham Board of Education, arguing that the school board had violated Title IX by retaliating against him for making an accusation of discriminatory practices. The *Jackson* case was thus unique because it raised the question of whether Title IX's implication of private right of action extended beyond direct victims of sex discrimination, to also protect those who report discrimination against others.

Both the federal district court and the appellate court determined that Jackson could not sue under Title IX because the legislation did not explicitly mention retaliation. They further stated that even if Title IX had mentioned retaliation, Jackson would still be ineligible to sue because he was only an indirect victim. On October 6, 2003, the Supreme Court agreed to hear the *Jackson* case. The Birmingham Board of Education maintained that the Supreme Court "should not interpret Title IX to prohibit retaliation because it was not on notice that it could be held liable for retaliating against those who complain of Title IX violations." The Court disagreed, however, maintaining that "funding recipients have been on notice that they could be subjected to private suits for intentional sex discrimination under Title IX since 1979," with *Cannon v. University of Chicago.* In a 5–4 vote, the Supreme Court reversed the decision of the lower courts, ruling that Title IX did offer protection from retaliation for individuals reporting sex discrimination. In handing down this decision, the Supreme Court established four principles that would affect the future of Title IX: (1) that its language should be broadly construed; (2) that retaliation for reporting discrimination is, itself, considered discrimination; (3) that guarding against retaliation is essential for ensuring Title IX's effectiveness; and (4) that the law protects indirect, as well as direct, victims of discrimination.

Further Reading

"For the Record: Title IX Dispute." Episode on Alabama Public Television, original air date December 7, 2004.

Jackson v. Birmingham Board of Education, 544 U.S. 167 (2005); 309 F.3d 1333 (11th Cir. 2002), *reversed and remanded.*

Lipka, Sara. "High Court Expands Protections of Title IX." *The Chronicle of Higher Education* 51.31 (April 8, 2005): A1 (available at http://chronicle.com/free/v51/i31/31a00101.htm).

National Women's Law Center. "Statement of Roderick Jackson" (http://www.nwlc.org/details.cfm?id=1905&section=newsroom).

National Women's Law Center. "Supreme Court's Decision in *Jackson v. Birmingham Board of Education* Enhances Protection of Title IX" (http://www.nwlc.org/pdf/FactSheet_JacksonSupremeCourt.pdf).

Javits Amendment

Proposed by New York Democratic Senator Jacob R. Javits in June 1974, the Javits Amendment, Section 844 of the Education Amendments of 1974, called for the recognition that the dollar amount spent on particular sports was not necessarily a fair metric for gauging equity and compliance with Title IX, because some sports programs cost more to support and maintain than others. For example, proponents of the Javits Amendment argued that the cost of maintaining a football team, which includes many players, much equipment, a field and stadium, and many coaches and officials, costs more than maintaining a track and field team. The Javits Amendment thus called for the addition of the following text to Title IX: "with respect to intercollegiate athletics activities reasonable provisions considering the nature of particular sports." After a period of public comment, the Javits Amendment was accepted and implemented in the July 1975 document *Final Regulations Concerning Title IX and Scholastic-Collegiate Sports.*

The **National Collegiate Athletic Association** (NCAA), however, was furious about both the Javits Amendment and the previous year's failed **Tower Amendment**, which would have exempted revenue-generating sports from Title IX compliance, because the wording of each of these amendments would add explicit mention of collegiate sports to the legislation, thus weakening the NCAA's argument that athletics departments should be considered exempt from Title IX regulations because they did not directly receive federal money. Furthermore, the organization claimed that the regulations were vague. Women's groups viewed the Javits Amendment as a significant victory over the NCAA for the same reason. Because its language caused sports and gender equity to be explicitly linked in a federal law, the amendment ensured that Title IX would be construed as pertaining to collegiate athletics, including to those sports that produced revenue.

Further Reading

Senate Conference Rep. No. 1026, 93rd Cong., 2nd Sess. 4271 (1974).

Suggs, Welch. *A Place on the Team: The Triumph and Tragedy of Title IX.* Princeton, NJ: Princeton University Press, 2005.

Jaynes, Betty F. (1945–)

Founding member of the **Women's Basketball Coaches Association** (WBCA) and former chair of the U.S. Girls' and Women's Basketball Rules Committee, Betty F. Jaynes was named the WBCA's first chief executive officer in September 1996. She now serves as a consultant and liaison for the organization, overseeing the WBCA's legislative role with the **National Collegiate Athletic Association** (NCAA).

Born in Covington, Georgia, Jaynes played basketball at Newton County High School, where she lettered all four years and was named an all-state player two years in a row. She also earned a starting spot on the 1963 Class AA state championship team. She went on to receive a Bachelor of Science in physical education from Georgia College in 1967 and a master's degree in physical education from the University of North Carolina-Greensboro the following year. Upon her graduation, Jaynes became a physical education professor at Madison College, now James Madison University. In 1970 she was appointed head women's basketball coach. While there, Jaynes led her team to win the 1975 **Association for Intercollegiate Athletics for Women** (AIAW) Virginia state championship. She was also involved in the development of the Kodak Women's All-America Basketball Team. Jaynes remained at James Madison University until 1982, when she resigned in order to focus on her duties as executive director of the newly formed WBCA.

In her role as the WBCA's executive director, Jaynes relocated the organization's offices to Atlanta, Georgia, in 1985. She served as executive director for fifteen years and was then appointed chief executive officer in September 1996. Under her leadership, the WBCA's membership increased from approximately 200 members to more than 5,000 members, hailing from all levels of girls' and women's basketball. Jaynes now serves as a consultant for the WBCA, regarding the NCAA and Title IX compliance. Jaynes credits the Title IX legislation for her place on many athletic boards and for the increased sports opportunities and scholarships now provided to women and girls. In 1991 Jaynes founded and served as the first president of the Georgia Women's Intersport Network (Ga-WIN), established to promote public awareness for women's sports and Title IX.

A longtime leader in women's basketball, Jaynes serves on the Women's Basketball Hall of Fame Board of Directors and was a trustee for the Naismith Memorial Basketball Hall of Fame from 1990 to 2006. She is also a trustee and former vice president of the **Women's Sports Foundation** (WSF). In 2000 Jaynes was inducted into the Women's Basketball Hall of Fame, and in 2006 she received the Naismith Memorial Basketball Hall of Fame's Bunn Lifetime Achievement Award. She was also inducted into the Georgia Sports Hall of Fame in May 2007.

Further Reading

Skaine, Rosemarie. *Women College Basketball Coaches*. Jefferson, NC: McFarland, 2001.
Women's Basketball Coaches Association Web site (http://www.wbca.org/).

Johnson, Mamie "Peanut" (September 27, 1935–)

Born in 1935 to Gentry Harrison and Della Belton Havelow of Ridgeway, South Carolina, Mamie "Peanut" Johnson was the second woman to play in professional baseball's Negro League. Desiring to play baseball as a young child, Johnson learned to pitch by wrapping rocks in twine and masking tape and throwing them at birds. In 1943 she enrolled at New York University, where she studied medicine and engineering. She tried out for a spot in the **All-American Girls Professional Baseball League** (AAGPBL), but because she was African American, she was not allowed to play. In 1953 a former player in the Negro League introduced Johnson to the manager of the Indianapolis Clowns, and that season she began pitching for the Clowns, a team that also included players Connie Morgan and **Toni Stone**. Johnson stayed with the league, earning $700 per month, until it ultimately folded in 1955. Johnson earned her nickname "Peanut" during her first game with the Clowns. A batter from the opposing team commented that she would not be able to strike him out since she was no bigger than a peanut—Johnson only weighed 100 pounds. Johnson did strike out the batter and was known from then on as "Peanut."

After retiring from baseball in 1955, Johnson worked as a nurse in Washington DC. Although some continue to believe that women were only allowed into the Negro League for publicity purposes, it cannot be denied that Johnson was a leader in breaking through society's gender barriers, almost twenty years before the passage of Title IX.

Further Reading

Everbach, Tracy. "Breaking Baseball Barriers: The 1953–1954 Negro League and Expansion of Women's Public Roles." *American Journalism* 22.1 (Winter 2005): 13–33.

Johnson, Mamie. *A Strong Right Arm: The Story of Mamie "Peanut" Johnson.* New York: Dial Books, 2002.

K

Facing serious budget constraints in 1993, the University of Illinois decided to cut four varsity teams, men's swimming and fencing and men's and women's diving, from its athletic program. The university considered seven criteria in deciding which sports to terminate: the availability of regional and national championships, the teams' records of success at the university, the level of interest and participation in particular sports at the high school level, the level of spectator interest, the conditions of university facilities, gender and ethnic issues, and the overall cost of the sports. Female enrollment at the university was 44 percent, but women composed only approximately 24 percent of the school's athlete population. In order to avoid a Title IX violation, the university attempted to move toward correcting this imbalance when making its decision about which teams to cut. The men's swim team, however, filed suit, claiming that the school had violated Title IX and the Equal Protection Amendment because it had eliminated only the men's swim team, rather than both the men's and women's swim teams. The district court ruled in favor of the University of Illinois, and the men's swim team appealed to the 7th Circuit Court, which upheld the lower court's decision. The 7th Circuit Court reasoned that it was not a Title IX violation to drop men's swimming because, even after eliminating the men's swim team, men's overall participation in the University of Illinois's athletics program was still disproportional to their representation in the student body.

Further Reading

Bonnette, Valerie McMurtrie. *Title IX and Intercollegiate Athletics: How It All Works—In Plain English.* San Diego, CA: Good Sports, Inc., 2004.

Kelley v. Board of Trustees, University of Illinois, 35 F.3d 265 (7th Cir. 1994), *cert. denied,* 513 U.S. 1128 (1995).

King, Billie Jean Moffitt (November 22, 1943–)

The winner of thirty-nine Grand Slam singles titles, twenty Wimbledon titles, and nearly 700 career victories, Billie Jean King is perhaps best remembered for beating fifty-five-year-old men's Wimbledon champion Bobby Riggs in a nationally televised "Battle of the Sexes" in 1973. Born in Long Beach, California, the eldest child of Bill, a firefighter, and Betty Moffitt, a homemaker. King's interest in sport began while playing baseball with her father and her younger brother Randy, who later became a professional baseball player, as well as while playing football with neighborhood friends. When she was eleven, King's parents enrolled her in a local recreational tennis program, and she fell in love with the sport. By sixteen she was taking private lessons and was ranked fourth nationally. At seventeen she and partner Karen Hantze became the youngest doubles team to win the Wimbledon title. In 1965 she married law student Larry King; in the same year, she first achieved a number one ranking.

Using her position as the number one female tennis player in the world as leverage, King worked tirelessly to promote women's sports. Among her goals was equal pay for women athletes. In 1971 she became the first woman athlete to earn more than $100,000 playing her sport, but when the male winner of the 1972 U.S. Open was paid $15,000 more than King had received for winning the women's U.S. Open championship, she declared that she would not play the next year, if the discrepancy in prize money persisted; in 1973 the U.S. Open offered equal prize money for its male and female winners.

In 1973, King founded *womenSports* magazine, which later became *Women's Sports and Fitness,* as well as establishing the **Women's Sports Foundation** (WSF) with former swimmer **Donna de Varona**. King was also the driving force behind the Virginia Slims women's professional tennis circuit, and she was the first president of the Women's Tennis Association in 1973. Shortly after, in 1974, she accepted a challenge from men's tennis champion Bobby Riggs. Riggs had stated that women's game was so inferior to men's that he could beat the top women players even though he was fifty-five years old, and he did manage to defeat Margaret Court. After declining several times, King finally accepted Riggs' challenge, and in front of more than 30,000 spectators and an estimated 50 million television viewers, she soundly defeated him in straight sets, 6–4, 6–3, 6–3. This victory became symbolic of female athletes' struggle to participate in sports on an equal footing with men.

So important was King to women's sports that she was named *Sports Illustrated*'s Sportswoman of the Year in 1972, designated the Associated Press's Female Athlete of the Year in 1967 and 1973, and inducted into the Women's Sports Hall of Fame in 1980 and the International Tennis Hall of Fame in 1987. King used her athletic ability to draw attention to a variety of women's issues, and in 1990 *Life* magazine named her one of the "100 Most Important Americans of the 20th Century." She retired from competitive play in 1983, but has since remained active. In addition to writing, announcing, and hosting tennis clinics, King has coached Olympic tennis players and served as the director of World Team Tennis. In 2002 she was named a Women in Sports and Events (WISE) Woman of the Year. King continues to champion women's athletics, speaking out on issues of sport, gender equity, and Title IX.

Further Reading

Hahn, James, and Lynn Hahn. *King! The Sports Career of Billie Jean King.* Mankato, MN: Crestwood House, 1987.

King, Billie Jean, and Kim Chapin. *Billie Jean.* London: W.H. Allen, 1975.

Kremer, Andrea (February 25, 1959–)

Andrea Kremer, a sports reporter for both ESPN and NBC Sports, was born in February 1959 in Philadelphia, Pennsylvania. As a young child, Kremer quickly became a fan of football. At eight years old, she created "press kits" for the upcoming Super Bowl. After graduating from high school, she enrolled in the University of Pennsylvania, where she pursued a career as a ballet dancer, performing with the Pennsylvania Ballet. After graduating in 1980 with a Bachelor of Arts degree, Kremer was hired as sports editor for the *Main Line Chronicle,* a weekly newspaper in Ardmore, Pennsylvania. While at *Main Line,* Kremer wrote an article on NFL Films, the company that produces movies of football highlights for the National Football League. With her mother's encouragement, Kremer sent her resume to the company and was hired as a producer in 1984. She also served as cohost for the company's *This Is the NFL* and earned an Emmy nomination for her television special "Autumn Ritual."

In 1989 Kremer left NFL Films to join ESPN as a Chicago-based correspondent. In 1994 she left Chicago for Los Angeles and began working on programs such as *SportsCenter, Sunday NFL Countdown,* and *Monday Night Countdown.* Kremer received an Emmy for her work on *Sunday NFL Countdown.* She also worked on ESPN's *Outside the Lines* series and hosted *Sunday Conversations,* a series of forty-five minute interviews with leading athletes. Named *P.O.V. Magazine*'s best female sportscaster in 1997, Kremer has covered every Super Bowl game since 1985. Most recently, in April 2006, Kremer joined NBC Sports as the sideline and feature reporter for *NBC Sunday Night Football.*

Further Reading

ESPN. "Andrea Kremer Biography" (http://media.espn.com/MediaZone/bios/Talent/KremerAndrea.html).

The Pennsylvania Gazette. "Alumni Profile: Andrea Kremer" (http://www.upenn.edu/gazette/0597/0597pro2.html).

Krone, Julieanne Louise (July 24, 1963–)

Jockey Julie Krone, the first woman to win a title at a major track, was born in Benton Harbor, Michigan, in July 1964, to Don and Judi Krone. Having learned to ride at a young age, Krone loved racing horses around the family's Michigan home and entering local riding competitions. After working a summer job at the Kentucky Derby's Churchill Downs, Krone left high school and moved to Tampa, Florida, with her grandparents, where she continued to ride at the Tampa Bay Downs racetrack. Shortly after moving to Tampa, she won her first race and went on to place first in nine of the forty-eight races held at the Tampa track.

It was at Tampa Bay Downs that Krone met agent Chick Lang, who encouraged her to ride in Baltimore's Pimlico race. Despite her success in Tampa, Krone still faced difficulty finding horses to ride. While the sport had officially been opened to women in 1968, many owners and trainers still believed that women should not be jockeys. Nevertheless, Krone relentlessly pursued her goal, traveling to various racetracks with the hope of convincing others that she was a capable jockey. She proved successful in the 1980s, winning almost 2,000 races.

After a brief suspension for marijuana possession in 1983, Krone returned to racing after a sixty-day suspension, only to break her back when she fell off her horse during a race. With a total of 324 wins in 1987, she ranked sixth among jockeys in America. Continuing her tradition of breaking gender barriers in horse racing, Krone recovered and went on to race in the Breeders' Cup at Churchill Downs, becoming the first woman ever to race in that event. By the end of 1988, Krone was both the top-ranked and the winningest female jockey in the United States. In 1993 she became the first woman to win a Triple Crown race. Krone continued racing until 1999, when injuries forced her to retire. In August 2000 she became the first female jockey to be inducted into the National Thoroughbred Racing Hall of Fame.

Further Reading

Callahan, Dorothy M. *Julie Krone: A Winning Jockey*. Minneapolis, MN: Dillon Press, 1990.
Krone, Julie, and Nancy Ann Richardson. *Riding for My Life*. Boston: Little, Brown, 1995.
Savage, Jeff. *Julie Krone, Unstoppable Jockey*. Minneapolis, MN: Lerner Publications, 1996.

L

Lieberman, Nancy Elizabeth (July 1, 1958–)

Born in Brooklyn, New York, to Jerome and Renne Lieberman, basketball player Nancy Lieberman began playing the sport at an early age. Though girls were not allowed to play basketball in the New York Public School Athletic League, Lieberman was undeterred, playing her sport whenever and wherever she could. She joined the Far Rockaway High School team and also played for the New York Chuckles in Harlem during the summer. While still in high school, she was selected to play on the U.S. Pan-American team. In 1976 she played for the U.S. Olympic team, at the age of only seventeen, and became the youngest basketball player ever to win an Olympic medal.

After high school, Lieberman enrolled at Old Dominion University in Virginia. Playing on the school's women's basketball team, she won three All-American titles, as well as two team national titles. She was also the first two-time winner of the Wade Trophy for outstanding female college basketball player and a recipient of the Broderick Award for basketball's top female player. After college, she played on the U.S. national team in the World Women's Basketball Championship in 1979.

In 1981 Lieberman signed a three-year contract with the **Women's Professional Basketball League** (WBL) to play for the Dallas Diamonds. Accepting this contract made her the first woman in professional basketball to sign for more than $100,000. In her first year with the Dallas Diamonds, she was named both All-Pro and Rookie of the Year. After the league folded in 1981, she worked as trainer and motivator for tennis great Martina Navratilova and wrote a book about women's basketball. In 1984 she joined the newly-created Women's American Basketball Association (WABA) as the first draft pick for the Dallas Diamonds. This league also folded, but Lieberman rebounded quickly, playing for the United States Basketball League in Massachusetts, and hence becoming the first woman to play in a men's professional basketball league.

When the **Women's National Basketball Association** (WNBA) was established in 1997, Lieberman played for the Phoenix Mercury during the league's first season. She then became the head coach and general manager of the WNBA's Detroit Shock for three seasons, before being named head coach of the National Women's Basketball League's Dallas Fury in 2004. Lieberman currently works as a basketball analyst for ESPN and conducts basketball camps for boys and girls during the summer.

Further Reading

Lieberman-Cline, Nancy. *Lady Magic: The Autobiography of Nancy Lieberman-Cline.* New York: Sagamore Publishing, 1991.

Lopez, Nancy Marie (January 6, 1957–)

Nancy Lopez, one of the most successful women golfers of all time, was born in Torrance, California, to Domingo, a body shop owner, and Marina Lopez, a homemaker, in January 1957. The family later moved to Roswell, New Mexico. Lopez was introduced to golf by her parents; her father played for fun, while her mother had taken up the sport to help alleviate a lung disorder. With little money for a babysitter, the couple would take their young daughter to the course with them. The family had to travel to Albuquerque to play, however, because no local courses permitted Mexican American golfers.

Having played since she was seven years old, Lopez won her first tournament at the age of nine. Just three years later, she won the New Mexico State Women's Amateur Championship. By the time she was a teenager, Lopez had become the highest rated amateur golfer in the world. Playing on her high school's all-male golf team, she was instrumental in helping the team win a state championship, and during her senior year, she placed second at the Women's Open, winning $7,040.

Lopez won an athletic scholarship to the University of Tulsa in Oklahoma, where her coach encouraged her to play in the U.S. Women's Open as an amateur; she finished in second place. During her sophomore year, her studies suffered, and she left school to concentrate on golf, joining the Ladies Professional Golf Association (LPGA) in 1977. Lopez won nine tournaments during her first full professional season and was named both Rookie of the Year and Player of the Year. By 1983 she had achieved a career earnings of a million dollars, and by 1987 she had won thirty-four tournaments, thus qualifying for induction into the LPGA Hall of Fame.

In 1997 Lopez won her last tournament—her forty-eighth career victory. In 2000 she established "The Nancy Lopez Award" to be presented each year to the best female amateur golfer. Also in 2000, she became a board member and spokesperson for the Albany, Georgia, chapter of The First Tee, an affiliate of the World Golf Foundation, which seeks to provide affordable access to golf for all, especially young people. Lopez also works as an editor for *Golf for Women* magazine and has established her own company, the Nancy Lopez Golf Company. She has received many honors, including the 1992 **Flo Hyman** Award and the 1998 Bob Jones Award, and in 1991 her elementary school was renamed Nancy Lopez Elementary School.

Further Reading

Hahn, James. *Nancy Lopez: Golfing Pioneer.* St. Paul, MN: EMC Corp., 1979.

Lopez, Nancy, and Peter Schwed. *The Education of a Woman Golfer.* New York: Simon and Schuster, 1979.

Lopiano, Donna (September 11, 1946–)

Donna Lopiano, executive director of the **Women's Sports Foundation** (WSF), was born in Stamford, Connecticut, in 1946. Unable to play Little League Baseball because she was a girl, Lopiano grew up determined to fight for equal opportunities for women in sport.

When she was fifteen years old, Lopiano began playing for the Raybestos Brakettes, a local women's softball team in Stratford, Connecticut. She was a pitcher with the team for the next ten years and was an American Softball Association (ASA) All-American nine times. She was also voted most valuable player three times in the ASA National Championships. Lopiano was inducted into the ASA Hall of Fame in 1983. In addition to softball, she also played basketball, volleyball, and field hockey, participating in twenty-six national championships.

Lopiano attended Southern Connecticut State University, graduating with a degree in physical education in 1968. She went on to receive both a master's degree and a doctorate from the University of Southern California. She took her first job in 1972, the same year Title IX was signed, as the assistant athletic director at Brooklyn College, where she coached both men's and women's volleyball. She then moved on to become the women's athletic director at the University of Texas at Austin in 1975. Under Lopiano's administration, the University of Texas won eighteen NCAA women's titles. In her seventeen-year tenure at the University of Texas, Lopiano's budget for women's programs increased from just $57,000 to more than $4 million. While at the University of Texas, Lopiano was twice named Administrator of the Year by the **National Association of Collegiate Women Athletic Administrators** (NACWAA).

Lopiano became the chief executive officer of the Women's Sports Foundation in 1992, the same year she received the **National Association for Girls and Women in Sport's** Guiding Woman in Sport Award. Named one of *Sporting*

News's 100 most influential people in sports, Lopiano has long been dedicated to promoting Title IX compliance in school athletics programs. *College Sports* magazine listed Lopiano as one of the country's fifty most influential people in college sports in 1997. Past president of the **Association of Intercollegiate Athletics for Women** (AIAW), Lopiano is the author of numerous books on women and sports, and she contributed to Jane Gottesman's 2001 project *Game Face: What Does a Female Athlete Look Like?* Honored with the Lifetime Achievement Award from the NACWAA, Lopiano has also served on the **National Collegiate Athletic Association**'s Gender Equity Task Force.

Further Reading

Johnson, Anne Janette. *Great Women in Sports*. Detroit, MI: Visible Ink Press, 1996.

Women's Sports Foundation. "Donna Lopiano Biography" (http://www.womenssports foundation.org/cgi-bin/iowa/contrib.html?record=3).

Lowrey v. Texas A&M University System dba Tarleton State (1997)

An employee of Tarleton State University since 1977, Jan Lowrey filed suit against the university in 1994 under Title IX, claiming that Tarleton was practicing sex discrimination in its employment of staff in its women's athletic programs. During her time at Tarleton, Lowrey served as a physical education instructor, head women's basketball coach, and women's athletic coordinator, but she was ultimately removed from the last position. In 1993 she applied for the position of athletic director but was not selected. Lowrey claimed that her dismissal from the position of women's athletic coordinator and her failure to be appointed athletic director were the result of her having served on a gender equity task force that was responsible for identifying Title VII and IX violations. She contended that the complaints she had lodged about inequities in Tarleton's athletic programs had led the school to retaliate against her. Her case established that Title IX does provide private right of action for individuals to sue on the basis of alleged retaliation for reporting Title IX violations.

Further Reading

Carpenter, Linda Jean, and R. Vivian Acosta. *Title IX*. Champaign, IL: Human Kinetics, 2005.

Lowrey v. Texas A&M University System, 117 F.3d 242 (5th Cir. 1997).

Ludtke, Melissa (1951–)

Sports journalist Melissa Ludtke, the first female reporter to be allowed into a men's locker room, was born in Iowa City, Iowa, in 1951, to James and Jean Ludtke. While growing up in Amherst, Massachusetts, Ludtke played several sports, including basketball, volleyball, and tennis. After high school, she went on to attend Mills College and Wellesley College, graduating from the latter with a degree in art history. Intent on obtaining a teaching certificate, Ludtke enrolled in Smith College in 1973. While at Smith, Ludtke's career plans changed, and she developed an interest in sports broadcasting.

In 1974 Ludtke was hired as a researcher for *Sports Illustrated* magazine. She soon began concentrating on baseball, writing a number of articles and stories on the sport. In 1977 Ludtke was assigned to cover the World Series, which featured the New York Yankees and the Los Angeles Dodgers. Though she had initially garnered permission to interview players in the locker room, Major League Baseball Commissioner Bowie Kuhn vetoed the decision and denied Ludtke access to the locker room. Ludtke and *Sports Illustrated* attempted to negotiate with Kuhn, but to no avail. Ludtke and Time Inc., publisher of *Sports Illustrated*, filed a lawsuit against Commissioner Kuhn and the Yankees, demanding that locker rooms be open to women reporters. In September of the following year, federal judge Constance Baker Motley ruled that all sports reporters, regardless of gender, should have equal access to locker rooms.

Ludtke left *Sports Illustrated* in 1979 to work as a researcher for CBS News and *Time* magazine. She is the author of the 1997 book *On Our Own: Unmarried Motherhood in America* and is currently the editor of *Nieman Reports*, a journal published by Harvard University's Nieman Foundation. Ludtke received the **Association for Women in Sports Media's** Mary Garber Pioneer Award in 2003.

Further Reading

Ludtke, Melissa, and Anne G. Ritchie. *Interviews with Melissa Ludtke*. Washington, DC: The Washington Press Club Foundation, 1994.

Ludtke v. Kuhn, 461 F. Supp. 86 (D.N.Y. 1978).

Washington Press Club Foundation. *Women in Journalism: Oral Histories of Pioneer Journalists*. Washington, DC: The Foundation, 1987–1994.

M

Mercer v. Duke University (1999)

In the fall of 1994, Yorktown Heights High School all-state football kicker Heather Sue Mercer tried out as a walk-on kicker for the Duke University football team. Mercer did not make the team, but she did become a team manager and also participated in practice sessions and drills. An excellent kicker, Mercer was chosen in 1995 by the football team's seniors to play in an intra-squad scrimmage. The game ended with Mercer kicking the winning field goal. The kick was later shown on ESPN, and head football coach Fred Goldsmith told both Mercer and the media that she had made the team. She was listed on the team roster filed with the NCAA and included in the team's yearbook; however, Mercer was not allowed to participate in any of the 1995 games. She was also not allowed to attend the team's summer camp or to don a uniform and sit on the sidelines with her teammates. In addition, she claimed that the head coach had made a number of offensive comments to her. Just before the 1996 season began, Mercer was dismissed from the team. In 1997 she sued Duke for a Title IX violation, claiming that she was removed from the team because she was a woman. She strengthened her claim by arguing that the coach had allowed less talented male kickers to remain on the team.

During the case's early hearings, the Duke lawyers won a dismissal, but Mercer appealed. The court hearing the appeal determined that it was acceptable for schools to have separate teams for men and women, if the activity was a contact sport, and also that schools were not required to allow women to try out for contact sports. However, the court also found that if a school did allow women to try out for a contact sport, then Title IX would apply. The case was remanded back to the trial court, where a jury found that Duke had discriminated against Mercer on the basis of gender. She was awarded $1 in compensatory damages and $2 million in punitive damages. Duke, however, appealed, and the Fourth Circuit Court of Appeals ruled that Title IX did not allow for punitive damages that were unsupported by compensatory damages, despite the fact that ten years earlier, the Supreme Court had made no exclusion in *Franklin* for the awarding of punitive damages under Title IX. Thus, the case concluded with Mercer being awarded her $1 in compensatory damages.

Further Reading.

Anderson, Paul M., and Karri Zwicker, eds. "Mercer v. Duke." *You Make the Call: National Sports Law Institute of Marquette University Law School Newsletter* 2.2 (Fall 1999) (available at http://law.marquette.edu/cgi-bin/site.pl?2130&pageID=497).

Carpenter, Linda Jean, and R. Vivian Acosta. *Title IX.* Champaign, IL: Human Kinetics, 2005.

Mercer v. Duke University, 190 F.3d 643 (4th Cir. 1999).

Mercer v. Duke: *The Verdict and Its Implications.* VHS. Duke Program in Public Law Luncheon Series, 2000.

Meyers, Ann Elizabeth (March 26, 1955–)

The first woman to sign a National Basketball Association (NBA) contract, Ann Meyers was born in March 1955 in San Diego, California, to Bob and Patricia Meyers. Already playing a variety of sports, including track and field, Meyers began playing basketball, while attending Sonora High School in La Habra, California. During her senior year in 1974, she became the first high school player to win a spot on the U.S. national team. Upon graduating from high school, Meyers was offered a full athletic scholarship to the University of California at Los Angeles (UCLA), making her the first woman to garner such an award from that university.

Coached by **Billie Moore**, Meyers became the first four-time All-American women's basketball player. While in college, she played on the U.S. women's Olympic basketball team in 1976, the first year that women's basketball was included as an Olympic event. As she concluded her career at UCLA, having scored more points than any other player in the history of the school's basketball program, Meyers was selected as the university's Athlete of the Year in 1978. That same year she also received the Broderick Award for outstanding women's college player, the Broderick Cup for outstanding woman athlete, and the Woman Athlete of the Year award from the **National Association for Girls and Women in Sport**. After her graduation, Meyers' number was retired, and her team jersey was placed in the Naismith Memorial Basketball Hall of Fame.

Meyers was the first player drafted by the **Women's Professional Basketball League** (WBL), and she made history in 1980, when she signed a contract with the NBA's Indiana Pacers, making her the first woman to sign an NBA contract. Although she ultimately failed to make the team, Meyers began a career as a broadcaster for the Pacers. She soon signed with the WBL's New Jersey Gems, where she was voted Most Valuable Player during her first season. While playing for the Gems, Meyers continued her sports broadcasting career, serving as a commentator for women's basketball games.

In 1986 Meyers married baseball's Don Drysdale, who died of a heart attack in 1993. The first woman to be inducted into the UCLA Athletics Hall of Fame, Meyers is currently a women's basketball analyst for CBS, NBC, and ESPN.

Further Reading

Hult, Joan S., and Marianna Trekell. *A Century of Women's Basketball: From Frailty to Final Four*. Reston, VA: National Association for Girls and Women in Sport, 1991.

Porter, Karra. *Mad Seasons: The Story of the First Women's Professional Basketball League, 1978–1981*. Lincoln, NE: University of Nebraska Press, 2006.

Miller, Cheryl DeAnne (January 3, 1964–)

Former basketball player and head coach of the **Women's National Basketball Association's** (WNBA) Phoenix Mercury, Cheryl Miller was born in Riverside, California, in January 1964, to Saul and Carrie Miller. Miller began playing basketball when she was a young girl, playing on the fifth grade boys' team. She went on to play for Riverside Polytechnic High School, where she set the California Interscholastic Federation's record for most career points. Miller was named an All-American four times by *Parade* magazine.

With scholarship offers from more than 200 schools across the country, Miller enrolled at the University of Southern California (USC) in 1983. After leading the Lady Trojans to the NCAA championships in both her freshman and sophomore years, Miller was selected most valuable player for each tournament. While at USC, Miller was a three-time winner of the Naismith College Player of the Year award. She also received the Wade Trophy and the Broderick Award, in addition to being named *Sports Illustrated*'s best player in the country. When she graduated in 1986, USC retired Miller's number, making her the first basketball player to receive that honor.

After college, Miller was drafted by several professional leagues, including the men's United States Basketball League (USBL). Because of knee injuries, however, Miller was unable to continue her professional career, which she concluded after playing in the 1986 Goodwill Games and the World Basketball Championships. Between 1986 and 1991, Miller worked as an assistant basketball coach at USC, as well as serving as a sports commentator for ABC. Named USC's head coach in 1993, she coached the Lady Trojans for two seasons.

In 1995 Miller began a broadcasting career with Turner Sports, covering NBA games for TNT and TBS Superstation. In 1996 she became the first woman to call a nationally-televised NBA game. From 1997 to 2000, Miller coached the WNBA's Phoenix Mercury. Citing fatigue, she resigned after the 2000 season, but she continues to work as a television analyst. Miller was inducted into the Women's Basketball Hall of Fame in 1999.

Further Reading

Nelson, Kelly. "Cheryl DeAnne Miller," in *The Scribner Encyclopedia of American Lives: Sports Figures.* New York: Charles Scribner's Sons, 2002.

Skaine, Rosemarie. *Women College Basketball Coaches.* Jefferson, NC: McFarland, 2001.

Mink, Patsy Matsu Takemoto (December 6, 1927–September 28, 2002)

Japanese American congressional representative and key figure in the writing of Title IX, Patsy Mink was born on Maui, Hawaii, in December 1927. She attended the University of Hawaii at Manoa and later transferred to the University of Nebraska. While there, Mink was forced to reside in a special dormitory for the university's non-Caucasian students. Refusing to accept this policy, Mink formed a coalition that ultimately brought an end to the university's discriminatory housing policy. Mink then returned to the University of Hawaii, where she received degrees in both zoology and chemistry, in preparation for attending medical school. Mink soon discovered, however, that none of the twenty medical schools to which she had applied accepted women. Committed to combating discrimination against women, Mink decided to attend law school instead. She was accepted to the University of Chicago's law school even though the school did not admit women, because the admissions committee misunderstood her application, believing "Patsy" to be a man's name. She received her law degree from the University of Chicago Law School in 1951.

After law school, Mink returned to Honolulu, where she opened a private practice. She was elected to the state house of representatives in 1956 and to the state senate in 1958 and 1962. She was elected to the U.S. House of Representatives in 1965, serving six consecutive terms as a Democrat from Hawaii, and becoming the first Asian American woman ever to be elected to the U.S. Congress. As a result of the discrimination she had faced, Mink was a strong advocate of equal educational opportunities for women and, along with Representative **Edith Green** and Senator **Birch Bayh**, she helped to draft the 1972 Title IX Amendment of the Higher Education Act. Mink also sponsored the Early Childhood Education Act and the 1973 **Women's Educational Equity Act**, which in addition to promoting equal education opportunities for girls and women, also provides funds to help educational institutions meet Title IX requirements. Mink went on to serve as Assistant Secretary of State under President Jimmy Carter and was also a founding member of the National Women's Political Caucus, an organization dedicated to increasing women's political engagement. In 2002, the year of Title IX's thirtieth anniversary, Mink

Rep. Patsy Mink (D-Hawaii) meets reporters on Capitol Hill Wednesday, November 5, 1997, to call on the Senate Judiciary Committee to support Bill Lann Lee's nomination to head the Justice Department's civil rights division. AP Images/Joe Marquette.

was honored by the National Organization for Women as a Woman of Vision. Upon her death in September 2002, President George W. Bush honored her by renaming the Title IX Amendment the Patsy T. Mink Equal Opportunity in Education Act.

Further Reading

Davidson, Sue. *A Heart in Politics: Jeannette Rankin and Patsy T. Mink*. Seattle: Seal Press, 1994.

Joint Resolution Recognizing the Contributions of Patsy Takemoto Mink. Washington, DC: U.S. Government Printing Office, 2002.

"Patsy Takemoto Mink" in *Women in Congress, 1917–1990*. Prepared under the direction of the Commission on the Bicentenary by the Office of the Historian, U.S. House of Representatives. Washington, DC: Government Printing Office, 1991.

Moore, Billie Jean (May 5, 1943–)

One of the first individuals to be inducted into the Women's Basketball Hall of Fame, basketball player and coach Billie Moore was born in Westmoreland, Kansas, in May 1943. Moore attended Washburn University, where she played both basketball and softball, and later earned a master's degree at Southern Illinois University at Carbondale in 1967. Two years later, she began coaching women's basketball at California State University at Fullerton. In her first season there, Moore coached her team to the **Association of Intercollegiate Athletics for Women's** (AIAW) national championship title. While at California State Fullerton, she coached her team to eight consecutive conference titles.

Moore's accomplishments in coaching women's college basketball paved the way for her to become head coach of the USA World University team in both 1973 and 1975; she was also named assistant coach of the USA Pan-American team in 1975. The following year, Moore was chosen as head coach for the 1976 U.S. Olympic women's basketball team. Under her coaching, the team won a silver medal in Montreal.

In 1977 Moore began coaching at University of California Los Angeles (UCLA), where she led her team to the AIAW national title in 1978, thus becoming the first coach to lead two schools to women's basketball national championships. She continued to coach at UCLA until her retirement, at the end of the 1992–1993 season. She has also helped to select players for almost every Olympic women's basketball team since 1976.

Moore was inducted into the Women's Basketball Hall of Fame in 1999. The following year, she became the tenth woman to be enshrined in the Naismith Memorial Basketball Hall of Fame. In March 2002, the Atlanta Tipoff Club presented Moore with the 2002 Naismith Women's Outstanding Contribution to Basketball Award, a prize honoring individuals who impact the game of basketball in a positive way. In addition to creating a "Talking Basketball" series of cassette tapes, Moore has also authored a book on women's basketball titled *Basketball, Theory and Practice*.

Further Reading

Hawkes, Nena Rey, and John F. Seggar. *Celebrating Women Coaches: A Biographical Dictionary*. Westport, CT: Greenwood, 2000.
Moore, Billie J., and John O. White. *Basketball, Theory and Practice*. Dubuque, IA: W.C. Brown Co., 1980.

Muldowney, Shirley (June 19, 1940–)

Drag racer Shirley Muldowney was born in Schenectady, New York, in June 1940. She began drag racing as a teenager, a pursuit she shared with her boyfriend, whom she married at the age of sixteen. The couple teamed up to race; she was the driver and he was the mechanic. After racing in local Funny Car competitions, she won her first major drag race in 1971 at Rockingham, North Carolina. She continued to participate in the Funny Car races for two more years. After surviving three crashes, Muldowney began racing Top Fuel dragsters, cars that were both safer and faster than the ones she had previously been driving.

In 1974 Muldowney became the first woman to qualify for a national race in the Top Fuel category; she was the first woman in America to be licensed to drive top fuel dragsters. Two years later, she also became the first woman to win at the Spring Nationals of the National Hot Rod Association (NHRA), as well as becoming the first woman to be named to the American Auto Racing Writers and Broadcasters Association's Auto Racing All-American Team. That same year, she also beat the six-second record on the quarter-mile track. In 1977 Muldowney won three national drag races, becoming the year's NHRA World Champion.

Despite her world championship title, Muldowney still faced challenges finding sponsorship. Because she was a female driver, she had to work disproportionately hard to prove her capabilities as a drag racer. Driving her pink car, Muldowney successfully broke the 1980 Gatornationals' quarter-mile track six-second record, clocking in at 5.075 seconds. After winning eleven races that year, she was awarded her second NHRA Top Fuel World Championship title, making her the first driver to win this title twice. Muldowney continued to take the drag racing world by storm, winning successive national races and setting new records. In 1982 she won her third World Championship. It was after this win that a film about her racing career, *Heart Like a Wheel*, was released. Muldowney served as creative consultant for the project.

With her career at its height, Muldowney's car crashed in 1984 at the Sanair Speedway in Montreal. Suffering multiple broken bones, she spent more than seven weeks in the hospital and underwent five operations. Despite her injuries, Muldowney still wanted to race. She made her comeback in January 1986, at the Firebird international Raceway in Phoenix, Arizona. In her debut race, she clocked in just a mere .03 seconds over her career-best. Over the course of the 1986 season, Muldowney lowered her times, ultimately achieving 5.42 seconds, the fastest time of her career. She continued to race until 1991.

Further Reading

Duden, Jane. *Shirley Muldowney*. Mankato, MN: Crestwood House, 1988.

Muldowney, Shirley, and Bill Stephens. *Shirley Muldowney's Tales from the Track*. Champaign, IL: Sports Publishing, 2005.

N

National Association for Girls and Women in Sport

With roots dating back to 1899, the National Association for Girls and Women in Sport (NAGWS) was established in 1974 as an organization dedicated to promoting opportunities for girls and women in sport. At an 1899 conference of the American Physical Education Association (APEA), the Women's Basket Ball Rules Committee was formed to examine different rules used for women's basketball and systemize them through the development of a rule book. In 1916 the APEA created the Standing Committee on Women's Athletics, which was responsible for developing guides and rule books for a variety of women's sports. In 1932 the Standing Committee on Women's Athletics was reorganized into the National Section on Women's Athletics. The group merged with the National Amateur Athletic Federation's Women's Division in 1940, and its name was changed to the National Section on Girls and Women's Sports in 1953. When it joined the American Alliance for Health, Physical Education, Recreation, and Dance (AAHPERD) five years later, its name was again changed, this time to the Division for Girls and Women's Sports. The division gained its present name when AAHPERD restructured in 1974, two years after the passage of Title IX.

Despite its many name changes, the goal of NAGWS has remained the same: "[to] promote opportunities for girls and women in sport through conferences, clinics, and advocacy programs that [focus] on teaching, coaching, and current issues concerning female athletics." NAGWS sponsors a number of programs and events to achieve its mission, including the **National Girls and Women in Sports Day** (NGWSD), Backyards and Beyond, and the Complete Athlete Program. Backyards and Beyond is a "grassroots program [that] promotes education, advocacy, implementation, and vigilance surrounding social justice issues that are relevant to girls and women in sport." The Complete Athlete Program, a joint effort with the Amateur Athletic Union Girls Basketball program, was designed to "provide a quality sports education program" that teaches not only the rules of the sport, but life skills, character development, and fair play, as well.

Since 1978 NAGWS has partnered with the **Women's Basketball Coaches Association** (WBCA) to present the Wade Trophy to female athletes who have "demonstrated their commitment to their sport, to their academic development, and to the importance of acting responsibly both on and off the basketball court." The award was established in honor of women's basketball coach **Margaret Wade**. NAGWS also presents several other accolades, including the Guiding Woman in Sport and Nell Jackson awards, to honor "those individuals who continue to make great efforts in the journey toward equality for all girls and women in sport."

Before Title IX, "appropriate" activities for girls were gymnastics, skating, dancing, and cheerleading. Today these activities are competitive events featuring both men and women. Photo from authors' private collection.

A sport available only to males until the 1920s, cheerleading is today a competitive sport for both males and females. Circulation for the *American Cheerleader* magazine is estimated at 200,000, and 62 percent of cheerleaders are involved in a second sport. UAB Archives, University of Alabama at Birmingham.

NAGWS serves as a resource center for individuals interested in women's and girls' sports, coaching, and education. The organization has been publishing the *Women in Sport and Physical Activity Journal* since 2004, and it also offers the online newsletter *GWS News*. In 1992 it published the *NAGWS Title IX Toolbox*, which features information about the legislation, news articles, and descriptions of various court cases, as well as information on how to evaluate programs for Title IX compliance and guidelines and lesson plans for educating others about Title IX.

Further Reading

Morgan, Kay. "NAGWS: 100 Years." *JOPERD: Journal of Physical Education, Recreation & Dance* 70.4 (April 1999): 19–23.

National Association for Girls and Women in Sport Web site (http://www.aahperd.org/nagws/).

National Association of Collegiate Women Athletics Administrators

An outgrowth of the **Association for Intercollegiate Athletics for Women** (AIAW), the National Association of Collegiate Women Athletic Administrators (NACWAA) was originally created as the Council of Collegiate Women Athletic Administrators in 1979, in order to promote increased opportunities for women in athletics. The organization took its present name in 1992 and has almost 2,000 members. The NACWAA is "dedicated to providing educational programs, professional and personal development opportunities, information exchange, and support services to enhance college athletics and to promote the growth, leadership, and success of women as athletics administrators, professional staff, coaches, and student-athletes." Past presidents of the organization include Judith Sweet of the NCAA and **Christine H. B. Grant** of the University of Iowa.

In 2002 NACWAA partnered with the **National Collegiate Athletics Association's** Committee on Women's Athletics to establish The Institute for Athletics Executives. Meeting annually in July, the Institute's goal is to increase opportunities for women to attain positions as athletic directors. NACWAA also hosts the NACWAA/HERS (Higher Education Resource Services) Institute for Administrative Advancement, which "prepares participants to work with issues [such as Title IX, gender equity, and diversity] currently facing intercollegiate athletics administrators." In March 2007, NACWAA was a cosponsor of "Title IX Hoopla: Celebrating 35 Years of Women & Sport" at the 2007 NCAA Women's Final Four games in Cleveland, Ohio. NACWAA maintains a special Title IX Committee to keep members apprised of legislative issues surrounding Title IX and gender equity.

Further Reading

National Association of Collegiate Women Athletic Administrators Web site (http://www.nacwaa.org/).

National Coalition for Women and Girls in Education

Formed in 1975, the National Coalition for Women and Girls in Education (NCWGE) was created to aid in the enforcement of Title IX, which had been implemented three years before. Upon discovering that compliance with Title IX was far from complete, delegates from a number of leading organizations, including the American Association of University Women (AAUW), the American Civil Liberties Union, the **National Women's Law Center** (NWLC), and the National Education Association (NEA), joined together to establish the NCWGE, with the hope that a unified voice would encourage enforcement of the legislation. NCWGE was indeed successful in its mission.

Today NCWGE comprises more than fifty separate organizations "dedicated to improving educational opportunities for girls and women." The coalition is committed to ensuring gender equity for women and girls of all ages. Over the years, NCWGE has issued a number of publications on the status of Title IX. In 2002, on the thirtieth anniversary of the legislation, NCWGE released *Title IX at 30: Report Card on Gender Equity*. This report evaluated the state of "gender equity in education in nine key areas: access to higher education, athletics, career education, employment, learning environment, math and science, sexual harassment, standardized testing, and treatment of pregnant and parenting students."

NCWGE continues to monitor federal programs and advocates for expanding Title IX into areas such as internships, job-training programs, and vocational education. In 2002 the coalition also worked with the Office of Educational Research and Improvement to gather information on student participation in secondary school athletics and vocational education programs. NCWGE also maintains an Athletics Task Force, chaired by the National Women's Law Center. Created to "ensure that women and girls receive equal opportunities in athletics at both the secondary school and college levels," the Athletic Task Force focuses on Title IX and gender equity in athletics.

Further Reading
National Coalition for Women and Girls in Education Web site (http://www.ncwge. org/index.htm).

National Collegiate Athletic Association

Growing out of the Intercollegiate Athletic Association of the United States (IAAUS), which was created in March 1906, the National Collegiate Athletic Association (NCAA) was established in 1910 to govern intercollegiate athletics at the campus, regional, and national levels. The NCAA held its first national championships for track and field in 1921. Walter Byers was appointed the organization's executive director in 1951 and remained in the position until he retired in October 1987. In 1952, the NCAA's national headquarters were moved to Kansas City, Missouri.

In 1965 the NCAA created a Special Committee on Women's Competition to discuss the issue of women's participation in the NCAA. In 1973, the year following the passage of Title IX, the NCAA granted permission for women to compete in its tournaments. Although women were allowed to compete in NCAA championships, the organization did not officially govern women's collegiate athletics. Until the early 1980s, women's collegiate athletics programs were under the jurisdiction of the **Association for Intercollegiate Athletics for Women** (AIAW). This changed in 1980, however, when the NCAA decided to offer women's championships in five select sports. At the NCAA Convention the following year, the organization voted to open four seats to women on the NCAA Council and to create women's sports committees. Institutions were given until August 1985 to determine whether they would remain members of the AIAW or join the NCAA. The AIAW filed a lawsuit against the NCAA in

1982, claiming that the latter had violated the Sherman Antitrust Act in an effort to monopolize women's college sports. The AIAW failed to prove violations of the Sherman Antitrust Act and lost the suit the following year.

When Title IX was passed in June 1972, the NCAA vehemently opposed the new law, insisting that the legislation would lead to the downfall of men's intercollegiate athletics programs. In 1974 Senator John Tower of Texas supported the NCAA's position and proposed an amendment that sought to exclude intercollegiate athletics from Title IX's authority. Although the **Tower Amendment** failed to pass, the NCAA did not quell its efforts to limit the power of Title IX. To this end, the organization filed a lawsuit against the U.S. Department of Health, Education, and Welfare (HEW) in 1976. The court dismissed the case in 1978.

In the 1980s, the NCAA began to take a more active role in promoting gender equity with the creation of a Committee on Women's Athletics, which was established to make policy recommendations and "promote equitable opportunities, fair treatment, and respect for all women in all aspects of intercollegiate athletics." Continuing in this vein, the NCAA has also hosted a number of Title IX/Gender Equity Forums and established a task force to evaluate the status of its member institutions, with respect to gender equity. Since 1991 the NCAA has awarded the NCAA Woman of the Year Award to a senior student athlete who exhibits excellence in athletics, academics, service, and leadership.

Further Reading

Crowley, Joseph N., David Pickle, and Rich Clarkson. *In the Arena: The NCAA's First Century.* Indianapolis, IN: NCAA, 2006.

National Collegiate Athletic Association Web site (http://www.ncaa.org/).

"NCAA Challenges Validity of HEW's Title IX." *NCAA News* 13.3, February 15, 1976, pp. 1, 3 (available at http://web1.ncaa.org/web_video/NCAANewsArchive/1976/19760215.pdf).

National Girls and Women in Sports Day

Chartered in 1986, National Girls and Women in Sports Day (NGWSD) is a joint effort coordinated by the National Girls and Women in Sports Coalition, which is composed of several leading women's and girls' organizations, including the **National Women's Law Center** (NWLC), the **Women's Sports Foundation** (WSF), the Girl Scouts of the USA, the American Association of University Women (AAUW), the YWCA, and Girls Incorporated. Initially organized by the Women's Sports Foundation in memory of the late Olympic volleyball player **Flora "Flo" Hyman,** who died in a tournament in Japan in January 1986, NGWSD was quickly designated a national day by Congress "to honor female athletic achievement and to recognize the importance of participation in sports and fitness for girls and women of all ages." The first NGWSD was held in

Washington DC, on February 4, 1987. Since then NGWSD has striven to acknowledge women and girls' struggle for equal access and opportunity in sports. NGWSD events are celebrated around the country each February to recognize female athletes and to encourage girls and women to participate in sports. NGWSD festivities in the nation's capital also include the presentation of the Women's Sports Foundation's Flo Hyman Award, given to the athlete who most exhibits the volleyball player's excellence of character.

Each year a contest is held to choose the theme for the upcoming NGWSD. Contest winners receive an all-expenses-paid trip to Washington DC, to participate in the event. Expressed in no more than six words, each year's chosen theme must "focus attention on issues involving girls and women in sports." Title IX of the 1972 Education Amendments was specifically commemorated in 2002, with the theme "Celebrating 30 Years of Title IX." NGWSD's mission is well-illustrated by its 2007 theme: "Throw Like a Girl—Lead Like a Champion!"

While NGWSD events only take place one day each year, the NGWSD organizers seek to encourage support for women and girls in sport that lasts throughout the year. In NGWSD's "10-Point Play" activity, teams are encouraged to outline tasks for ten consecutive days that will "change the world" for the girls who will follow in the footsteps of today's female athletes. NGWSD leaders also provide individuals with a sample letter to distribute to their local and state governments, requesting an official proclamation of the importance of sports for girls and women. NGWSD community action kits, posters, and certificates are also available to individuals, teams, and classes, free of charge.

Now in its twenty-first year, NGWSD continues to honor past accomplishments, as well as to promote and raise awareness of sports for girls and women. Organizations such as the American Association of University Women (AAUW) take part in NGWSD activities as a way to "refocus attention on the importance of active support for girls and women in athletics and the enforcement of laws such as Title IX that guarantee equal opportunity and ban sex discrimination in education and athletic programs."

Further Reading

National Girls and Women in Sports Day Web site (http://www.aahperd.org/ngwsd central/).

Women's Sports Foundation Web site (http://www.womenssportsfoundation.org/).

National Women's Law Center

Dedicated to working on behalf of women and girls to address a variety of issues, the National Women's Law Center was established in 1972, the same year that Title IX was signed into law. Originally created as the Women's Rights Project of the Center for Law and Social Policy, the National Women's Law Center became an independent organization in 1981. The organization addresses laws affecting women's and girls' education, employment, economic security, and health and is dedicated to "protect[ing] and advanc[ing] the progress of women and girls at work, in school, and in virtually every aspect of their lives." It has initiated a number of programs to address these issues.

The Center's education program focuses on the strong enforcement of Title IX and on generating increased opportunities for women and girls to achieve gender equity in education. The Center is especially concerned with "training women and girls for today's technology-oriented workplace." It has compiled numerous resources dealing with gender equity in education, including single-sex education, math and science curricula, and career and technical education; examples are state-by-state "report cards" and legal guides. The Center also maintains a list of resources on Title IX and athletics, such as the 2005 Clarification to Title IX, information on related legal cases, and a guide that can help individuals to determine whether a school is in compliance with Title IX. In 1988 the Center led a national alliance in support of the Civil Rights Restoration Act, which stipulates that Title IX applies to all educational programs within an institution, including athletics, if that institution receives federal funds. The Center also chairs the **National Coalition for Women and Girls in Education**'s Athletics Task Force.

In 1997 alone, the Center filed more than twenty-five charges against colleges and universities, claiming sex discrimination in sports scholarships and failure to comply with Title IX. In 1999 the Center won the landmark case *Davis v. Monroe County Board of Education*, which holds schools responsible under Title IX for student-to-student sexual harassment. In 2002 the Center was pleased to find that only thirty colleges and universities had a disparity of more than $6 million between scholarships for male and female athletes. In 2006 it was successful in obtaining an agreement with Maryland's Prince George's County Public Schools that would bring the school system's sports programs into full compliance with Title IX. The agreement, which ensures that each school in the county provides "equal athletic participation opportunities and benefits" to male and female students, is a model for school districts across the nation.

Headquartered in Washington DC, the Center has received a number of awards for its continued leadership in advocating gender equity. The Center has issued a number of publications pertaining to Title IX, including *Keeping Score: Girls' Participation in High School Athletics in Massachusetts*; *Check It Out: Is the Playing Field Level for Women and Girls at Your School?*; and *Breaking Down Barriers: A Legal Guide to Title IX*. The Center has received the Myra Sadker Equity Award, for its role in promoting equity in education, and the **Women's Sports Foundation**'s Billie Jean King Contribution Award, for its efforts in supporting Title IX in court and working to effect gender equity in sports.

Further Reading

National Women's Law Center Web site (http://www.nwlc.org/).

National Wrestling Coaches Association v. U.S. Department of Education (2004)

In 2002 the National Wrestling Coaches Association (NWCA), the Committee to Save Bucknell Wrestling, the Marquette Wrestling Club, the Yale Wrestling Association, and the College Sports Council filed suit against the U.S. Department of Education, alleging that Title IX's Three-Part Test and the Department of Education's interpretation of the legislation were discriminatory to men's athletics and particularly harmful to men's wrestling. Instead of suing an individual school for cutting men's teams, as had often occurred in previous cases, the NWCA chose to sue the Department of Education for creating the regulations.

In response, the Department of Education filed a motion to dismiss the case on the grounds that the plaintiffs did not have standing to sue the Department of Education and that they could not tie their injuries to Title IX's regulations. The court agreed with the Department of Education, and the case was dismissed. The NWCA appealed, but the lower court's ruling was upheld. The court stated in its ruling that no part of Title IX's Three-Part Test requires—or even suggests—that schools cut men's teams or male players in order to comply with the law; it also noted that most schools do not choose to achieve compliance through this means, instead opting to increase opportunities for women's participation. In addition, the court concluded that the NWCA was unable to show that the schools' decisions to cut their men's wrestling programs had been the direct result of Title IX, arguing that eliminations could have conceivably occurred for a number of reasons, including budget pressures or low participation.

Further Reading

Epstein, Adam. "Stand or Fall: Wrestlers Continue to Grapple with Defeat." *JOPERD: Journal of Physical Education, Recreation, & Dance* 75.9 (Nov./Dec. 2004): 7–8.

National Wrestling Coaches Association v. Department of Education, 366 F.3d 930 (D.D.C. 2004).

Neal v. Board of Trustees of the California State Universities (1999)

In 1993 the California chapter of the National Organization for Women (Cal-NOW) won a Title IX lawsuit that resulted in the entire California State system being declared in violation of Title IX. The judge who presided over the case ordered the individual schools of the Cal State system to achieve parity, within a 5 percent margin, between their proportions of male-to-female students and male-to-female athletes, as well as in their scholarship spending, and to achieve a discrepancy of no more than 10 percent between their budgets for men's and women's programs. The wrestling coach at California State University at Bakersfield (CSUB), T. J. Kerr, actively addressed the challenge by creating a women's wrestling club. Women composed 63 percent of the student body at CSUB, but only 49 percent of its athlete population—thus, the proportions were still not within 5 percent of each other.

Facing budgetary constraints in 1995, in an effort to meet the mandate resulting from the *Cal-NOW* case, the CSUB administration decided to implement roster management (i.e. the practice of limiting the size of teams), with the goal of preventing the need to eliminate some men's teams altogether. The wrestling team was capped at twenty-seven members. Eventually, however, CSUB decided to eliminate the program entirely. In response, a group of twenty male and eight female wrestlers led by Stephen Neal, filed suit in 1996, claiming that the practice of roster management constituted a violation of Title IX.

The district court agreed with the plaintiffs that limiting the number of players on a team in order to meet the requirements of the *Cal-NOW* order was indeed a violation of Title IX. CSUB appealed, and the 9th Circuit Court reversed the lower court's decision. The Circuit Court found that a school can attempt to achieve compliance in any way it deems necessary, including placing limits on the number of students of the overrepresented gender who can participate in a sport. Thus, roster management was determined not to be a violation of Title IX.

Further Reading

Bonnette, Valerie McMurtrie. *Title IX and Intercollegiate Athletics: How It All Works—In Plain English*. San Diego, CA: Good Sports, Inc., 2004.

Carpenter, Linda Jean, and R. Vivian Acosta. *Title IX*. Champaign, IL: Human Kinetics, 2005.

Neal v. Board of Trustees of the California State Universities, 198 F.3d 763 (9th Cir. 1999).

Nelson, Mariah Burton (April 1956–)

Journalist and former basketball player Mariah Burton Nelson was born in Blue Bell, Pennsylvania, in April 1956. When she was sixteen years old, her family moved to Phoenix, Arizona. While attending Arcadia High School, Nelson lettered in five sports and also played for the Arizona Phoenix Dusters of the **Amateur Athletic Union** (AAU). After high school, she enrolled at Stanford University, where she continued to play basketball. She was the team's captain and leading scorer all four years. Nelson graduated from Stanford in 1978 with a degree in psychology. After college Nelson went on to play in a French basketball league, and then later returned to the United States, where she played for the New Jersey Gems, of the short-lived **Women's Professional Basketball**

League (WBL). She also continued her education, receiving a master's degree in public health from San Jose State University in 1983.

Nelson is a former weekly columnist for *The Washington Post*, and she also served as an editor for *Women's Sports and Fitness* magazine. In 1988 she received the **Women's Sports Foundation**/Miller Lite Journalism Award for her work on sports and gender issues. Her first book, *Are We Winning Yet? How Women Are Changing Sports and Sports Are Changing Women*, published in 1991, received the Amateur Athletic Foundation's Book Award in 1992. In 1995 Nelson was honored with the National Organization for Women's award for excellence in sports writing. The following year, she was presented with the Guiding Woman in Sport Award from the **National Association of Girls and Women in Sport** (NAGWS). The author of several books, including *We Are All Athletes: Bringing Courage, Confidence, and Peak Performance into Our Everyday Lives* and *The Stronger Women Get, the More Men Love Football*, Nelson frequently lectures to organizations around the country. In May 2006, Nelson became executive director of the American Association for Physical Activity and Recreation.

Further Reading

Nelson, Mariah Burton. *We Are All Athletes: Bringing Courage, Confidence, and Peak Performance into Our Everyday Lives*. Arlington, VA: Dare Press, 2002.

North Haven Board of Education v. Bell (1982)

In 1978 tenured school teacher Elaine Dove filed a complaint with the U.S. Department of Health, Education, and Welfare (HEW) stating that the North Haven (Connecticut) Board of Education had violated Title IX by refusing to allow her to return to work after her year-long maternity leave. HEW initiated an investigation into the school board's polices for dealing with hiring, leaves of absence, tenure, and seniority. The board refused to cooperate with HEW, stating that Title IX only applied to students and was never intended to regulate employment practices. HEW then notified the board that it was considering initiating enforcement proceedings. In response, the school board filed suit against HEW.

In addition to its investigation of the North Haven Board of Education, HEW was also investigating the Trumbull (Connecticut) Board of Education, based on a complaint issued by Linda Potz, a school guidance counselor. According to Potz, the Trumbull board had discriminated against her based on gender, in terms of job assignments and working conditions, ultimately refusing to renew her contract. On appeal, both the North Haven and Trumbull cases were combined, and Dove's complaint had resulted in two much broader issues being raised: Was Title IX applicable to employees and did Congress provide implied approval of HEW's authority to enforce Title IX regulations?

Regarding the first issue, the Supreme Court determined that Title IX did indeed cover employees. The Court based its decision on Title IX's statutory language, which consistently refers to "person(s)," rather than to specific groups, such as students. The Court also cited language in Subpart E of the legislation stating that "No person, shall, on the basis of sex . . . be subjected to discrimination in employment." The Court also reviewed the legislative history of Title IX, including the 1970 hearings that led to its development, and found that much of the testimony that had occurred had concerned employment issues.

Regarding the second issue, the Court found that Congress did, in fact, provide implied consent for the HEW to enforce Title IX regulations. The Court noted that whenever Congress had been faced with the decision of whether to support a regulation, the body had assented. Furthermore, it noted that Congress had had plenty of opportunities to revisit and revise the regulations, but had declined to do so; this discovery supported the Court's belief that Congress approved of the regulations. Thus, the *North Haven* case both affirmed HEW's enforcement authority and established that employees could seek redress for discrimination under Title IX, as well as Title VII.

The Court's decision on this case, however, was not unanimous. The dissenting opinion concerned the issue of federal dollars, rather than the issues of legislative history and intent of Title IX. The dissent argued that, since Dove's unit did not receive any federal money, she was not covered by Title IX. While this dissenting opinion had no effect on the case, it would come to have a powerful impact two years later, in **Grove City College v. Bell** (1984).

Further Reading

North Haven Board of Education v. Bell, 456 U.S. 512 (1982).

Zirkel, Perry A., Sharon Nalbone Richardson, and Steven S. Goldberg. *A Digest of Supreme Court Decisions Affecting Education*. Bloomington, IN: Phi Delta Kappa Educational Foundation, 2001.

Nyad, Diana (August 22, 1949–)

Swimmer Diana Nyad was born in New York City in August 1949, to William Sneed and Lucy Curtis. Raised in Florida, Nyad began swimming at an early age. She trained with Jack Nelson, an Olympic coach, and soon became known for her backstroke. She was a state champion in both the 100-meter and 200-meter backstroke races by the time she was twelve years old. She had hoped to enter the 1968 Olympics, but was unable to compete because of illness. She then turned to marathon swimming, entering a ten-mile marathon in Hamilton, Ontario, in 1970. In her first professional marathon, Nyad broke the women's world record. Five years later, she set another record, swimming the twenty-eight miles around Manhattan in seven hours and fifty-seven minutes.

Throughout her swimming career, Nyad continued to set world records. In 1978 she attempted to swim from Cuba to Florida but was derailed by a storm. Though unable to complete her swim from Cuba, Nyad set the world record for swimming the 102.5 miles from Bimini Island to Jupiter, Florida, in twenty-seven hours and thirty-eight minutes in 1979. Nyad set a number of records, including the women's world record for swimming Argentina's twenty-six-mile-long Parana River. She held the world record for the longest swim until 1997. Nyad was inducted into the National Women's Hall of Fame in 1986 and the International Swimming Hall of Fame in 2003.

During the 1980s, Nyad began a career in television and radio, working for ABC and CNBC. She is currently the host of National Public Radio's *The Savvy Traveler*, for which she received the Miller Lite National Journalism Award, and she also serves as a sports correspondent for Fox Sports News.

Further Reading

Gould, Toni S. *Diana Nyad*. New York: Walker, 1983.

Nyad, Diana. *Other Shores*. New York: Random House, 1978.

P

Patrick, Danica Sue (March 25, 1982–)

Race car driver Danica Patrick was born in Beloit, Washington, in March 1982, to T.J. and Bev Patrick. Patrick became interested in racing after her younger sister entered her first go-kart race. She began her career in 1992, racing go-karts and winning several national championships. When she was sixteen years old, Patrick moved to England and began participating in races, such as the Formula Ford and Formula Vauxhall series. In 2000 she finished second in Britain's Formula Ford Festival, the best finish ever made by a woman or by an American.

Patrick returned to the United States in 2002, when she signed a contract to race with the Rahal Letterman Racing team. Racing in the 2003 Toyota Atlantic Series, she placed third and became the first woman to finish that high in the event. In May 2005, following in the footsteps of **Janet Guthrie**, Patrick became the fourth woman ever to race in the Indianapolis 500. Finishing in fourth place, the best performance ever by a female driver, Patrick was named Rookie of the Year for both the Indianapolis 500 and the Indy Racing League.

In addition to her racing career, Patrick is also the host of several television programs for Spike TV. Born ten years after the passage of Title IX, Patrick has truly benefited from the opportunities the legislation created for women.

Further Reading
Patrick, Danica. *Danica: Crossing the Line*. New York: Simon & Schuster, 2006.

Pederson v. Louisiana State University (2000)

In 1994 two groups of female athletes filed suit against Louisiana State University (LSU), claiming that the university had denied them equal opportunity to participate in college sports, to receive scholarships, and to access to benefits and services. The athletes also charged that the university discriminated against women, with regard to coaches' salaries. The first group, led by Beth Pederson, wanted the school to develop a women's soccer program, and the second group sought the addition of a fast-pitch softball team. Pederson also intended to establish a putative class, or a group of entities that have suffered a common wrong, of all female athletes enrolled since 1993. LSU argued that if the school were indeed in violation of Title IX, it was not intentional.

The district court ruling in the case found that LSU had failed all three portions of the Three-Part Test of Title IX compliance. LSU had failed part one, the issue of proportionality, because women composed 49 percent of the student body, but only 29 percent of the student athlete population. The school had not added any women's teams in over fourteen years, thus failing part two, which involves demonstrating a history of upgrading or adding women's teams. Finally, because there were two groups asking for two different teams to be established, the university was deemed to have failed part three, which specifies that schools must accommodate the interests and abilities of students. However, the district court also declared these violations to have been unintentional, meaning that damages could not be awarded; it thus denied the plaintiffs' motion to create a putative class. The plaintiffs appealed to the 5th Circuit Court.

The 5th Circuit upheld the district court's decision that LSU had indeed violated Title IX, but it reversed both the ruling that school had violated the law unintentionally and the lower court's denial of the motion to create a putative class. Based on the statements of university employees, the 5th Circuit Court found that LSU had intended to treat women differently than men, and that by intentionally discriminating against a protected class, the school had intentionally violated Title IX.

Further Reading

Bonnette, Valerie McMurtrie. *Title IX and Intercollegiate Athletics: How It All Works—In Plain English*. San Diego, CA: Good Sports, Inc., 2004.

Mitten, Matthew J., and Paul M. Anderson, eds. "*Pederson v. Louisiana State University.*" *You Make the Call: National Sports Law Institute of Marquette University Law School Newsletter* 1.3 (Summer 2000) (available at http://law.marquette.edu/cgi-bin/site.pl?2130&pageID=494).

Pederson v. Louisiana State University, 213 F.3d 858 (5th Cir. 2000).

R

Roberts, Robin (1960–)

Sports broadcaster and former basketball player Robin Roberts was born in Tuskegee, Alabama, in 1960. After graduating as her high school's salutatorian, Roberts enrolled at Southeastern Louisiana University (SLU), where she received a basketball scholarship, an opportunity that she credits to Title IX. While at SLU, Roberts earned recognition as the university's third all-time highest scorer. In addition to playing basketball, Roberts also served as sports director for a local radio station. She graduated cum laude from SLU, with a degree in communications in 1983. After her graduation, Roberts continued her involvement with sports broadcasting. She was employed at several television stations in Mississippi before moving to Nashville, Tennessee, where she worked as both a sports anchor and a reporter for WSMV-TV. While there, Roberts received *Nashville Scene*'s Sportscaster of the Year Award in 1987.

The following year, Roberts moved to Atlanta, Georgia, to work as a sports reporter for WAGA-TV. In February 1990, Roberts began working for ESPN, as a play-by-play commentator and contributor to programs such as *SportsCenter* and *NFL Prime Time*. In addition to covering the 1996 and 1998 Olympics, Roberts also hosted the network's **Women's National Basketball Association** (WNBA) games, as well as both men's and women's college basketball games. In June 1999, Roberts began hosting ESPN Classic's *Vintage NBA*, which highlighted a different athlete each week. In June 1995, she also began contributing to ABC's *Good Morning America* and ABC Sports' *Wide World of Sports*.

A highly acclaimed journalist, Roberts was named to the advisory board for the **Women's Sports Foundation** (WSF) in 1991, and she received the 1993 Excellence in Sports Journalism Award for Broadcast Media from Northeastern

University's School of Journalism and Center for the Study of Sport in Society. In 1996 the Women in Sports and Events (WISE) presented the first Robin Roberts Sports Journalism Scholarship at the NCAA Women's Final Four, and that same year, Roberts received the Distinguished Achievement Award in Broadcasting from the University of Georgia's broadcasting association DiGamma Kappa. Two years later, she was named one of WISE's 1998 Women of the Year. One of *Basketball Times'* Five Most Intriguing People in College Basketball, Roberts was also recognized as one of the NCAA's 100 Most Influential Student-Athletes in the organization's history in April 2006.

Further Reading

Roberts, Robin. *Basketball Year: What It's Like to Be a Woman Pro.* Brookfield, CT: Millbrook Press, 2000.

Roberts v. Colorado State Board of Agriculture (1993)

Facing a budget deficit, Colorado State University's (CSU) athletic department decided to eliminate men's baseball and women's fast-pitch softball. Members of the softball team filed suit in 1992, claiming that dropping the softball program violated Title IX and requesting that the program be reinstated. Upon investigation, the district court found that CSU had added eleven women's programs, but that all of them had been added before 1977, and that the institution had also eliminated three other women's sports. Thus, CSU had initially shown an effort to improve women's athletics, but this effort had not been consistent and ongoing, as required by part two of the Title IX's Three-Part Test of compliance. The school failed the proportionality and full accommodation portions of the test, as well.

As a result, CSU was found to be in violation of Title IX and was ordered to reinstate the softball program. CSU appealed the district court's decision, arguing that it had not violated Title IX and that the district court had no authority to order the school to reinstate a particular program. The 20th Circuit Court, however, affirmed the district court's decision, determining that a court can indeed order a school to reinstate a specific sport in order for it to accommodate the interests and abilities of students.

Further Reading

Bonnette, Valerie McMurtrie. *Title IX and Intercollegiate Athletics: How It All Works—In Plain English.* San Diego, CA: Good Sports, Inc., 2004.

Roberts v. Colorado State Board of Agriculture, 998 F.2d 824 (10th Cir. 1993), *cert. denied*, 510 U.S. 1004 (1993).

S

Stone, Toni (1921–November 2, 1996)

Negro League baseball player Toni Stone was born Marcenia Lyle in 1921, in St. Paul, Minnesota. In 1932, as a teenager, she enrolled in a baseball school run by Gabby Street, a former major league catcher for the St. Louis Cardinals. In the mid-1940s, she moved to San Francisco, California, and took the name Toni Stone. While in San Francisco, Stone first played for a local American Legion team, and then joined an African American barnstorming team known as the San Francisco Sea Lions. While on a trip to Louisiana with the Sea Lions, Stone accepted an offer to join the New Orleans Black Pelicans.

In 1949 Stone again switched teams, this time playing for the Negro League's New Orleans Creoles. She remained with the team until 1953, when she signed with the Indianapolis Clowns. While playing for the Clowns, Stone was reportedly the highest paid baseball player in the minor leagues, earning $12,000 during the 1953 season. In 1954 she was traded to the Kansas City Monarchs. Stone retired after just one season with the Monarchs, and the Negro League disbanded the following year.

After her retirement, Stone worked as a nurse and continued to play baseball in Oakland, California, where she settled with her husband Aurelium Alberga. Stone was inducted into the International Women's Sports Hall of Fame in 1985. She died of heart failure in 1996.

Further Reading

Berlage, Gai. *Women in Baseball: The Forgotten History*. Westport, CT: Praeger, 1994.

Everbach, Tracy. "Breaking Baseball Barriers: The 1953–1954 Negro League and the Expansion of Women's Roles." *American Journalism* 22.1 (Winter 2005): 13–33.

Summitt, Patricia "Pat" Sue Head (June 14, 1952–)

Pat Summitt, head coach of the Lady Volunteers at the University of Tennessee (UT), was born in 1952 in Henrietta, Tennessee, to James and Hazel Head. Summitt played basketball as a young child, but the first high school she attended in Henrietta did not have a girls' basketball team. The family moved to a neighboring town so that she could play on the girls' team at Cheatham County High School in Ashland City. As a freshman, she played forward on the varsity team.

After graduating from high school in the fall of 1970, Summitt enrolled at the University of Tennessee at Martin, one of the few colleges that offered a women's basketball program. Two years later, she led the team to the first national basketball championships of the **Association of Intercollegiate Athletics for Women** (AIAW). The following year, in 1973, she was captain of the U.S. team at the World University Games in Moscow. In 1976 Summitt was chosen to be on the U.S. Olympic team, playing in the first Olympics in which women's basketball was included as an event.

After injuring her knee during her senior year, Summitt graduated from college in 1974, with a degree in physical education, and enrolled at the University of Tennessee at Knoxville to earn her master's degree in the same field. While there, she received a graduate assistantship to coach the university's women's basketball team. In her first coaching season, Summitt coached the team to a record sixteen wins and eight losses. Since then, she has gone on to lead the Lady Volunteers to multiple national championships, as well as to appearances in both AIAW and **National Collegiate Athletic Association** (NCAA) Final Four games. After coaching the U.S. Junior National Team in the Pan-American Games in 1977, Summitt was selected as assistant coach of the 1980 U.S. Olympic team. By the next Olympics, in 1984, she had been named head coach of the U.S. women's team.

In 1983 Summitt was named Coach of the Year by the **Women's Basketball Coaches Association** (WBCA). Six years later, she was presented with the Basketball Hall of Fame's John Bunn Award for excellence in coaching, making her the first female coach to receive this distinction. She was inducted into the International Women's Sports Hall of Fame in 1990. By 1991 Summitt had become the third winningest coach in America. In 1997 she became the first female coach ever to be featured on the cover of *Sports Illustrated* magazine. Two years later, she was honored as one of Women in Sports and Events (WISE) Women of the Year. In 2005 Summitt became the winningest coach in the history of NCAA basketball. In April 2007, in her thirty-third year at the University of Tennessee, she led the Lady Volunteers to the team's seventh NCAA national championship title.

Tennessee coach Pat Summitt holds the basketball net, and her son Tyler Summitt holds the championship trophy, after winning the NCAA Women's national championship college basketball game Tuesday, April 3, 2007, in Cleveland, Ohio. Tennessee defeated Rutgers 59–46. AP Images/Amy Sancetta.

Further Reading

Coach Summitt Web site (http://www.coachsummitt.com/).

Summitt, Pat Head. *Raise the Roof: The Inspiring Inside Story of the Tennessee Lady Vols' Undefeated 1997–98 Season.* New York: Broadway Books, 1998.

T

Teague, Bertha Frank (September 17, 1906–June 13, 1991)

Known as "Mrs. Basketball of Oklahoma," Bertha Teague was born in Carthage, Missouri, in September 1906, to road contractor John Frank. She graduated from high school in 1923, and married James E. Teague the following year. The couple moved to Cairo, Oklahoma, where Teague became a first-grade teacher. Although she had never formally played the sport herself, Teague began coaching the girls' basketball team at Byng High School in Ada, Oklahoma, in 1927. Upon graduating from Oklahoma State University in 1932, Teague continued her coaching position at Byng. While there, she led the team to compete in fifteen Oklahoma state championship games, winning eight games and taking second place in the other seven games. Between 1936 and 1939, Teague's team experienced a streak of ninety-eight consecutive wins. During her tenure at Byng, her teams won so many games that she held the record for most wins at the girls' high school level until 1991.

Teague was one of the founders of the Oklahoma High School Girls Basketball Coaches Association in 1962. That same year, she wrote *Basketball for Girls*, in which she described her philosophy and coaching methods. Teague strongly believed that sport was a healthy activity for women and girls.

Teague was named the 1966 National Basketball Committee Coach of the Year and the 1967 Oklahoma Girls Basketball Coach of the Year. She also founded the Bertha Teague Mid-America Girls Basketball Tournament, the first girls' basketball camp in the Southwest, and in 1985, she became one of the first three women to be inducted into the Naismith Memorial Basketball Hall of Fame.

Further Reading

Teague, Bertha. *Basketball for Girls*. New York: Ronald Press, Co., 1962.

Tower Amendment

Proposed by Republican Senator John Tower of Texas in 1974, the Tower Amendment suggested that revenue-producing sports should be excluded from compliance with Title IX. Tower's argument was that revenue-producing sports supported not only themselves, but entire athletic departments as well, and therefore that forcing these sports to comply with Title IX would hurt all programs in athletics departments. Tower further argued that the authors of Title IX had never intended for the law to apply to sports, and that by forcing colleges to add women's sports, money would be diverted from the programs that fans paid to see, such as football, thus lessening the quality of the revenue-producing sports and causing schools to lose money, since fewer fans would pay to attend a lower quality events. A key issue in the amendment was that it defined revenue-producing sports in name only; a given instance of a program did not actually have to generate any revenue in order to qualify. The amendment meant that if sports such as football or men's basketball were labeled as revenue producing, then they could be excluded, when determining whether inequities existed. Thus, schools would only have to show that equity existed between women's sports and smaller, less influential, less well-funded men's sports, such as wrestling and swimming. The Tower Amendment never made it out of committee, and its failure signaled that all sports were to be treated equally and were subject to the regulations of Title IX. The issue of revenue-producing sports has continued to resurface throughout the history of Title IX, however, as exemplified by the case of *Blair v. Washington State University* (1987). *See also:* Javits Amendment.

Further Reading

Suggs, Welch. *A Place on the Team: The Triumph and Tragedy of Title IX*. Princeton, NJ: Princeton University Press, 2005.

V

Sportscaster Lesley Visser was born in September 1953, in Quincy, Massachusetts. While in high school, Visser was the captain of both the field hockey and basketball teams and was named best athlete during her sophomore year. After receiving a grant from the Carnegie Foundation in 1974 and graduating with a degree in English from Boston College in 1975, Visser began working as a sportswriter for the *Boston Globe*. While there, she became the first woman beat writer for the NFL in 1976, writing for the New England Patriots. She was named best woman sportscaster in the nation in 1983.

In 1984 Visser left the *Boston Globe* to join CBS Sports' *The NFL Today*. In addition to her work on *The NFL Today*, she also covered baseball, basketball, and the Olympics. In 1989 Visser went to Berlin to cover the fall of the Berlin Wall for CBS News. She focused her coverage specifically on how sports would change in East Germany after reunification. Visser set another record in 1992, when she became the first woman to cover the Super Bowl's postgame ceremonies.

In 1995 Visser left CBS and began working for both ABC Sports and ESPN. While at ABC, she became the first woman to host Monday Night Football. Returning to CBS in 2000, Visser became the first female sportscaster to carry the Olympic Torch in 2004; the International Olympic Committee bestowed this honor for her pioneering career in sports journalism. She is currently a commentator for ESPN's SportsCenter and NFL Gameday.

Although she began her career at a time when female reporters were typically not allowed in men's locker rooms or on sidelines, Visser became a highly acclaimed journalist, winning the **Women's Sports Foundation**'s journalism award in 1992, receiving the first Mary Garber Pioneer Award from the

Association for Women in Sports Media (AWSM) in 1999, and being named one of Women in Sports and Events (WISE) Women of the Year in 2002 for her work as a broadcaster with CBS sports. In August 2006, Visser was honored by the Pro Football Hall of Fame, which presented her with its Pete Rozelle Radio-Television Award, making her the first woman to receive this distinction.

Further Reading

Lesley Visser Web site (http://www.lesleyvisser.com/).

W

Wade, Lily Margaret (December 31, 1912–February 16, 1995)

Basketball coach and player Margaret Wade was born in McCool, Mississippi, in December 1912, to Robert and Bittie Wade. Growing up in Cleveland, Mississippi, Wade played basketball at Cleveland High School, where she was an All-Conference player two years in a row. She enrolled at Delta State Teachers College in 1929, where she continued to play on the school's team for three years, serving as captain for two of them. Before the beginning of her last season, however, the college eliminated its women's basketball program, believing that the sport was too strenuous for women.

After graduating from college, Wade went on to play professionally with the Tupelo Red Wings, leading the team to the Southern Championship. When a knee injury ended her career after just two seasons, she began coaching high school basketball teams in 1933. Wade continued to coach high school teams in both Georgia and Mississippi for the next twenty-one years.

In 1959 Wade returned to Delta State University as the school's first Director of the Women's Physical Education Department. Forty-one years after disbanding its women's basketball program, the university reestablished it in 1973, and Wade, at the age of sixty, was appointed head coach. Wade's teams garnered immediate success; she led them to three consecutive **Association of Intercollegiate Athletics for Women** (AIAW) national championships.

Wade retired in 1979. Established in her honor, the Margaret Wade Trophy is now awarded each year to the top women's college basketball player. Wade was the first woman to be inducted to the Mississippi Sport Hall of Fame and the first women's college basketball coach to be inducted into the Naismith Memorial Basketball Hall of Fame. The first woman to be bestowed with the Naismith Women's Outstanding Contributions to Basketball award, Wade was truly a pioneer in the development of women's basketball. She died in February 1995, at the age of eighty-three.

Further Reading

Hawkes, Nena Ray, and John F. Seggar. *Celebrity Women Coaches: A Biographical Dictionary*. Westport, CT: Greenwood, 2000.

Wade, Margaret, and Mel Hankinson. *Basketball*. Cleveland, MS: Delta State University, 1980.

Waldman, Suzyn "Georgie Girl" (1947–)

Sports journalist Suzyn Waldman, the first female play-by-play announcer for a Major League Baseball team, was born in Boston, Massachusetts in 1947 to Phillip and Jeanne Waldman. Waldman attended the New England Conservatory of Music and later graduated with a degree in economics from Simmons College. She then began a career acting and singing on Broadway before eventually transitioning into sports reporting.

In 1987 she became a broadcaster for New York's WFAN all-sports radio station. Covering games for the New York Yankees and the New York Knicks, Waldman remained with WFAN for fifteen years, hosting a daily sports talk show, until she joined the YES network. In 1995, at a game between the Texas Rangers and the New York Yankees, she became the first woman to announce the play-by-play for a nationally televised baseball broadcast. In 2005 Waldman accepted a job as color commentator for the Yankees on WCBS-AM radio, becoming the first woman to hold such a position.

In 1999 Waldman played an instrumental role in resolving the fourteen-year feud between Yankee's coach Yogi Berra and owner George Steinbrenner, receiving a Heroes Award from the Thurman Munson Foundation for her efforts. Named New York's Sportscaster of the Year in 1996, Waldman also received the 1999 Star Award from the American Women in Radio and TV organization.

Further Reading

Doren, Kim, and Charlie Jones. *You Go Girl!: Winning the Woman's Way*. Kansas City, MO: Andrew McMeel Publishers, 2000.

White, Nera Dyson (November 15, 1935–)

Women's basketball pioneer Nera Dyson White was born in Macon County, Tennessee, in November 1935, to Horace and Lois White. White played on the Macon County High School girls' basketball team in Lafayette, Tennessee, serving as her team's captain for two years and earning the title of most valuable player in 1954. After high school, she enrolled at George Peabody College for Teachers. Because the college did not have a women's basketball team, White began playing on an amateur team sponsored by the Nashville Business College, part of the **Amateur Athletic Union** (AAU), in 1955.

Between 1955 and 1969, White led the Nashville Business College team to ten AAU national championships. She was designated an All-American in her first AAU tournament. White was named the conference's most valuable player. A frequent member of the United States All-Star team, she played basketball around the world, including at the World Basketball Championship in Rio de Janeiro, Brazil, in 1957, where she was named the World's Best Player. She led the team to a gold medal in the tournament and was voted Best Woman Player in the World. Called "Queen of the Hardwood" by Amateur Athletic Magazine in 1969, White was named AAU All-American fifteen consecutive times, thus setting a record in women's basketball. She was also named the AAU's most valuable player nine times. White retired from basketball in 1969. She has been elected to both the Tennessee Sports Hall of Fame and the Women's Basketball Hall of Fame.

In addition to playing basketball, White also played softball and was on a number of state and regional teams. Playing on the American Softball Association (ASA) Fast Pitch teams in both 1959 and 1965, White was the first woman to run around the bases in just ten seconds. She continued playing softball even after she retired from basketball. In 1980 she was named an All-American for slow-pitch softball.

One of the best female basketball players of all time, White was one of the first three women to be inducted into the Naismith Basketball Hall of Fame and was ranked seventh on *Sports Illustrated*'s list of the fifty best sports figures in Tennessee.

Further Reading

Douchant, Mike. *Encyclopedia of College Basketball*. New York: Gale Research, 1995.

Women's Basketball Coaches Association

Committed to promoting the sport of women's basketball, the Women's Basketball Coaches Association (WBCA) was formed in 1981. During the 1981 summer Olympic Festival in Syracuse, New York, a number of women's basketball coaches, including **Patricia "Pat" Summitt** and C. Vivian Stringer, met to discuss the lack of an organization exclusively for coaches of women's basketball. The budding group named Jill Hutchinson, head coach of the Illinois State University women's basketball team, as president. **Betty F. Jaynes**, head women's basketball coach at James Madison University from 1970 to 1982, was appointed the organization's executive director. Originally located in Wayne, Pennsylvania, Jaynes moved the WBCA offices to Atlanta, Georgia, in 1985.

The WBCA actively seeks to defend the rights of women and girls of all ages in a variety of areas. To achieve this objective, the WBCA closely follows federal legislative action on Title IX, conducts research on women's salaries, and monitors all **National Collegiate Athletic Association** (NCAA) regulations, as well as legislation concerning high school, junior/community college, and National Association for Intercollegiate Athletics (NAIA) basketball programs. In 1994 and 1997, the association conducted two surveys of women basketball coaches in all divisions. The organization has also established the Rights, Equity & Fairness (R.E.F.) Program, designed to protect women's basketball coaches' rights during the hiring and firing processes, to offer emotional support for coaches who have lost their jobs, and to maintain a resource center for coaches who are seeking jobs or are in need of legal assistance.

In 2005 the WBCA partnered with Minute Maid/Coca-Cola to sponsor "The Art of Women's Basketball" art print contest. In conjunction with the NCAA Women's Final Four, middle and high school students entered original drawings that illustrated "the gracefulness, strength, passion, and competitiveness of women's basketball." Each year the WBCA also hosts the Nike "So You Want to be a Coach" program. Over the course of two-and-a-half days, this workshop "provide[s] an educational and professional foundation for minority female basketball players in order to better prepare them for entering the coaching profession" and seeks to generate interest in coaching among minority players. Having had just over 200 members when it was initially established, the WBCA now boasts more than 5,000 members from all levels of women's basketball.

Further Reading

Women's Basketball Coaches Association Web site (http://www.wbca.org/).

Women's Educational Equity Act

The Women's Educational Equity Act (WEEA) of 1974, sponsored by Representative **Patsy T. Mink** and Senator Walter F. Mondale, was passed by Congress as part of the Special Projects Act of the Education Amendments of 1974. Under this act, the U.S. Department of Education awarded grants and contracts in order to support activities, events, and organizations that would provide educational equity for girls and women. WEEA activities included creating textbooks and educational materials, offering training for educators, generating research, and increasing opportunities for women and girls in education. One of the primary concerns of WEEA was to support Title IX.

To oversee the WEEA program and make recommendations about gender equity in education, the National Advisory Council on Women's Education Programs (NACWEP) was established as part of the Department of Education in 1975. The council was composed of seventeen individuals appointed by the president; the chair of the Civil Rights Commission; the director of the Women's Bureau of the Department of Labor; and the director of the Women's Action Program of the Department of Health, Education, and Welfare (HEW). In addition to both students and university administrators, members of NACWEP included the director of the National Organization for Women's Legal Defense and Education Fund's Project on Equal Education Rights and the director of the Association of American Colleges' Project on the Status and Education of Women.

Before it was officially dissolved in 1988, NACWEP produced several reports on the status of education for women and Title IX. In 1978 the council published *The Unenforced Law: Title IX Activity by Federal Agencies Other Than HEWS*, a study finding that most agencies were ignoring the legislation. In *The Half Full, Half Empty Glass* (1981), NACWEP reported on developments occurring since Title IX's passage. When WEEA was reauthorized in 1978, NACWEP played a key role in drafting the revision to include "grants for projects to assist state and local school districts to implement Title IX."

One of the organizations funded by WEEA was the Education Development Center's WEEA Equity Resource Center, based in Newton, Massachusetts. In its more than twenty-year history, the center conducted research on gender equity and produced a number of educational and classroom materials on both Title IX and gender equity. Established in 1977, the center's funding contract ended in 2003.

Over the years, the Women's Educational Equity Act was incorporated into several different amendments and has been under the management of various agencies. NACWEP was abolished with the 1988 Hawkins-Stafford Amendments. WEEA has most recently been incorporated into the No Child Left Behind Act. Since it began in 1974, WEEA has funded more than 700 programs.

Further Reading

United States General Accounting Office. *Women's Educational Equity Act: A Review of Program Goals and Strategies Needed*. Report to Congressional Requestors. Washington, DC: General Accounting Office, 1994.

Women's Equity Action League

The Women's Equity Action League (WEAL) was founded in Cleveland, Ohio, in 1968 by Elizabeth Boyer, who also served as the organization's first president, in conjunction with other local members of the National Organization for Women (NOW). WEAL was "dedicated to improving the status and lives of all women primarily through education, litigation, and legislation." In addition to promoting equal employment and economic opportunities for women, the organization also sought to enforce antidiscrimination laws and to encourage more young women to pursue careers in science, technology, and medicine.

Just one year after it was established, WEAL had members in twenty-two states across the country. In 1971 the organization began issuing the *WEAL Washington Report*, a review of federal legislation relevant to women. The following year, WEAL members actively supported the passage of Title IX and the equal rights amendment. WEAL was particularly involved in promoting Title IX in the 1970s and 1980s. In 1974 WEAL joined several other organizations, including NOW and the National Education Association (NEA), in filing a complaint against the U.S. Department of Health, Education, and Welfare (HEW); the Office of Civil Rights (OCR); the U.S. Department of Labor; and the Office of Federal Contract Compliance, claiming that the last entity had failed to enforce antidiscrimination laws. Three years later, a district court judge ordered OCR to investigate the discrimination charges. In March 1982, WEAL and the other organizations declared that OCR was not complying with the order. The original 1977 order was then amended to require all OCR investigations to determine an institution's compliance.

Between 1975 and 1983, WEAL maintained the Sports Project Referral and Information Network (SPRINT), through which the organization "collected and distributed information on women and girls in sports, particularly in educational institutions, and monitored legal and political developments, model programs, and trends in women's physical education and athletics." SPRINT also published *In the Running*, a newsletter on women's sports events. In addition, WEAL also issued several other publications on Title IX and women's sports.

By the late 1980s, WEAL was unable to maintain its funding. The organization was dissolved in 1989.

Further Reading

Women's Equity Action League Archives. Arthur and Elizabeth Schlesinger Library on the History of Women in America, Radcliffe Institute for Advanced Study, Harvard University.

Women's National Basketball Association

The Women's National Basketball Association (WNBA) was formed on April 24, 1996, by the Board of Governors of the men's National Basketball Association (NBA). Although it was not the first women's basketball league, the WNBA was the first to have the full support of the NBA. Additionally, the WNBA and the American Basketball League (ABL) were the first leagues to market women's basketball as a competitive athletic competition, rather than simply a sideshow to accompany men's basketball.

When the WNBA was first conceptualized, NBA officials decided to hold women's games during the summer, instead of synchronizing them with the men's games, which were held during the fall and winter. WNBA creators wanted the women's teams to complement the men's in both name and uniform. The league initially consisted of only eight teams. The WNBA appointed women's basketball pioneers **Val Ackerman** and **Carol Blazejowski** to serve as its president and vice president, respectively. Hoping to capitalize on the success of the 1996 Olympic team, the WNBA signed three Olympic team members as its first players: Rebecca Lobo, Lisa Leslie, and Sheryl Swoopes, who was pregnant at the time the contracts were signed. All three players became spokespersons for the newly formed league.

The WNBA began its first season in June 1997, with its first game, a match between the New York Liberty and the Los Angeles Sparks, being held on June 21, 1997. President Val Ackerman tossed up the ceremonial first ball to begin the game. When the league's rival, the ABL, folded in 1999, many of its players joined the WNBA. Additional teams were added to the roster during the first season, and by 2000 the league had doubled its number of teams. The league held its first all-star game, televised on ESPN, in July 1999; more than 18,000 people were in attendance.

When Ackerman resigned her position in February 2005 to become the president of USA Basketball, NBA Commissioner David Stern appointed Donna Orender, a former player in the Women's Professional Basketball League (WBL), as the new president of the WNBA. During the 2006 season, the league's tenth, the WBNA announced the formation of the All-Decade Team, which would be composed of individuals who had made the greatest contributions to the sport of women's basketball and to the WNBA.

Further Reading

Ennis, Lisa A. "Crashing the Boards: The WNBA and the Evolution of an Image," in *Basketball in America: From the Playgrounds to Jordan's Game and Beyond*, ed. Bob Batchelor, Binghamton, NY: Haworth Press, 2005, pp. 231–242.

Whiteside, Kelly. *WNBA: A Celebration: Commemorating the Birth of a League*. New York: HarperHorizon, 1998.

Women's National Basketball Association Web site (http://www.wnba.com/).

Women's Sports Foundation

The Women's Sports Foundation (WSF) was founded in 1974 by tennis star **Billie Jean King** and former Olympic swimmer **Donna de Varona**. For more than thirty years, the WSF has attempted to "advance the lives of girls and women through sports and physical activity." Since its inception, the organization has envisioned a world where "no one underestimates the sports ability of a person simply because of gender or appearance" and where "there is extensive interest in, and quality media coverage of, women in sports."

The WSF has developed a number of programs and events to raise awareness of women's sports and to celebrate the many accomplishments of female

Athletic scholarship funding for women was practically nonexistent before Title IX, but today more than $400 million in scholarships is available to female athletes. Photo from authors' private collection.

athletes in the United States. The WSF provides information on sports, athletes, fitness, current issues such as Title IX and gender equity, sports careers, and scholarships, in addition to a variety of other topics. In pursuit of its mission, the WSF has created many services. One example is Geena Takes Aim, a program led by actress Geena Davis, which seeks "to empower girls and young women to know their rights in sport and to teach them practical ways to deal with situations they face which may not be fair." Geena Takes Aim provides a Title IX library, online assessment tools to determine whether schools are compliant, and a guide to assessing gender equity in schools. Another example is the It Takes a Team! Educational Campaign for Lesbian, Gay, Bisexual and Transgender Issues in Sport program, which strives to eliminate homophobia—a barrier to sport participation for both women and men. Initiated by tennis player Martina Navratilova in 1996, It Takes a Team! is a collaborative project between several organizations, including the **National Collegiate Athletic Association** (NCAA). In 2002 the group published an educational resource kit for coaches and sports programs alike. The WSF also sponsors GoGirlGo!, an educational program dedicated to encouraging a million young girls, ages eight to eighteen, to engage in physical activity. Featuring an action center, lounge, gym, and school, as well as star athletes and four GoGirl characters, the GoGirlGo! program promotes good health, sports, and physical activity in fun and interactive ways. The program received a Gold Award from the National Health Information organization in both 2004 and 2006.

Over the years, the WSF has established several awards to honor individuals who have made a difference in women's sports. In addition to the Coach of the Year Award, the Flo Hyman Award, and the Sportswoman of the Year Award, the WSF has recently established the Billies, which celebrate positive media representations of women in sports. Recipients of these awards in 2006 included journalist **Christine Brennan** and the exhibit "*Game Face: What Does a Female Athlete Look Like?*" The WSF also sponsors the traveling photography exhibit SuperWomen and a speakers' bureau. The organization also offers over $500,000 in grants to be awarded to eligible programs each year.

Further Reading
GoGirlGo! Web site (http://www.gogirlgo.com/).
Women's Sports Foundation Web site (http://www.womenssportsfoundation.org/).

Woodard, Lynette (August 12, 1959–)

Lynette Woodard, the first female member of the Harlem Globetrotters, was born in Wichita, Kansas, to Lugene and Dorothy Woodard. She began playing basketball while attending Wichita North High School. After graduating from high school in 1977, Woodard enrolled at the University of Kansas, where she joined the women's basketball team. Leading both her team and the nation with over twenty-five points per game, she was ultimately named freshman player of the year by both *Street and Smith* and *Basketball Weekly*. During her junior year, she was invited to play on the U.S. team at the 1979 World University Games. In 1981 she was awarded the Wade Trophy and the Broderick Award, in recognition of her role in women's college basketball. Woodard was also a four-time All-American and the first woman to receive the **National Collegiate Athletic Association's** Top V Award, a distinction given to the top five college athletes in the country.

Upon graduating from college with a degree in speech communications and human relations, Woodard played on the U.S. national team for the 1983 Pan-American Games and the World University Games. The next year, she was named captain of the U.S. Olympic team, leading the team to win America's first Olympic gold medal for women's basketball.

Woodard joined the Harlem Globetrotters in October 1985, becoming the first female member of the team. While on the team, she worked to promote opportunities for women basketball players, beyond playing for college teams. She was named the **Women's Sports Foundation's** Professional Sportswoman of the Year in 1986. After leaving the Globetrotters in 1987, Woodard played in Italian and Japanese leagues until 1992. She returned to the United States in 1992, when she was named athletic director for the Kansas City school system.

In 1997 Woodard joined the newly founded **Women's National Basketball Association** (WNBA), playing for the Cleveland Rockers. She also played for the league's Detroit Shock before returning to the University of Kansas as an assistant coach. Woodard was inducted into the International Sports Hall of Fame, and she was also named one of the 100 greatest female athletes by *Sports Illustrated for Women* magazine.

Further Reading
Newman, Matthew. *Lynette Woodard*. Mankato, MN: Crestwood House, 1986.

Appendices

Subtitle B Regulations of the Offices of the Department of Education

Chapter 1 Office for Civil Rights, Department of Education

Part 106 Nondiscrimination on the Basis of Sex in Education Programs or Activities Receiving Federal Financial Assistance

Subpart A—Introduction

Subpart B—Coverage

Subpart C—Discrimination on the Basis of Sex in Admission and Recruitment Prohibited

106.21 Admission.
106.22 Preference in admission.
106.23 Recruitment.

Subpart D—Discrimination on the Basis of Sex in Education Programs or Activities Prohibited

106.31 Education programs or activities.
106.32 Housing.
106.33 Comparable facilities.
106.34 Access to course offerings.
106.35 Access to schools operated by LEAs.
106.36 Counseling and use of appraisal and counseling materials.
106.37 Financial assistance.
106.38 Employment assistance to students.
106.39 Health and insurance benefits and services.
106.40 Marital or parental status.
106.41 Athletics.
106.42 Textbooks and curricular material.

Subpart E—Discrimination on the Basis of Sex in Employment in Education Programs or Activities Prohibited

106.51 Employment.
106.52 Employment criteria.
106.53 Recruitment.
106.54 Compensation.
106.55 Job classification and structure.
106.56 Fringe benefits.
106.57 Marital or parental status.
106.58 Effect of State or local law or other requirements.
106.59 Advertising.
106.60 Pre-employment inquiries.
106.61 Sex as a bona-fide occupational qualification.

Subpart F—Procedures [Interim]

106.71 Procedures.
Subject Index to Title IX Preamble and Regulation
Appendix A to Part 106—Guidelines for Eliminating Discrimination and Denial of Services on the Basis of Race, Color, National Origin, Sex, and Handicap in Vocational Education Programs
Authority: 20 U.S.C. 1681 *et seq.*, unless otherwise noted.
Source: 45 FR 30955, May 9, 1980, unless otherwise noted.

Subpart A—Introduction

106.1 Purpose and effective date.

The purpose of this part is to effectuate title IX of the Education Amendments of 1972, as amended by Pub. L. 93–568, 88 Stat. 1855 (except sections 904 and 906 of those Amendments) which is designed to eliminate (with certain exceptions) discrimination on the basis of sex in any education program or activity receiving Federal financial assistance, whether or not such program or activity is offered or sponsored by an educational institution as defined in this part. This part is also intended to effectuate section 844 of the Education Amendments of 1974, Pub. L. 93–380, 88 Stat. 484. The effective date of this part shall be July 21, 1975.

(Authority: Secs. 901, 902, Education Amendments of 1972, 86 Stat. 373, 374; 20 U.S.C. 1681, 1682, as amended by Pub. L. 93–568, 88 Stat. 1855, and sec. 844, Education Amendments of 1974, 88 Stat. 484, Pub. L. 93380)

106.2 Definitions.

As used in this part, the term:

(a) *Title IX* means title IX of the Education Amendments of 1972, Pub. L. 92–318, as amended by section 3 of Pub. L. 93–568, 88 Stat. 1855, except sections 904 and 906 thereof; 20 U.S.C. 1681, 1682, 1683, 1685, 1686.

(b) *Department* means the Department of Education.

(c) *Secretary* means the Secretary of Education.

(d) *Assistant Secretary* means the Assistant Secretary for Civil Rights of the Department.

(e) *Reviewing Authority* means that component of the Department delegated authority by the Secretary to appoint, and to review the decisions of, administrative law judges in cases arising under this part.

(f) *Administrative law judge* means a person appointed by the reviewing authority to preside over a hearing held under this part.

(g) *Federal financial assistance* means any of the following, when authorized or extended under a law administered by the Department:

    (1) A grant or loan of Federal financial assistance, including funds made available for:

        (i) The acquisition, construction, renovation, restoration, or repair of a building or facility or any portion thereof; and

        (ii) Scholarships, loans, grants, wages or other funds extended to any entity for payment to or on behalf of students admitted to that entity, or extended directly to such students for payment to that entity.

    (2) A grant of Federal real or personal property or any interest therein, including surplus property, and the proceeds of the sale or transfer of such property, if the Federal share of the fair market value of the property is not, upon such sale or transfer, properly accounted for to the Federal Government.

    (3) Provision of the services of Federal personnel.

    (4) Sale or lease of Federal property or any interest therein at nominal consideration or at consideration reduced for the purpose of assisting the recipient or in recognition of public interest to be served thereby, or

permission to use Federal property or any interest therein without consideration.

(5) Any other contract, agreement, or arrangement which has as one of its purposes the provision of assistance to any education program or activity, except a contract of insurance or guaranty.

(h) *Program or activity* and *program* means all of the operations of—

(1) (i) A department, agency, special purpose district, or other instrumentality of a State or local government; or

(ii) The entity of a State or local government that distributes such assistance and each such department or agency (and each other State or local government entity) to which the assistance is extended, in the case of assistance to a State or local government;

(2) (i) A college, university, or other postsecondary institution, or a public system of higher education; or

(ii) A local educational agency (as defined in 20 U.S.C. 8801), system of vocational education, or other school system;

(3) (i) An entire corporation, partnership, other private organization, or an entire sole proprietorship—

(A) If assistance is extended to such corporation, partnership, private organization, or sole proprietorship as a whole; or

(B) Which is principally engaged in the business of providing education, health care, housing, social services, or parks and recreation; or

(ii) The entire plant or other comparable, geographically separate facility to which Federal financial assistance is extended, in the case of any other corporation, partnership, private organization, or sole proprietorship; or

(4) Any other entity that is established by two or more of the entities described in paragraph (h)(1), (2), or (3) of this section; any part of which is extended Federal financial assistance.

(Authority: 20 U.S.C. 1687)

(i) *Recipient* means any State or political subdivision thereof, or any instrumentality of a State or political subdivision thereof, any public or private agency, institution, or organization, or other entity, or any person, to whom Federal financial assistance is extended directly or through another recipient and which operates an education program or activity which receives such assistance, including any subunit, successor, assignee, or transferee thereof.

(j) *Applicant* means one who submits an application, request, or plan required to be approved by a Department official, or by a recipient, as a condition to becoming a recipient.

(k) *Educational institution* means a local educational agency (LEA) as defined by section 1001(f) of the Elementary and Secondary Education Act of 1965 (20 U.S.C. 3381), a preschool, a private elementary or secondary school, or an applicant or recipient of the type defined by paragraph (l), (m), (n), or (o) of this section.

(l) *Institution of graduate higher education* means an institution which:
  (1) Offers academic study beyond the bachelor of arts or bachelor of science degree, whether or not leading to a certificate of any higher degree in the liberal arts and sciences; or
  (2) Awards any degree in a professional field beyond the first professional degree (regardless of whether the first professional degree in such field is awarded by an institution of undergraduate higher education or professional education); or
  (3) Awards no degree and offers no further academic study, but operates ordinarily for the purpose of facilitating research by persons who have received the highest graduate degree in any field of study.

(m) *Institution of undergraduate higher education* means:
  (1) An institution offering at least two but less than four years of college level study beyond the high school level, leading to a diploma or an associate degree, or wholly or principally creditable toward a baccalaureate degree; or
  (2) An institution offering academic study leading to a baccalaureate degree; or
  (3) An agency or body which certifies credentials or offers degrees, but which may or may not offer academic study.

(n) *Institution of professional education* means an institution (except any institution of undergraduate higher education) which offers a program of academic study that leads to a first professional degree in a field for which there is a national specialized accrediting agency recognized by the Secretary.

(o) *Institution of vocational education* means a school or institution (except an institution of professional or graduate or undergraduate higher education) which has as its primary purpose preparation of students to pursue a technical, skilled, or semiskilled occupation or trade, or to pursue study in a technical field, whether or not the school or institution offers certificates, diplomas, or degrees and whether or not it offers fulltime study.

(p) *Administratively separate unit* means a school, department or college of an educational institution (other than a local educational agency) admission to which is independent of admission to any other component of such institution.

(q) *Admission* means selection for part-time, full-time, special, associate, transfer, exchange, or any other enrollment, membership, or matriculation in or at an education program or activity operated by a recipient.

(r) *Student* means a person who has gained admission.

(s) *Transition plan* means a plan subject to the approval of the Secretary pursuant to section 901(a)(2) of the Education Amendments of 1972, under which an educational institution operates in making the transition from being an educational institution which admits only students of one sex to being one which admits students of both sexes without discrimination.

(Authority: Secs. 901, 902, Education Amendments of 1972, 86 Stat. 373, 374; 20 U.S.C. 1681, 1682)

[45 FR 30955, May 9, 1980; 45 FR 37426, June 3, 1980]

106.3 Remedial and affirmative action and self-evaluation.

(a) *Remedial action.* If the Assistant Secretary finds that a recipient has discriminated against persons on the basis of sex in an education program or activity, such recipient shall take such remedial action as the Assistant Secretary deems necessary to overcome the effects of such discrimination.

(b) *Affirmative action.* In the absence of a finding of discrimination on the basis of sex in an education program or activity, a recipient may take affirmative action to overcome the effects of conditions which resulted in limited participation therein by persons of a particular sex. Nothing herein shall be interpreted to alter any affirmative action obligations which a recipient may have under Executive Order 11246.

(c) *Self-evaluation.* Each recipient education institution shall, within one year of the effective date of this part:

    (1) Evaluate, in terms of the requirements of this part, its current policies and practices and the effects thereof concerning admission of students, treatment of students, and employment of both academic and non-academic personnel working in connection with the recipient's education program or activity;

    (2) Modify any of these policies and practices which do not or may not meet the requirements of this part; and

    (3) Take appropriate remedial steps to eliminate the effects of any discrimination which resulted or may have resulted from adherence to these policies and practices.

(d) *Availability of self-evaluation and related materials.* Recipients shall maintain on file for at least three years following completion of the evaluation required under paragraph (c) of this section, and shall provide to the Assistant Secretary upon request, a description of any modifications made pursuant to paragraph (c)(ii) of this section and of any remedial steps taken pursuant to paragraph (c)(iii) of this section.

(Authority: Secs. 901, 902, Education Amendments of 1972, 86 Stat. 373, 374; 20 U.S.C. 1681, 1682)

106.4 Assurance required.

(a) *General.* Every application for Federal financial assistance shall as condition of its approval contain or be accompanied by an assurance from the applicant or recipient, satisfactory to the Assistant Secretary, that the education program or activity operated by the applicant or recipient and to which this part applies will be operated in compliance with this. An assurance of compliance with this part shall not be satisfactory to the Assistant Secretary if the applicant or recipient to whom such assurance applies fails to commit itself to take whatever remedial action is necessary in accordance with § 106.3(a) to eliminate existing discrimination on the basis of sex or to eliminate the effects of past discrimination whether occurring prior or subsequent to the submission to the Assistant Secretary of such assurance.

(b) *Duration of obligation.*

    (1) In the case of Federal financial assistance extended to provide real property or structures thereon, such assurance shall obligate the recipient or,

in the case of a subsequent transfer, the transferee, for the period during which the real property or structures are used to provide an education program or activity.

(2) In the case of Federal financial assistance extended to provide personal property, such assurance shall obligate the recipient for the period during which it retains ownership or possession of the property.

(3) In all other cases such assurance shall obligate the recipient for the period during which Federal financial assistance is extended.

(c) *Form.* The Director will specify the form of the assurances required by paragraph (a) of this section and the extent to which such assurances will be required of the applicant's or recipient's subgrantees, contractors, subcontractors, transferees, or successors in interest.

(Authority: Secs. 901, 902, Education Amendments of 1972, 86 Stat. 373, 374; 20 U.S.C. 1681, 1682)

[45 FR 30955, May 9, 1980, as amended at 45 FR 86298, Dec. 30, 1980]

106.5 Transfers of property.

If a recipient sells or otherwise transfers property financed in whole or in part with Federal financial assistance to a transferee which operates any education program or activity, and the Federal share of the fair market value of the property is not upon such sale or transfer properly accounted for to the Federal Government both the transferor and the transferee shall be deemed to be recipients, subject to the provisions of subpart B of this part.

(Authority: Secs. 901, 902, Education Amendments of 1972, 86 Stat. 373, 374; 20 U.S.C. 1681, 1682)

106.6 Effect of other requirements.

(a) *Effect of other Federal provisions.* The obligations imposed by this part are independent of, and do not alter, obligations not to discriminate on the basis of sex imposed by Executive Order 11246, as amended; sections 704 and 855 of the Public Health Service Act (42 U.S.C. 292d and 298b–2); Title VII of the Civil Rights Act of 1964 (42 U.S.C. 2000e *et seq.*); the Equal Pay Act (29 U.S.C. 206 and 206(d)); and any other Act of Congress or Federal regulation.

(Authority: Secs. 901, 902, 905, Education Amendments of 1972, 86 Stat. 373, 374, 375; 20 U.S.C. 1681, 1682, 1685)

(b) *Effect of State or local law or other requirements.* The obligation to comply with this part is not obviated or alleviated by any State or local law or other requirement which would render any applicant or student ineligible, or limit the eligibility of any applicant or student, on the basis of sex, to practice any occupation or profession.

(c) *Effect of rules or regulations of private organizations.* The obligation to comply with this part is not obviated or alleviated by any rule or regulation of any organization, club, athletic or other league, or association which would render any applicant or student ineligible to participate or limit the eligibility or participation of any applicant or student, on the basis of sex, in any education program or activity operated by a recipient and which receives Federal financial assistance.

(Authority: Secs. 901, 902, Education Amendments of 1972, 86 Stat. 373, 374; 20 U.S.C. 1681, 1682)

106.7 Effect of employment opportunities.

The obligation to comply with this part is not obviated or alleviated because employment opportunities in any occupation or profession are or may be more limited for members of one sex than for members of the other sex.

(Authority: Secs. 901, 902, Education Amendments of 1972, 86 Stat. 373, 374; 20 U.S.C. 1681, 1682)

106.8 Designation of responsible employee and adoption of grievance procedures.

(a) *Designation of responsible employee.* Each recipient shall designate at least one employee to coordinate its efforts to comply with and carry out its responsibilities under this part, including any investigation of any complaint communicated to such recipient alleging its noncompliance with this part or alleging any actions which would be prohibited by this part. The recipient shall notify all its students and employees of the name, office address and telephone number of the employee or employees appointed pursuant to this paragraph.

(b) *Complaint procedure of recipient.* A recipient shall adopt and publish grievance procedures providing for prompt and equitable resolution of student and employee complaints alleging any action which would be prohibited by this part.

(Authority: Secs. 901, 902, Education Amendments of 1972, 86 Stat. 373, 374; 20 U.S.C. 1681, 1682)

106.9 Dissemination of policy.

(a) *Notification of policy.*

(1) Each recipient shall implement specific and continuing steps to notify applicants for admission and employment, students and parents of elementary and secondary school students, employees, sources of referral of applicants for admission and employment, and all unions or professional organizations holding collective bargaining or professional agreements with the recipient, that it does not discriminate on the basis of sex in the educational program or activity which it operates, and that it is required by title IX and this part not to discriminate in such a manner. Such notification shall contain such information, and be made in such manner, as the Assistant Secretary finds necessary to apprise such persons of the protections against discrimination assured them by title IX and this part, but shall state at least that the requirement not to discriminate in the education program or activity extends to employment therein, and to admission thereto unless Subpart C does not apply to the recipient, and that inquiries concerning the application of title IX and this part to such recipient may be referred to the employee designated pursuant to § 106.8, or to the Assistant Secretary.

(2) Each recipient shall make the initial notification required by paragraph (a)(1) of this section within 90 days of the effective date of this part or of

the date this part first applies to such recipient, whichever comes later, which notification shall include publication in:

(i)   Local newspapers;

(ii) Newspapers and magazines operated by such recipient or by student, alumnae, or alumni groups for or in connection with such recipient; and

(iii) Memoranda or other written communications distributed to every student and employee of such recipient.

(b) *Publications.*

(1)   Each recipient shall prominently include a statement of the policy described in paragraph (a) of this section in each announcement, bulletin, catalog, or application form which it makes available to any person of a type, described in paragraph (a) of this section, or which is otherwise used in connection with the recruitment of students or employees.

(2)   A recipient shall not use or distribute a publication of the type described in this paragraph which suggests, by text or illustration, that such recipient treats applicants, students, or employees differently on the basis of sex except as such treatment is permitted by this part.

(c) *Distribution.* Each recipient shall distribute without discrimination on the basis of sex each publication described in paragraph (b) of this section, and shall apprise each of its admission and employment recruitment representatives of the policy of nondiscrimination described in paragraph (a) of this section, and require such representatives to adhere to such policy.

(Authority: Secs. 901, 902, Education Amendments of 1972, 86 Stat. 373, 374; 20 U.S.C. 1681, 1682)

Subpart B—Coverage

106.11 Application.

Except as provided in this subpart, this part 106 applies to every recipient and to the education program or activity operated by such recipient which receives Federal financial assistance.

(Authority: Secs. 901, 902, Education Amendments of 1972, 86 Stat. 373, 374; 20 U.S.C. 1681, 1682)

[45 FR 86298, Dec. 30, 1980]

106.12 Educational institutions controlled by religious organizations.

(a) *Application.* This part does not apply to an educational institution which is controlled by a religious organization to the extent application of this part would not be consistent with the religious tenets of such organization.

(b) *Exemption.* An educational institution which wishes to claim the exemption set forth in paragraph (a) of this section, shall do so by submitting in writing to the Assistant Secretary a statement by the highest ranking official of the institution, identifying the provisions of this part which conflict with a specific tenet of the religious organization.

(Authority: Secs. 901, 902, Education Amendments of 1972, 86 Stat. 373, 374; 20 U.S.C. 1681, 1682)

106.13 Military and merchant marine educational institutions.

This part does not apply to an educational institution whose primary purpose is the training of individuals for a military service of the United States or for the merchant marine.

(Authority: Secs. 901, 902, Education Amendments of 1972, 86 Stat. 373, 374; 20 U.S.C. 1681, 1682)

106.14 Membership practices of certain organizations.

(a) *Social fraternities and sororities.* This part does not apply to the membership practices of social fraternities and sororities which are exempt from taxation under section 501(a) of the Internal Revenue Code of 1954, the active membership of which consists primarily of students in attendance at institutions of higher education.

(b) *YMCA, YWCA, Girl Scouts, Boy Scouts and Camp Fire Girls.* This part does not apply to the membership practices of the Young Men's Christian Association, the Young Women's Christian Association, the Girl Scouts, the Boy Scouts and Camp Fire Girls.

(c) *Voluntary youth service organizations.* This part does not apply to the membership practices of voluntary youth service organizations which are exempt from taxation under section 501(a) of the Internal Revenue Code of 1954 and the membership of which has been traditionally limited to members of one sex and principally to persons of less than nineteen years of age.

(Authority: Secs. 901, 902, Education Amendments of 1972, 86 Stat. 373, 374; 20 U.S.C. 1681, 1682; sec. 3(a) of P.L. 93–568, 88 Stat. 1862 amending Sec. 901)

106.15 Admissions.

(a) Admissions to educational institutions prior to June 24, 1973, are not covered by this part.

(b) *Administratively separate units.* For the purposes only of this section, §§ 106.16 and 106.17, and subpart C, each administratively separate unit shall be deemed to be an educational institution.

(c) *Application of subpart C.* Except as provided in paragraphs (d) and (e) of this section, subpart C applies to each recipient. A recipient to which subpart C applies shall not discriminate on the basis of sex in admission or recruitment in violation of that subpart.

(d) *Educational institutions.* Except as provided in paragraph (e) of this section as to recipients which are educational institutions, subpart C applies only to institutions of vocational education, professional education, graduate higher education, and public institutions of undergraduate higher education.

(e) *Public institutions of undergraduate higher education.* Subpart C does not apply to any public institution of undergraduate higher education which traditionally and continually from its establishment has had a policy of admitting only students of one sex.

(Authority: Secs. 901, 902, Education Amendments of 1972, 86 Stat. 373, 374; 20 U.S.C. 1681, 1682)

[45 FR 30955, May 9, 1980, as amended at 45 FR 86298, Dec. 30, 1980]

106.16 Educational institutions eligible to submit transition plans.

(a) *Application*. This section applies to each educational institution to which subpart C applies which:

(1) Admitted only students of one sex as regular students as of June 23, 1972; or

(2) Admitted only students of one sex as regular students as of June 23, 1965, but thereafter admitted as regular students, students of the sex not admitted prior to June 23, 1965.

(b) *Provision for transition plans*. An educational institution to which this section applies shall not discriminate on the basis of sex in admission or recruitment in violation of subpart C unless it is carrying out a transition plan approved by the Secretary as described in § 106.17, which plan provides for the elimination of such discrimination by the earliest practicable date but in no event later than June 23, 1979.

(Authority: Secs. 901, 902, Education Amendments of 1972, 86 Stat. 373, 374; 20 U.S.C. 1681, 1682)

106.17 Transition plans.

(a) *Submission of plans*. An institution to which § 106.16 applies and which is composed of more than one administratively separate unit may submit either a single transition plan applicable to all such units, or a separate transition plan applicable to each such unit.

(b) *Content of plans*. In order to be approved by the Secretary a transition plan shall:

(1) State the name, address, and Federal Interagency Committee on Education (FICE) Code of the educational institution submitting such plan, the administratively separate units to which the plan is applicable, and the name, address, and telephone number of the person to whom questions concerning the plan may be addressed. The person who submits the plan shall be the chief administrator or president of the institution, or another individual legally authorized to bind the institution to all actions set forth in the plan.

(2) State whether the educational institution or administratively separate unit admits students of both sexes, as regular students and, if so, when it began to do so.

(3) Identify and describe with respect to the educational institution or administratively separate unit any obstacles to admitting students without discrimination on the basis of sex.

(4) Describe in detail the steps necessary to eliminate as soon as practicable each obstacle so identified and indicate the schedule for taking these steps and the individual directly responsible for their implementation.

(5) Include estimates of the number of students, by sex, expected to apply for, be admitted to, and enter each class during the period covered by the plan.

(c) *Nondiscrimination*. No policy or practice of a recipient to which § 106.16 applies shall result in treatment of applicants to or students of such recipient in violation of subpart C unless such treatment is necessitated by an obstacle identified in paragraph (b) (3) of this section and a schedule for eliminating that obstacle has been provided as required by paragraph (b) (4) of this section.

(d) *Effects of past exclusion.* To overcome the effects of past exclusion of students on the basis of sex, each educational institution to which § 106.16 applies shall include in its transition plan, and shall implement, specific steps designed to encourage individuals of the previously excluded sex to apply for admission to such institution. Such steps shall include instituting recruitment which emphasizes the institution's commitment to enrolling students of the sex previously excluded.

(Authority: Secs. 901, 902, Education Amendments of 1972, 86 Stat. 373, 374; 20 U.S.C. 1681, 1682)

Subpart C—Discrimination on the Basis of Sex in Admission and Recruitment Prohibited

106.21 Admission.

(a) *General.* No person shall, on the basis of sex, be denied admission, or be subjected to discrimination in admission, by any recipient to which this subpart applies, except as provided in §§ 106.16 and 106.17.

(b) *Specific prohibitions.*

(1) In determining whether a person satisfies any policy or criterion for admission, or in making any offer of admission, a recipient to which this subpart applies shall not:

(i) Give preference to one person over another on the basis of sex, by ranking applicants separately on such basis, or otherwise;

(ii) Apply numerical limitations upon the number or proportion of persons of either sex who may be admitted; or

(iii) Otherwise treat one individual differently from another on the basis of sex.

(2) A recipient shall not administer or operate any test or other criterion for admission which has a disproportionately adverse effect on persons on the basis of sex unless the use of such test or criterion is shown to predict validly success in the education program or activity in question and alternative tests or criteria which do not have such a disproportionately adverse effect are shown to be unavailable.

(c) *Prohibitions relating to marital or parental status.* In determining whether a person satisfies any policy or criterion for admission, or in making any offer of admission, a recipient to which this subpart applies:

(1) Shall not apply any rule concerning the actual or potential parental, family, or marital status of a student or applicant which treats persons differently on the basis of sex;

(2) Shall not discriminate against or exclude any person on the basis of pregnancy, childbirth, termination of pregnancy, or recovery therefrom, or establish or follow any rule or practice which so discriminates or excludes;

(3) Shall treat disabilities related to pregnancy, childbirth, termination of pregnancy, or recovery therefrom in the same manner and under the same policies as any other temporary disability or physical condition; and

(4)   Shall not make pre-admission inquiry as to the marital status of an applicant for admission, including whether such applicant is "Miss or Mrs." A
recipient may make pre-admission inquiry as to the sex of an applicant for
admission, but only if such inquiry is made equally of such applicants of
both sexes and if the results of such inquiry are not used in connection
with discrimination prohibited by this part.

(Authority: Secs. 901, 902, Education Amendments of 1972, 86 Stat. 373, 374;
20 U.S.C. 1681, 1682)

106.22 Preference in admission.

A recipient to which this subpart applies shall not give preference to applicants for
admission, on the basis of attendance at any educational institution or other school
or entity which admits as students only or predominantly members of one sex, if the
giving of such preference has the effect of discriminating on the basis of sex in
violation of this subpart.

(Authority: Secs. 901, 902, Education Amendments of 1972, 86 Stat. 373, 374;
20 U.S.C. 1681, 1682)

106.23 Recruitment.

(a) *Nondiscriminatory recruitment.* A recipient to which this subpart applies shall
not discriminate on the basis of sex in the recruitment and admission of
students. A recipient may be required to undertake additional recruitment
efforts for one sex as remedial action pursuant to § 106.3(a), and may choose to
undertake such efforts as affirmative action pursuant to § 106.3(b).

(b) *Recruitment at certain institutions.* A recipient to which this subpart applies shall not
recruit primarily or exclusively at educational institutions, schools or entities
which admit as students only or predominantly members of one sex, if such actions
have the effect of discriminating on the basis of sex in violation of this subpart.

(Authority: Secs. 901, 902, Education Amendments of 1972, 86 Stat. 373, 374;
20 U.S.C. 1681, 1682)

**Subpart D—Discrimination on the Basis of Sex in Education Programs or
Activities Prohibited**

106.31 Education programs or activities.

(a) *General.* Except as provided elsewhere in this part, no person shall, on the basis of
sex, be excluded from participation in, be denied the benefits of, or be subjected to
discrimination under any academic, extracurricular, research, occupational training, or other education program or activity operated by a recipient which receives
Federal financial assistance. This subpart does not apply to actions of a recipient
in connection with admission of its students to an education program or activity
of (1) a recipient to which subpart C does not apply, or (2) an entity, not a recipient, to which subpart C would not apply if the entity were a recipient.

(b) *Specific prohibitions.* Except as provided in this subpart, in providing any aid,
benefit, or service to a student, a recipient shall not, on the basis of sex:

(1)   Treat one person differently from another in determining whether such
person satisfies any requirement or condition for the provision of such aid,
benefit, or service;

(2) Provide different aid, benefits, or services or provide aid, benefits, or services in a different manner;

(3) Deny any person any such aid, benefit, or service;

(4) Subject any person to separate or different rules of behavior, sanctions, or other treatment;

(5) Apply any rule concerning the domicile or residence of a student or applicant, including eligibility for in-state fees and tuition;

(6) Aid or perpetuate discrimination against any person by providing significant assistance to any agency, organization, or person which discriminates on the basis of sex in providing any aid, benefit or service to students or employees;

(7) Otherwise limit any person in the enjoyment of any right, privilege, advantage, or opportunity.

(c) *Assistance administered by a recipient educational institution to study at a foreign institution.* A recipient educational institution may administer or assist in the administration of scholarships, fellowships, or other awards established by foreign or domestic wills, trusts, or similar legal instruments, or by acts of foreign governments and restricted to members of one sex, which are designed to provide opportunities to study abroad, and which are awarded to students who are already matriculating at or who are graduates of the recipient institution; *Provided,* a recipient educational institution which administers or assists in the administration of such scholarships, fellowships, or other awards which are restricted to members of one sex provides, or otherwise makes available reasonable opportunities for similar studies for members of the other sex. Such opportunities may be derived from either domestic or foreign sources.

(d) *Aid, benefits or services not provided by recipient.*

(1) This paragraph applies to any recipient which requires participation by any applicant, student, or employee in any education program or activity not operated wholly by such recipient, or which facilitates, permits, or considers such participation as part of or equivalent to an education program or activity operated by such recipient, including participation in educational consortia and cooperative employment and student-teaching assignments.

(2) Such recipient:

(i) Shall develop and implement a procedure designed to assure itself that the operator or sponsor of such other education program or activity takes no action affecting any applicant, student, or employee of such recipient which this part would prohibit such recipient from taking; and

(ii) Shall not facilitate, require, permit, or consider such participation if such action occurs.

(Authority: Secs. 901, 902, Education Amendments of 1972, 86 Stat. 373, 374; 20 U.S.C. 1681, 1682)

[45 FR 30955, May 9, 1980, as amended at 47 FR 32527, July 28, 1982]

106.32 Housing.

(a) *Generally.* A recipient shall not, on the basis of sex, apply different rules or regulations, impose different fees or requirements, or offer different services or benefits related to housing, except as provided in this section (including housing provided only to married students).

(b) *Housing provided by recipient.*

(1) A recipient may provide separate housing on the basis of sex.

(2) Housing provided by a recipient to students of one sex, when compared to that provided to students of the other sex, shall be as a whole:

(i) Proportionate in quantity to the number of students of that sex applying for such housing; and

(ii) Comparable in quality and cost to the student.

(c) *Other housing.*

(1) A recipient shall not, on the basis of sex, administer different policies or practices concerning occupancy by its students of housing other than provided by such recipient.

(2) A recipient which, through solicitation, listing, approval of housing, or otherwise, assists any agency, organization, or person in making housing available to any of its students, shall take such reasonable action as may be necessary to assure itself that such housing as is provided to students of one sex, when compared to that provided to students of the other sex, is as a whole:

(i) Proportionate in quantity and

(ii) Comparable in quality and cost to the student.

A recipient may render such assistance to any agency, organization, or person which provides all or part of such housing to students only of one sex.

(Authority: Secs. 901, 902, 907, Education Amendments of 1972, 86 Stat. 373, 374, 375; 20 U.S.C. 1681, 1682, 1686)

106.33 Comparable facilities.

A recipient may provide separate toilet, locker room, and shower facilities on the basis of sex, but such facilities provided for students of one sex shall be comparable to such facilities provided for students of the other sex.

(Authority: Secs. 901, 902, Education Amendments of 1972, 86 Stat. 373, 374)

106.34 Access to classes and schools.

A recipient shall not provide any course or otherwise carry out any of its education program or activity separately on the basis of sex, or require or refuse participation therein by any of its students on such basis, including health, physical education, industrial, business, vocational, technical, home economics, music, and adult education courses.

(a) With respect to classes and activities in physical education at the elementary school level, the recipient shall comply fully with this section as expeditiously as possible but in no event later than one year from the effective date of this regulation. With respect to physical education classes and activities at the secondary and post-secondary levels, the recipient shall comply fully with this section as expeditiously as possible but in no event later than three years from the effective date of this regulation.

(b) This section does not prohibit grouping of students in physical education classes and activities by ability as assessed by objective standards of individual performance developed and applied without regard to sex.

(c) This section does not prohibit separation of students by sex within physical education classes or activities during participation in wrestling, boxing, rugby, ice hockey, football, basketball and other sports the purpose or major activity of which involves bodily contact.

(d) Where use of a single standard of measuring skill or progress in a physical education class has an adverse effect on members of one sex, the recipient shall use appropriate standards which do not have such effect.

(e) Portions of classes in elementary and secondary schools which deal exclusively with human sexuality may be conducted in separate sessions for boys and girls.

(f) Recipients may make requirements based on vocal range or quality which may result in a chorus or choruses of one or predominantly one sex.

(Authority: Secs. 901, 902, Education Amendments of 1972, 86 Stat. 373, 374; 20 U.S.C. 1681, 1682)

106.35 Access to institutions of vocational education.

A recipient which is a local educational agency shall not, on the basis of sex, exclude any person from admission to:

(a) Any institution of vocational education operated by such recipient; or

(b) Any other school or educational unit operated by such recipient, unless such recipient otherwise makes available to such person, pursuant to the same policies and criteria of admission, courses, services, and facilities comparable to each course, service, and facility offered in or through such schools.

(Authority: Secs. 901, 902, Education Amendments of 1972, 86 Stat. 373, 374; 20 U.S.C. 1681, 1682)

[71 FR 62543, Oct. 25, 2006]

106.36 Counseling and use of appraisal and counseling materials.

(a) *Counseling.* A recipient shall not discriminate against any person on the basis of sex in the counseling or guidance of students or applicants for admission.

(b) *Use of appraisal and counseling materials.* A recipient which uses testing or other materials for appraising or counseling students shall not use different materials for students on the basis of their sex or use materials which permit or require different treatment of students on such basis unless such different materials cover the same occupations and interest areas and the use of such different materials is shown to be essential to eliminate sex bias. Recipients shall develop and use internal procedures for ensuring that such materials do not discriminate on the basis of sex. Where the use of a counseling test or other instrument results in a substantially disproportionate number of members of one sex in any particular course of study or classification, the recipient shall take such action as is necessary to assure itself that such disproportion is not the result of discrimination in the instrument or its application.

(c) *Disproportion in classes*. Where a recipient finds that a particular class contains a substantially disproportionate number of individuals of one sex, the recipient shall take such action as is necessary to assure itself that such disproportion is not the result of discrimination on the basis of sex in counseling or appraisal materials or by counselors.

(Authority: Secs. 901, 902, Education Amendments of 1972, 86 Stat. 373, 374; 20 U.S.C. 1681, 1682)

106.37 Financial assistance.

(a) *General*. Except as provided in paragraphs (b) and (c) of this section, in providing financial assistance to any of its students, a recipient shall not:

    (1) On the basis of sex, provide different amount or types of such assistance, limit eligibility for such assistance which is of any particular type or source, apply different criteria, or otherwise discriminate;

    (2) Through solicitation, listing, approval, provision of facilities or other services, assist any foundation, trust, agency, organization, or person which provides assistance to any of such recipient's students in a manner which discriminates on the basis of sex; or

    (3) Apply any rule or assist in application of any rule concerning eligibility for such assistance which treats persons of one sex differently from persons of the other sex with regard to marital or parental status.

(b) *Financial aid established by certain legal instruments*.

    (1) A recipient may administer or assist in the administration of scholarships, fellowships, or other forms of financial assistance established pursuant to domestic or foreign wills, trusts, bequests, or similar legal instruments or by acts of a foreign government which requires that awards be made to members of a particular sex specified therein; *Provided,* That the overall effect of the award of such sex-restricted scholarships, fellowships, and other forms of financial assistance does not discriminate on the basis of sex.

    (2) To ensure nondiscriminatory awards of assistance as required in paragraph (b)(1) of this section, recipients shall develop and use procedures under which:

        (i) Students are selected for award of financial assistance on the basis of nondiscriminatory criteria and not on the basis of availability of funds restricted to members of a particular sex;

        (ii) An appropriate sex-restricted scholarship, fellowship, or other form of financial assistance is allocated to each student selected under paragraph (b)(2)(i) of this section; and

        (iii) No student is denied the award for which he or she was selected under paragraph (b)(2)(i) of this section because of the absence of a scholarship, fellowship, or other form of financial assistance designated for a member of that student's sex.

(c) *Athletic scholarships*.

    (1) To the extent that a recipient awards athletic scholarships or grants-in-aid, it must provide reasonable opportunities for such awards for members of

each sex in proportion to the number of students of each sex participating in interscholastic or intercollegiate athletics.

(2) Separate athletic scholarships or grants-in-aid for members of each sex may be provided as part of separate athletic teams for members of each sex to the extent consistent with this paragraph and § 106.41.

(Authority: Secs. 901, 902, Education Amendments of 1972, 86 Stat. 373, 374; 20 U.S.C. 1681, 1682; and Sec. 844, Education Amendments of 1974, Pub. L. 93–380, 88 Stat. 484)

106.38 Employment assistance to students.

(a) *Assistance by recipient in making available outside employment.* A recipient which assists any agency, organization or person in making employment available to any of its students:

(1) Shall assure itself that such employment is made available without discrimination on the basis of sex; and

(2) Shall not render such services to any agency, organization, or person which discriminates on the basis of sex in its employment practices.

(b) *Employment of students by recipients.* A recipient which employs any of its students shall not do so in a manner which violates subpart E of this part.

(Authority: Secs. 901, 902, Education Amendments of 1972, 86 Stat. 373, 374; 20 U.S.C. 1681, 1682)

106.39 Health and insurance benefits and services.

In providing a medical, hospital, accident, or life insurance benefit, service, policy, or plan to any of its students, a recipient shall not discriminate on the basis of sex, or provide such benefit, service, policy, or plan in a manner which would violate Subpart E of this part if it were provided to employees of the recipient. This section shall not prohibit a recipient from providing any benefit or service which may be used by a different proportion of students of one sex than of the other, including family planning services. However, any recipient which provides full coverage health service shall provide gynecological care.

(Authority: Secs. 901, 902, Education Amendments of 1972, 86 Stat. 373, 374; 20 U.S.C. 1681, 1682)

106.40 Marital or parental status.

(a) *Status generally.* A recipient shall not apply any rule concerning a student's actual or potential parental, family, or marital status which treats students differently on the basis of sex.

(b) *Pregnancy and related conditions.*

(1) A recipient shall not discriminate against any student, or exclude any student from its education program or activity, including any class or extracurricular activity, on the basis of such student's pregnancy, child-birth, false pregnancy, termination of pregnancy or recovery therefrom, unless the student requests voluntarily to participate in a separate portion of the program or activity of the recipient.

(2) A recipient may require such a student to obtain the certification of a physician that the student is physically and emotionally able to continue

participation so long as such a certification is required of all students for other physical or emotional conditions requiring the attention of a physician.

(3)   A recipient which operates a portion of its education program or activity separately for pregnant students, admittance to which is completely voluntary on the part of the student as provided in paragraph (b)(1) of this section shall ensure that the separate portion is comparable to that offered to non-pregnant students.

(4)   A recipient shall treat pregnancy, childbirth, false pregnancy, termination of pregnancy and recovery therefrom in the same manner and under the same policies as any other temporary disability with respect to any medical or hospital benefit, service, plan or policy which such recipient administers, operates, offers, or participates in with respect to students admitted to the recipient's educational program or activity.

(5)   In the case of a recipient which does not maintain a leave policy for its students, or in the case of a student who does not otherwise qualify for leave under such a policy, a recipient shall treat pregnancy, childbirth, false pregnancy, termination of pregnancy and recovery therefrom as a justification for a leave of absence for so long a period of time as is deemed medically necessary by the student's physician, at the conclusion of which the student shall be reinstated to the status which she held when the leave began.

(Authority: Secs. 901, 902, Education Amendments of 1972, 86 Stat. 373, 374; 20 U.S.C. 1681, 1682)

106.41 Athletics.

(a)   *General*. No person shall, on the basis of sex, be excluded from participation in, be denied the benefits of, be treated differently from another person or otherwise be discriminated against in any interscholastic, intercollegiate, club or intramural athletics offered by a recipient, and no recipient shall provide any such athletics separately on such basis.

(b)   *Separate teams*. Notwithstanding the requirements of paragraph (a) of this section, a recipient may operate or sponsor separate teams for members of each sex where selection for such teams is based upon competitive skill or the activity involved is a contact sport. However, where a recipient operates or sponsors a team in a particular sport for members of one sex but operates or sponsors no such team for members of the other sex, and athletic opportunities for members of that sex have previously been limited, members of the excluded sex must be allowed to try-out for the team offered unless the sport involved is a contact sport. For the purposes of this part, contact sports include boxing, wrestling, rugby, ice hockey, football, basketball and other sports the purpose or major activity of which involves bodily contact.

(c)   *Equal opportunity*. A recipient which operates or sponsors interscholastic, intercollegiate, club or intramural athletics shall provide equal athletic opportunity for members of both sexes. In determining whether equal opportunities are available the Director will consider, among other factors:

(1)   Whether the selection of sports and levels of competition effectively accommodate the interests and abilities of members of both sexes;

(2) The provision of equipment and supplies;

(3) Scheduling of games and practice time;

(4) Travel and per diem allowance;

(5) Opportunity to receive coaching and academic tutoring;

(6) Assignment and compensation of coaches and tutors;

(7) Provision of locker rooms, practice and competitive facilities;

(8) Provision of medical and training facilities and services;

(9) Provision of housing and dining facilities and services;

(10) Publicity.

Unequal aggregate expenditures for members of each sex or unequal expenditures for male and female teams if a recipient operates or sponsors separate teams will not constitute noncompliance with this section, but the Assistant Secretary may consider the failure to provide necessary funds for teams for one sex in assessing equality of opportunity for members of each sex.

(d) *Adjustment period.* A recipient which operates or sponsors interscholastic, intercollegiate, club or intramural athletics at the elementary school level shall comply fully with this section as expeditiously as possible but in no event later than one year from the effective date of this regulation. A recipient which operates or sponsors interscholastic, intercollegiate, club or intramural athletics at the secondary or post-secondary school level shall comply fully with this section as expeditiously as possible but in no event later than three years from the effective date of this regulation.

(Authority: Secs. 901, 902, Education Amendments of 1972, 86 Stat. 373, 374; 20 U.S.C. 1681, 1682; and Sec. 844, Education Amendments of 1974, Pub. L. 93–380, 88 Stat. 484)

106.42 Textbooks and curricular material.

Nothing in this regulation shall be interpreted as requiring or prohibiting or abridging in any way the use of particular textbooks or curricular materials.

(Authority: Secs. 901, 902, Education Amendments of 1972, 86 Stat. 373, 374; 20 U.S.C. 1681, 1682)

106.43 Standards for measuring skill or progress in physical education classes.

If use of a single standard of measuring skill or progress in physical education classes has an adverse effect on members of one sex, the recipient shall use appropriate standards that do not have that effect.

(Authority: 20 U.S.C. 1681, 1682)

[71 FR 62543, Oct. 25, 2006]

Subpart E—Discrimination on the Basis of Sex in Employment in Education Programs or Activities Prohibited

106.51 Employment.

(a) *General.*

(1) No person shall, on the basis of sex, be excluded from participation in, be denied the benefits of, or be subjected to discrimination in employment, or recruitment, consideration, or selection therefor, whether full-time or

part-time, under any education program or activity operated by a recipient which receives Federal financial assistance.

(2) A recipient shall make all employment decisions in any education program or activity operated by such recipient in a nondiscriminatory manner and shall not limit, segregate, or classify applicants or employees in any way which could adversely affect any applicant's or employee's employment opportunities or status because of sex.

(3) A recipient shall not enter into any contractual or other relationship which directly or indirectly has the effect of subjecting employees or students to discrimination prohibited by this subpart, including relationships with employment and referral agencies, with labor unions, and with organizations providing or administering fringe benefits to employees of the recipient.

(4) A recipient shall not grant preferences to applicants for employment on the basis of attendance at any educational institution or entity which admits as students only or predominantly members of one sex, if the giving of such preferences has the effect of discriminating on the basis of sex in violation of this part.

(b) *Application.* The provisions of this subpart apply to:

(1) Recruitment, advertising, and the process of application for employment;

(2) Hiring, upgrading, promotion, consideration for and award of tenure, demotion, transfer, layoff, termination, application of nepotism policies, right of return from layoff, and rehiring;

(3) Rates of pay or any other form of compensation, and changes in compensation;

(4) Job assignments, classifications and structure, including position descriptions, lines of progression, and seniority lists;

(5) The terms of any collective bargaining agreement;

(6) Granting and return from leaves of absence, leave for pregnancy, childbirth, false pregnancy, termination of pregnancy, leave for persons of either sex to care for children or dependents, or any other leave;

(7) Fringe benefits available by virtue of employment, whether or not administered by the recipient;

(8) Selection and financial support for training, including apprenticeship, professional meetings, conferences, and other related activities, selection for tuition assistance, selection for sabbaticals and leaves of absence to pursue training;

(9) Employer-sponsored activities, including those that are social or recreational; and

(10) Any other term, condition, or privilege of employment.

(Authority: Secs. 901, 902, Education Amendments of 1972, 86 Stat. 373, 374; 20 U.S.C. 1681, 1682)

106.52 Employment criteria.

A recipient shall not administer or operate any test or other criterion for any employment opportunity which has a disproportionately adverse effect on persons on the basis of sex unless:

(a) Use of such test or other criterion is shown to predict validly successful performance in the position in question; and

(b) Alternative tests or criteria for such purpose, which do not have such disproportionately adverse effect, are shown to be unavailable.

(Authority: Secs. 901, 902, Education Amendments of 1972, 86 Stat. 373, 374; 20 U.S.C. 1681, 1682)

106.53 Recruitment.

(a) *Nondiscriminatory recruitment and hiring.* A recipient shall not discriminate on the basis of sex in the recruitment and hiring of employees. Where a recipient has been found to be presently discriminating on the basis of sex in the recruitment or hiring of employees, or has been found to have in the past so discriminated, the recipient shall recruit members of the sex so discriminated against so as to overcome the effects of such past or present discrimination.

(b) *Recruitment patterns.* A recipient shall not recruit primarily or exclusively at entities which furnish as applicants only or predominantly members of one sex if such actions have the effect of discriminating on the basis of sex in violation of this subpart.

(Authority: Secs. 901, 902, Education Amendments of 1972, 86 Stat. 373, 374; 20 U.S.C. 1681, 1682)

106.54 Compensation.

A recipient shall not make or enforce any policy or practice which, on the basis of sex:

(a) Makes distinctions in rates of pay or other compensation;

(b) Results in the payment of wages to employees of one sex at a rate less than that paid to employees of the opposite sex for equal work on jobs the performance of which requires equal skill, effort, and responsibility, and which are performed under similar working conditions.

(Authority: Secs. 901, 902, Education Amendments of 1972, 86 Stat. 373, 374; 20 U.S.C. 1681, 1682)

106.55 Job classification and structure.

A recipient shall not:

(a) Classify a job as being for males or for females;

(b) Maintain or establish separate lines of progression, seniority lists, career ladders, or tenure systems based on sex; or

(c) Maintain or establish separate lines of progression, seniority systems, career ladders, or tenure systems for similar jobs, position descriptions, or job requirements which classify persons on the basis of sex, unless sex is a bonafide occupational qualification for the positions in question as set forth in § 106.61.

(Authority: Secs. 901, 902, Education Amendments of 1972, 86 Stat. 373, 374; 20 U.S.C. 1681, 1682)

106.56 Fringe benefits.

(a) *Fringe benefits defined.* For purposes of this part, *fringe benefits* means: Any medical, hospital, accident, life insurance or retirement benefit, service, policy or plan, any profit-sharing or bonus plan, leave, and any other benefit or service of employment not subject to the provision of § 106.54.

(b) *Prohibitions*. A recipient shall not:

(1) Discriminate on the basis of sex with regard to making fringe benefits available to employees or make fringe benefits available to spouses, families, or dependents of employees differently upon the basis of the employee's sex;

(2) Administer, operate, offer, or participate in a fringe benefit plan which does not provide either for equal periodic benefits for members of each sex, or for equal contributions to the plan by such recipient for members of each sex; or

(3) Administer, operate, offer, or participate in a pension or retirement plan which establishes different optional or compulsory retirement ages based on sex or which otherwise discriminates in benefits on the basis of sex.

(Authority: Secs. 901, 902, Education Amendments of 1972, 86 Stat. 373, 374; 20 U.S.C. 1681, 1682)

106.57 Marital or parental status.

(a) *General*. A recipient shall not apply any policy or take any employment action:

(1) Concerning the potential marital, parental, or family status of an employee or applicant for employment which treats persons differently on the basis of sex; or

(2) Which is based upon whether an employee or applicant for employment is the head of household or principal wage earner in such employee's or applicant's family unit.

(b) *Pregnancy*. A recipient shall not discriminate against or exclude from employment any employee or applicant for employment on the basis of pregnancy, childbirth, false pregnancy, termination of pregnancy, or recovery therefrom.

(c) *Pregnancy as a temporary disability*. A recipient shall treat pregnancy, childbirth, false pregnancy, termination of pregnancy, and recovery therefrom and any temporary disability resulting therefrom as any other temporary disability for all job related purposes, including commencement, duration and extensions of leave, payment of disability income, accrual of seniority and any other benefit or service, and reinstatement, and under any fringe benefit offered to employees by virtue of employment.

(d) *Pregnancy leave*. In the case of a recipient which does not maintain a leave policy for its employees, or in the case of an employee with insufficient leave or accrued employment time to qualify for leave under such a policy, a recipient shall treat pregnancy, childbirth, false pregnancy, termination of pregnancy and recovery therefrom as a justification for a leave of absence without pay for a reasonable period of time, at the conclusion of which the employee shall be reinstated to the status which she held when the leave began or to a comparable position, without decrease in rate of compensation or loss of promotional opportunities, or any other right or privilege of employment.

(Authority: Secs. 901, 902, Education Amendments of 1972, 86 Stat. 373, 374; 20 U.S.C. 1681, 1682)

106.58 Effect of State or local law or other requirements.

(a) *Prohibitory requirements*. The obligation to comply with this subpart is not obviated or alleviated by the existence of any State or local law or other requirement which imposes prohibitions or limits upon employment of members of one sex which are not imposed upon members of the other sex.

(b) *Benefits.* A recipient which provides any compensation, service, or benefit to members of one sex pursuant to a State or local law or other requirement shall provide the same compensation, service, or benefit to members of the other sex.

(Authority: Secs. 901, 902, Education Amendments of 1972, 86 Stat. 373, 374; 20 U.S.C. 1681, 1682)

106.59 Advertising.

A recipient shall not in any advertising related to employment indicate preference, limitation, specification, or discrimination based on sex unless sex is a *bona-fide* occupational qualification for the particular job in question.

(Authority: Secs. 901, 902, Education Amendments of 1972, 86 Stat. 373, 374; 20 U.S.C. 1681, 1682)

106.60 Pre-employment inquiries.

(a) *Marital status.* A recipient shall not make pre-employment inquiry as to the marital status of an applicant for employment, including whether such applicant is "Miss or Mrs."

(b) *Sex.* A recipient may make pre-employment inquiry as to the sex of an applicant for employment, but only if such inquiry is made equally of such applicants of both sexes and if the results of such inquiry are not used in connection with discrimination prohibited by this part.

(Authority: Secs. 901, 902, Education Amendments of 1972, 86 Stat. 373, 374; 20 U.S.C. 1681, 1682)

106.61 Sex as a bona-fide occupational qualification.

A recipient may take action otherwise prohibited by this subpart provided it is shown that sex is a bona-fide occupational qualification for that action, such that consideration of sex with regard to such action is essential to successful operation of the employment function concerned. A recipient shall not take action pursuant to this section which is based upon alleged comparative employment characteristics or stereotyped characterizations of one or the other sex, or upon preference based on sex of the recipient, employees, students, or other persons, but nothing contained in this section shall prevent a recipient from considering an employee's sex in relation to employment in a locker room or toilet facility used only by members of one sex.

(Authority: Secs. 901, 902, Education Amendments of 1972, 86 Stat. 373, 374; 20 U.S.C. 1681, 1682)

Subpart F—Procedures [Interim]

106.71 Procedures.

The procedural provisions applicable to title VI of the Civil Rights Act of 1964 are hereby adopted and incorporated herein by reference. These procedures may be found at 34 CFR 100.6–100.11 and 34 CFR, part 101.

(Authority: Secs. 901, 902, Education Amendments of 1972, 86 Stat. 373, 374; 20 U.S.C. 1681, 1682)

Source: http://www.ed.gov/policy/rights/reg/ocr/edlite-34cfr106.html.

Appendix B: A Policy Interpretation: Title IX and Intercollegiate Athletics

Federal Register, Vol.44, No. 239—Tuesday, Dec. 11, 1979

Intercollegiate athletics policy interpretation; provides more specific factors to be reviewed by OCR under program factors listed at Section 106.41 Of the Title IX regulation; explains OCR's approach to determining compliance in inter-collegiate athletics; adds two program factors, recruitment and support services to be reviewed; clarifies requirement for athletic scholarships—34 C.F.R. Section 106.37(C). The document contains dated references, and footnote 6 is out of date; however, the policy is still current.

Department of Health, Education, and Welfare
Office for Civil Rights
Office of the Secretary
45 CFR Part 26

Title IX of the Education Amendments of 1972; a Policy Interpretation; Title IX and Intercollegiate Athletics

Agency: Office for Civil Rights, Office of the Secretary, HEW.

Action: Policy interpretation.

Summary: The following Policy Interpretation represents the Department of Health, Education, and Welfare's interpretation of the intercollegiate athletic provisions of Title IX of the Education Amendments of 1972 and its implementing regulation. Title IX prohibits educational programs and institutions funded or otherwise supported by the Department from discriminating on the basis of sex. The Department published a proposed Policy Interpretation for public comment on December 11, 1978. Over 700 comments reflecting a broad range of opinion were received. In addition, HEW staff visited eight universities during June and July, 1979, to see how the proposed policy and other suggested alternatives would apply in actual practice at individual campuses. The final Policy Interpretation reflects the many comments HEW received and the results of the individual campus visits

Effective Date: December 11, 1979

For Further Information Contact: Colleen O'Connor, 330 Independence Avenue, Washington, D.C. (202) 245-6671

Supplementary Information:

I. Legal Background

A. The Statute

Section 901(a) of Title IX of the Education Amendments of 1972 provides:

- No person in the United States shall, on the basis of sex, be excluded from participation in, be denied the benefits of, or be subjected to discrimination under any education program or activity receiving Federal financial assistance.

Section 844 of the Education Amendments of 1974 further provides:

- The Secretary of [of HEW] shall prepare and publish proposed regulations implementing the provisions of Title IX of the Education Amendments of 1972 relating to the prohibition of sex discrimination in federally assisted education programs which shall include with respect to intercollegiate athletic activities reasonable provisions considering the nature of particular sports.

Congress passed Section 844 after the Conference Committee deleted a Senate floor amendment that would have exempted revenue-producing athletics from the jurisdiction of Title IX.

B. The Regulation

The regulation implementing Title IX is set forth, in pertinent part, in the Policy Interpretation below. It was signed by President Ford on May 27, 1975, and submitted to the Congress for review pursuant to Section 431(d)(1) of the General Education Provisions Act (GEPA).

During this review, the House Subcommittee on Postsecondary Education held hearings on a resolution disapproving the regulation. The Congress did not disapprove the regulation within the 45 days allowed under GEPA, and it therefore became effective on July 21, 1975.

Subsequent hearings were held in the Senate Subcommittee on Education on a bill to exclude revenues produced by sports to the extent they are used to pay the costs of those sports. The Committee, however, took no action on this bill.

The regulation established a three year transition period to give institutions time to comply with its equal athletic opportunity requirements. That transition period expired on July 21, 1978.

II. Purpose of Policy Interpretation

By the end of July 1978, the Department had received nearly 100 complaints alleging discrimination in athletics against more than 50 institutions of higher education. In attempting to investigate these complaints, and to answer questions from the university community, the Department determined that it should provide further guidance on what constitutes compliance with the law. Accordingly, this Policy Interpretation explains the regulation so as to provide a framework within which the complaints can be resolved, and to provide institutions of higher education with additional guidance on the requirements for compliance with Title IX in intercollegiate athletic programs.

III. Scope of Application

This Policy Interpretation is designed specifically for intercollegiate athletics. However, its general principles will often apply to club, intramural, and interscholastic athletic programs, which are also covered by regulation. Accordingly, the Policy Interpretation may be used for guidance by the administrators of such programs when appropriate.

This policy interpretation applies to any public or private institution, person or other entity that operates an educational program or activity which receives or benefits from financial assistance authorized or extended under a law administered by the Department. This includes educational institutions whose students participate in HEW funded or guaranteed student loan or assistance programs. For further information see definition of "recipient" in Section 86.2 of the Title IX regulation.

IV. Summary of Final Policy Interpretation

The final Policy Interpretation clarifies the meaning of "equal opportunity" in intercollegiate athletics. It explains the factors and standards set out in the law and regulation which the Department will consider in determining whether an institution's intercollegiate athletics program complies with the law and regulations. It also provides guidance to assist institutions in determining whether any disparities which may exist between men's and women's programs are justifiable and nondiscriminatory. The Policy Interpretation is divided into three sections:

- Compliance in Financial Assistance (Scholarships) Based on Athletic Ability: Pursuant to the regulation, the governing principle in this area is that all such assistance should be available on a substantially proportional basis to the number of male and female participants in the institution's athletic program.

- Compliance in Other Program Areas (Equipment and supplies; games and practice times; travel and per diem, coaching and academic tutoring; assignment and compensation of coaches and tutors; locker rooms, and practice and competitive facilities; medical and training facilities; housing and dining facilities; publicity; recruitment; and support services): Pursuant to the regulation, the governing principle is that male and female athletes should receive equivalent treatment, benefits, and opportunities.

- Compliance in Meeting the Interests and Abilities of Male and Female Students: Pursuant to the regulation, the governing principle in this area is that the athletic interests and abilities of male and female students must be equally effectively accommodated.

V. Major Changes to Proposed Policy Interpretation

The final Policy Interpretation has been revised from the one published in proposed form on December 11, 1978. The proposed Policy Interpretation was based on a two-part approach. Part I addressed equal opportunity for participants in athletic programs. It required the elimination of discrimination in financial support and other benefits and opportunities in an institution's existing athletic program. Institutions could establish a presumption of compliance if they could demonstrate that:

- "Average per capita" expenditures for male and female athletes were substantially equal in the area of "readily financially measurable" benefits and opportunities or, if not, that any disparities were the result of nondiscriminatory factors, and

- Benefits and opportunities for male and female athletes, in areas which are not financially measurable, "were comparable."

Part II of the proposed Policy Interpretation addressed an institution's obligation to accommodate effectively the athletic interests and abilities of women as well as men on a continuing basis. It required an institution either

- To follow a policy of development of its women's athletic program to provide the participation and competition opportunities needed to accommodate the growing interests and abilities of women, or

- To demonstrate that it was effectively (and equally) accommodating the athletic interests and abilities of students, particularly as the interests and abilities of women students developed.

While the basic considerations of equal opportunity remain, the final Policy Interpretation sets forth the factors that will be examined to determine an institution's actual, as opposed to presumed, compliance with Title IX in the area of intercollegiate athletics.

The final Policy Interpretation does not contain a separate section on institutions' future responsibilities. However, institutions remain obligated by the Title IX regulation to accommodate effectively the interests and abilities of male and female students with regard to the selection of sports and levels of competition available. In most cases, this will entail development of athletic programs that substantially expand opportunities for women to participate and compete at all levels.

The major reasons for the change in approach are as follows:

(1) Institutions and representatives of athletic program participants expressed a need for more definitive guidance on what constituted compliance than the discussion of a presumption of compliance provided. Consequently the final Policy Interpretation explains the meaning of "equal athletic opportunity" in such a way as to facilitate an assessment of compliance.

(2) Many comments reflected a serious misunderstanding of the presumption of compliance. Most institutions based objections to the proposed Policy Interpretation in part on the assumption that failure to provide compelling justifications for disparities in per capita expenditures would have automatically resulted in a finding of noncompliance. In fact, such a failure would only have deprived an institution of the benefit of the presumption that it was in compliance with the law. The Department would still have had the burden of demonstrating that the institution was actually engaged in unlawful discrimination. Since the purpose of issuing a policy interpretation was to clarify the regulation, the Department has determined that the approach of stating actual compliance factors would be more useful to all concerned.

(3) The Department has concluded that purely financial measures such as the per capita test do not in themselves offer conclusive documentation of discrimination, except where the benefit or opportunity under review, like a scholarship, is itself financial in nature. Consequently, in the final Policy Interpretation, the Department has detailed the factors to be considered in assessing actual compliance. While per capita breakdowns and other devices to examine expenditure patterns will be used as tools of analysis in the Department's investigative process, it is achievement of "equal opportunity" for which recipients are responsible and to which the final Policy Interpretation is addressed.

A description of the comments received, and other information obtained through the comment/consultation process, with a description of Departmental action in response to the major points raised, is set forth at Appendix "B" to this document.

VI. Historic Patterns of Intercollegiate Athletics Program Development and Operations

In its proposed Policy Interpretation of December 11, 1978, the Department published a summary of historic patterns affecting the relative status of men's and women's athletic programs. The Department has modified that summary to reflect additional information obtained during the comment and consultation process. The summary is set forth at Appendix A to this document.

VII. The Policy Interpretation

This Policy Interpretation clarifies the obligations which recipients of Federal aid have under Title IX to provide equal opportunities in athletic programs. In particular, this Policy Interpretation provides a means to assess an institution's compliance with the equal opportunity requirements of the regulation which are set forth at 45 CFR 88.37(c) and 88.4a(c).

A. Athletic Financial Assistance (Scholarships)

1. The Regulation. Section 86.37(c) of the regulation provides:
   - [Institutions] must provide reasonable opportunities for such award (of financial assistance) for member of each sex in proportion to the number of students of each sex participating in inter-collegiate athletics.

2. The Policy—The Department will examine compliance with this provision of the regulation primarily by means of a financial comparison to determine whether proportionately equal amounts of financial assistance (scholarship aid) are available to men's and women's athletic programs. The Department will measure compliance with this standard by dividing the amounts of aid available for the members of each sex by the numbers of male or female participants in the athletic program and comparing the results. Institutions may be found in compliance if this comparison results in substantially equal amounts or if a resulting disparity can be explained by adjustments to take into account legitimate, nondiscriminatory factors. Two such factors are:

   a. At public institutions, the higher costs of tuition for students from out-of-state may in some years be unevenly' distributed between men's and women's programs. These differences will be considered nondiscriminatory if they are not the result of policies or practices which disproportionately limit the availability of out-of-state scholarships to either men or women.

   b. An institution may make reasonable professional decisions concerning the awards most appropriate for program development. For example, team development initially may require spreading scholarships over as much as a full generation [four years) of student athletes. This may result in the award of fewer scholarships in the first few years than would be necessary to create proportionality between male and female athletes.

3. Application of the Policy—

   a. This section does not require a proportionate number of scholarships for men and women or individual scholarships of equal dollar value. It does mean that the total amount of scholarship aid made available to men and women must be substantially proportionate to their participation rates.

   b. When financial assistance is provided in forms other than grants, the distribution of non-grant assistance will also be compared to determine whether equivalent benefits are proportionately available to male and female athletes. A disproportionate amount of work-related aid or loans in the assistance made available to the members of one sex, for example, could constitute a violation of Title IX.

4. Definition—For purposes of examining compliance with this Section, the participants will be defined as those athletes:

a. Who are receiving the institutionally-sponsored support normally provided to athletes competing at the institution involved, e.g., coaching, equipment, medical and training room services, on a regular basis during a sport's season; and

b. Who are participating in organized practice sessions and other team meetings and activities on a regular basis during a sport's season: and

c. Who are listed on the eligibility or squad lists maintained for each sport, or

d. Who, because of injury, cannot meet a, b, or c above but continue to receive financial aid on the basis of athletic ability.

B. **Equivalence in Other Athletic Benefits and Opportunities**

1. The Regulation C The Regulation requires that recipients that operate or sponsor interscholastic, intercollegiate, club or intramural athletics. "provide equal athletic opportunities for members of both sexes." In determining whether an institution is providing equal opportunity in intercollegiate athletics the regulation requires the Department to consider, among others, the following factors:

(1)
(2) Provision and maintenance of equipment and supplies;
(3) Scheduling of games and practice times;
(4) Travel and per diem expenses;
(5) Opportunity to receive coaching and academic tutoring;
(6) Assignment and compensation of coaches and tutors;
(7) Provision of locker rooms, practice and competitive facilities;
(8) Provision of medical and training services and facilities;
(9) Provision of housing and dining services and facilities; and
(10) Publicity

Section 86.41(c) also permits the Director of the Office for Civil Rights to consider other factors in the determination of equal opportunity. Accordingly, this Section also addresses recruitment of student athletes and provision of support services.

This list is not exhaustive. Under the regulation, it may be expanded as necessary at the discretion of the Director of the Office for Civil Rights.

2. The Policy—The Department will assess compliance with both the recruitment and the general athletic program requirements of the regulation by comparing the availability, quality and kinds of benefits, opportunities, and treatment afforded members of both sexes. Institutions will be in compliance if the compared program components are equivalent, that is, equal or equal in effect. Under this standard, identical benefits, opportunities, or treatment are not required, provided the overall effects of any differences is negligible.

If comparisons of program components reveal that treatment, benefits, or opportunities are not equivalent in kind, quality or availability, a finding of compliance may still be justified if the differences are the result of nondiscriminatory factors. Some of the factors that may justify these differences are as follows:

a. Some aspects of athletic programs may not be equivalent for men and women because of unique aspects of particular sports or athletic activities. This type of distinction was called for by the "Javits' Amendment" to Title IX which instructed HEW to make "reasonable (regulatory) provisions considering the nature of particular sports" in intercollegiate athletics.

Generally, these differences will be the result of factors that are inherent to the basic operation of specific sports. Such factors may include rules of play, nature/replacement of equipment, rates of injury resulting from participation, nature of facilities required for competition, and the maintenance/upkeep requirements of those facilities. For the most part, differences involving such factors will occur in programs offering football, and consequently these differences will favor men. If sport-specific needs are met equivalently in both men's and women's programs, however, differences in particular program components will be found to be justifiable.

b. Some aspects of athletic programs may not be equivalent for men and women because of legitimately sex-neutral factors related to special circumstances of a temporary nature. For example, large disparities in recruitment activity for any particular year may be the result of annual fluctuations in team needs for first-year athletes. Such differences are justifiable to the extent that they do not reduce overall equality of opportunity.

c. The activities directly associated with the operation of a competitive event in a single-sex sport may, under some circumstances, create unique demands or imbalances in particular program components. Provided any special demands associated with the activities of sports involving participants of the other sex are met to an equivalent degree, the resulting differences may be found nondiscriminatory. At many schools, for example, certain sports, notably football and men's basketball, traditionally draw large crowds. Since the costs of managing an athletic event increase with crowd size, the overall support made available for event management to men's and women's programs may differ in degree and kind. These differences would not violate Title IX if the recipient does not limit the potential for women's athletic events to rise in spectator appeal and if the levels of event management support available to both programs are based on sex-neutral criteria (e.g.. facilities used, projected attendance, and staffing needs).

d. Some aspects of athletic programs may not be equivalent for men and women because institutions are undertaking voluntary affirmative actions to overcome effects of historical conditions that have limited participation in athletics by the members of one sex. This is authorized at '86.3(b) of the regulation.

3. Application of the Policy-General Athletic Program Components C
   a. Equipment and Supplies ('86.41(c)(2)). Equipment and supplies include but are not limited to uniforms, other apparel, sport-specific equipment

and supplies, general equipment and supplies, instructional devices, and conditioning and weight training equipment.

Compliance will be assessed by examining, among other factors, the equivalence for men and women of:

(1) The quality of equipment and supplies:

(2) The amount of equipment and supplies;

(3) The suitability of equipment and supplies:

(4) The maintenance and replacement of the equipment and supplies; and

(5) The availability of equipment and supplies.

b. Scheduling of Games and Practice Times ('86.41(c)(3)). Compliance will be assessed by examining, among other factors, the equivalence for men and women of:

(1) The number of competitive events per sport;

(2) The number and length of practice opportunities;

(3) The time of day competitive events are scheduled;

(4) The time of day practice opportunities are scheduled; and

(5) The opportunities to engage in available pre-season and post-season competition.

c. Travel and Per Diem Allowances ('86.41(c)(4)). Compliance will be assessed by examining, among other factors, the equivalence for men and women of:

(1) Modes of transportation;

(2) Housing furnished during travel:

(3) Length of stay before and after competitive events:

(4) Per diem allowances: and

(5) Dining arrangements.

d. Opportunity to Receive Coaching and Academic Tutoring ('86.41(c)(5)).

(1) Coaching Compliance will be assessed by examining, among other factors:

(a) Relative availability of full-time coaches:

(b) Relative availability of part-time and assistant coaches; and

(c) Relative availability of graduate assistants.

(2) Academic tutoring-Compliance will be assessed by examining, among other factors, the equivalence for men and women of:

(a) The availability of tutoring; and

(b) Procedures and criteria for obtaining tutorial assistance.

e. Assignment and Compensation of Coaches and Tutors ('86.41(c)(6)). In general, a violation of Section 86.41(c)(6) will be found only where compensation or assignment policies or practices deny male and female athletes coaching of equivalent quality, nature, or availability.

Nondiscriminatory factors can affect the compensation of coaches. In determining whether differences are caused by permissible factors, the range and nature of duties, the experience of individual coaches, the number of participants for particular sports, the number of assistant coaches supervised, and the level of competition will be considered.

Where these or similar factors represent valid differences in skill, effort, responsibility or working conditions they may, in specific circumstances, justify differences in compensation. Similarly, there may be unique situations in which a particular person may possess such an outstanding record of achievement as to justify an abnormally high salary.

(1) Assignment of Coaches—Compliance will be assessed by examining, among other factors, the equivalence for men's and women's coaches of:

(a) Training, experience, and other professional qualifications;

(b) Professional standing.

(2) Assignment of Tutors—Compliance will be assessed by examining, among other factors, the equivalence for men's and women's tutors of:

(a) Tutor qualifications;

(b) Training, experience, and other qualifications.

(3) Compensation of Coaches—Compliance will be assessed by examining, among other factors, the equivalence for men's and women's coaches of:

(a) Rate of compensation (per sport, per season);

(b) Duration of contracts;

(c) Conditions relating to contract renewal;

(d) Experience;

(e) Nature of coaching duties performed;

(f) Working conditions; and

(g) Other terms and conditions of employment.

(4) Compensation of Tutors—Compliance will be assessed by examining, among other factors, the equivalence for men's and women's tutors of:

(a) Hourly rate of payment by nature subjects tutored;

(b) Pupil loads per tutoring season;

(c) Tutor qualifications;

(d) Experience;

(e) Other terms and conditions of employment.

f. Provision of Locker Rooms, Practice and Competitive Facilities ('86.41(c)(7)). Compliance will be assessed by examining, among other factors, the equivalence for men and women of:

(1) Quality and availability of the facilities provided for practice and competitive events;

(2) Exclusivity of use of facilities provided for practice and competitive events;

(3) Availability of locker rooms;

(4) Quality of locker rooms;

(5) Maintenance of practice and competitive facilities; and

(6) Preparation of facilities for practice and competitive events.

g. Provision of Medical and Training Facilities and Services ('86.41(c)(8)). Compliance will be assessed by examining, among other factors, the equivalence for men and women of:

(1) Availability of medical personnel and assistance;

(2) Health, accident and injury insurance coverage;

(3) Availability and quality of weight and training facilities;

(4) Availability and quality of conditioning facilities; and

(5) Availability and qualifications of athletic trainers.

h. Provision of Housing and Dining Facilities and Services ('86.41(c)(9)). Compliance will be assessed by examining, among other factors, the equivalence for men and women of:

(1) Housing provided;

(2) Special services as part of housing arrangements (e.g., laundry facilities, parking space, maid service).

i. Publicity ('86.41(c)(10)). Compliance will be assessed by examining, among other factors, the equivalence for men and women of:

(1) Availability and quality of sports information personnel;

(2) Access to other publicity resources for men's and women's programs; and

(3) Quantity and quality of publications and other promotional devices featuring men's and women's programs.

4. Application of the Policy—Other Factors ('86.41(c)).

a. Recruitment of Student Athletes. The athletic recruitment practices of institutions often affect the overall provision of opportunity to male and female athletes. Accordingly, where equal athletic opportunities are not present for male and female students, compliance will be assessed by examining the recruitment practices of the athletic programs for both sexes to determine whether the provision of equal opportunity will require modification of those practices.

Such examinations will review the following factors:

(1) Whether coaches or other professional athletic personnel in the programs serving male and female athletes are provided with substantially equal opportunities to recruit;

(2) Whether the financial and other resources made available for recruitment in male and female athletic programs are equivalently adequate to meet the needs of each program; and

(3) Whether the differences in benefits, opportunities, and treatment afforded prospective student athletes of each sex have a disproportionately limiting effect upon the recruitment of students of either sex.

b. Provision of Support Services. The administrative and clerical support provided to an athletic program can affect the overall provision of opportunity to male and female athletes, particularly to the extent that the provided services enable coaches to perform better their coaching functions.

In the provision of support services, compliance will be assessed by examining, among other factors, the equivalence of:

(1) The amount of administrative assistance provided to men's and women's programs;

(2) The amount of secretarial and clerical assistance provided to men's and women's programs.

5. Overall Determination of Compliance. The Department will base its compliance determination under '86.41(c) of the regulation upon an examination of the following:

a. Whether the policies of an institution are discriminatory in language or effect; or

b. Whether disparities of a substantial and unjustified nature exist in the benefits, treatment, services, or opportunities afforded male and female athletes in the institution's program as a whole; or

c. Whether disparities in benefits, treatment, services, or opportunities in individual segments of the program are substantial enough in and of themselves to deny equality of athletic opportunity.

C. Effective Accommodation of Student Interests and Abilities.

1. The Regulation. The regulation requires institutions to accommodate effectively the interests and abilities of students to the extent necessary to provide equal opportunity in the selection of sports and levels of competition available to members of both sexes.

Specifically, the regulation, at '86.41(c)(1), requires the Director to consider, when determining whether equal opportunities are available.

Whether the selection of sports and levels of competition effectively accommodate the interests and abilities of members of both sexes.

Section 86.41(c) also permits the Director of the Office for Civil Rights to consider other factors in the determination of equal opportunity. Accordingly, this section also addresses competitive opportunities in terms of the competitive team schedules available to athletes of both sexes.

2. The Policy. The Department will assess compliance with the interests and abilities section of the regulation by examining the following factors:

a. The determination of athletic interests and abilities of students;

b. The selection of sports offered; and

c. The levels of competition available including the opportunity for team competition.

3. Application of the Policy C Determination of Athletic Interests and Abilities.

Institutions may determine the athletic interests and abilities of students by nondiscriminatory methods of their choosing provided:

a. The processes take into account the nationally increasing levels of women's interests and abilities;

b. The methods of determining interest and ability do not disadvantage the members of an underrepresented sex;

c. The methods of determining ability take into account team performance records; and

d. The methods are responsive to the expressed interests of students capable of intercollegiate competition who are members of an underrepresented sex.

4. Application of the Policy—Selection of Sports.

In the selection of sports, the regulation does not require institutions to integrate their teams nor to provide exactly the same choice of sports to men and women. However, where an institution sponsors a team in a particular sport for members of one sex, it may be required either to permit the excluded sex to try out for the team or to sponsor a separate team for the previously excluded sex.

a. Contact Sports—Effective accommodation means that if an institution sponsors a team for members of one sex in a contact sport, it must do so for members of the other sex under the following circumstances:

(1) The opportunities for members of the excluded sex have historically been limited; and

(2) There is sufficient interest and ability among the members of the excluded sex to sustain a viable team and a reasonable expectation of intercollegiate competition for that team.

b. Non-Contact Sports—Effective accommodation means that if an institution sponsors a team for members of one sex in a non-contact sport, it must do so for members of the other sex under the following circumstances:

(1) The opportunities for members of the excluded sex have historically been limited;

(2) There is sufficient interest and ability among the members of the excluded sex to sustain a viable team and a reasonable expectation of intercollegiate competition for that team; and

(3) Members of the excluded sex do not possess sufficient skill to be selected for a single integrated team, or to compete actively on such a team if selected.

5. Application of the Policy—Levels of Competition.

In effectively accommodating the interests and abilities of male and female athletes, institutions must provide both the opportunity for individuals of each sex to participate in intercollegiate competition, and for athletes of each sex to have competitive team schedules which equally reflect their abilities.

a. Compliance will be assessed in any one of the following ways:

(1) Whether intercollegiate level participation opportunities for male and female students are provided in numbers substantially proportionate to their respective enrollments; or

(2) Where the members of one sex have been and are underrepresented among intercollegiate athletes, whether the institution can show a

history and continuing practice of program expansion which is demonstrably responsive to the developing interest and abilities of the members of that sex; or

(3) Where the members of one sex are underrepresented among intercollegiate athletes, and the institution cannot show a continuing practice of program expansion such as that cited above, whether it can be demonstrated that the interests and abilities of the members of that sex have been fully and effectively accommodated by the present program.

b. Compliance with this provision of the regulation will also be assessed by examining the following:

(1) Whether the competitive schedules for men's and women's teams, on a program-wide basis, afford proportionally similar numbers of male and female athletes equivalently advanced competitive opportunities; or

(2) Whether the institution can demonstrate a history and continuing practice of upgrading the competitive opportunities available to the historically disadvantaged sex as warranted by developing abilities among the athletes of that sex.

c. Institutions are not required to upgrade teams to intercollegiate status or otherwise develop intercollegiate sports absent a reasonable expectation that intercollegiate competition in that sport will be available within the institution's normal competitive regions. Institutions may be required by the Title IX regulation to actively encourage the development of such competition, however, when overall athletic opportunities within that region have been historically limited for the members of one sex.

6. Overall Determination of Compliance.

The Department will base its compliance determination under '86.41(c) of the regulation upon a determination of the following:

a. Whether the policies of an institution are discriminatory in language or effect; or

b. Whether disparities of a substantial and unjustified nature in the benefits, treatment, services, or opportunities afforded male and female athletes exist in the institution's program as a whole; or

c. Whether disparities in individual segments of the program with respect to benefits, treatment, services, or opportunities are substantial enough in and of themselves to deny equality of athletic opportunity.

VIII. The Enforcement Process

The process of Title IX enforcement is set forth in ' 88.71 of the Title IX regulation, which incorporates by reference the enforcement procedures applicable to Title VI of the Civil Rights Act of 1964. The enforcement process prescribed by the regulation is supplemented by an order of the Federal District Court, District of Columbia, which establishes time frames for each of the enforcement steps.

According to the regulation, there are two ways in which enforcement is initiated:

- Compliance Reviews—Periodically the Department must select a number of recipients (in this case, colleges and universities which operate intercollegiate athletic programs) and conduct investigations to determine whether recipients are complying with Title IX. (45 CFR 80.7(a))

- Complaints—The Department must investigate all valid (written and timely) complaints alleging discrimination on the basis of sex in a recipient's programs. (45 CFR 80.7(b))

The Department must inform the recipient (and the complainant, if applicable) of the results of its investigation. If the investigation indicates that a recipient is in compliance, the Department states this, and the case is closed. If the investigation indicates noncompliance, the Department outlines the violations found.

The Department has 90 days to conduct an investigation and inform the recipient of its findings, and an additional 90 days to resolve violations by obtaining a voluntary compliance agreement from the recipient. This is done through negotiations between the Department and the recipient, the goal of which is agreement on steps the recipient will take to achieve compliance. Sometimes the violation is relatively minor and can be corrected immediately. At other times, however, the negotiations result in a plan that will correct the violations within a specified period of time. To be acceptable, a plan must describe the manner in which institutional resources will be used to correct the violation. It also must state acceptable time tables for reaching interim goals and full compliance. When agreement is reached, the Department notifies the institution that its plan is acceptable. The Department then is obligated to review periodically the implementation of the plan.

An institution that is in violation of Title IX may already be implementing a corrective plan. In this case, prior to informing the recipient about the results of its investigation, the Department will determine whether the plan is adequate. If the plan is not adequate to correct the violations (or to correct them within a reasonable period of time) the recipient will be found in noncompliance and voluntary negotiations will begin. However, if the institutional plan is acceptable, the Department will inform the institution that although the institution has violations, it is found to be in compliance because it is implementing a corrective plan. The Department, in this instance also, would monitor the progress of the institutional plan. If the institution subsequently does not completely implement its plan, it will be found in noncompliance.

When a recipient is found in noncompliance and voluntary compliance attempts are unsuccessful, the formal process leading to termination of Federal assistance will be begun. These procedures, which include the opportunity for a hearing before an administrative law judge, are set forth at 45 CFR 80.8-80.11 and 45 CFR Part 81.

IX. Authority

(Secs. 901, 902, Education Amendments of 1972, 86 Stat. 373, 374, 20 U.S.C. 1681, 1682; sec. 844, Education Amendments of 1974, Pub. L. 93-380, 88 Stat. 612; and 45 CFR Part 86)

Dated December 3, 1979.

Roma Stewart,

Director, Office for Civil Rights, Department of Health, Education, and Welfare.

Dated December 4, 1979.

Patricia Roberts Harris,

Secretary, Department of Health, Education, and Welfare.

Appendix A—Historic Patterns of Intercollegiate Athletics Program Development

1. Participation in intercollegiate sports has historically been emphasized for men but not women. Partially as a consequence of this, participation rates of women are far below those of men. During the 1977–78 academic year women students accounted for 48 percent of the national undergraduate enrollment (5,496,000 of 11,267,000 students). Yet, only 30 percent of the intercollegiate athletes are women.

   The historic emphasis on men's intercollegiate athletic programs has also contributed to existing differences in the number of sports and scope of competition offered men and women. One source indicates that, on the average, colleges and universities are providing twice the number of sports for men as they are for women.

2. Participation by women in sports is growing rapidly. During the period from 1971–1978, for example, the number of female participants in organized high school sports increased from 294,000 to 2,083,000 C an increase of over 600 percent. In contrast, between Fall 1971 and Fall 1977, the enrollment of females in high school decreased from approximately 7,600,000 to approximately 7,150,000 a decrease of over 5 percent.

   The growth in athletic participation by high school women has been reflected on the campuses of the nation's colleges and universities. During the period from 1971 to 1976 the enrollment of women in the nation's institutions of higher education rose 52 percent, from 3,400,000 to 5,201,000. During this same period, the number of women participating in intramural sports increased 108 percent from 276,167 to 576,167. In club sports, the number of women participants increased from 16,386 to 25,541 or 55 percent. In intercollegiate sports, women's participation increased 102 percent from 31,852 to 64,375. These developments reflect the growing interest of women in competitive athletics, as well as the efforts of colleges and universities to accommodate those interests.

3. The overall growth of women's intercollegiate programs has not been at the expense of men's programs. During the past decade of rapid growth in women's programs, the number of intercollegiate sports available for men has remained stable, and the number of male athletes has increased slightly. Funding for men's programs has increased from $1.2 to $2.2 million between 1970–1977 alone.

4. On most campuses, the primary problem confronting women athletes is the absence of a fair and adequate level of resources, services, and benefits. For example, disproportionately more financial aid has been made available for male athletes than for female athletes. Presently, in institutions that are members of both the National Collegiate Athletic Association (NCAA) and the Association for Intercollegiate Athletics for Women (AIAW), the average annual

scholarship budget is $39,000. Male athletes receive $32,000 or 78 percent of this amount, and female athletes receive $7,000 or 22 percent, although women are 30 percent of all the athletes eligible for scholarships.

Likewise, substantial amounts have been provided for the recruitment of male athletes, but little funding has been made available for recruitment of female athletes.

Congressional testimony on Title IX and subsequent surveys indicates that discrepancies also exist in the opportunity to receive coaching and in other benefits and opportunities, such as the quality and amount of equipment, access to facilities and practice times, publicity, medical and training facilities, and housing and dining facilities.

5. At several institutions, intercollegiate football is unique among sports. The size of the teams, the expense of the operation, and the revenue produced distinguish football from other sports, both men's and women's. Title IX requires that "an institution of higher education must comply with the prohibition against sex discrimination imposed by that title and its implementing regulations in the administration of any revenue producing intercollegiate athletic activity." However, the unique size and cost of football programs have been taken into account in developing this Policy Interpretation.

Appendix B—Comments and Responses

The Office for Civil Rights (OCR) received over 700 comments and recommendations in response to the December 11, 1978 publication of the proposed Policy Interpretation. After the formal comment period, representatives of the Department met for additional discussions with many individuals and groups including college and university officials, athletic associations, athletic directors, women's rights organizations and other interested parties. HEW representatives also visited eight universities in order to assess the potential of the proposed Policy Interpretation and of suggested alternative approaches for effective enforcement of Title IX.

The Department carefully considered all information before preparing the final policy. Some changes in the structure and substance of the Policy Interpretation have been made as a result of concerns that were identified in the comment and consultation process.

Persons who responded to the request for public comment were asked to comment generally and also to respond specifically to eight questions that focused on different aspects of the proposed Policy Interpretation.

Question No. 1: Is the description of the current status and development of intercollegiate athletics for men and women accurate? What other factors should be considered?

Comment A: Some commentors noted that the description implied the presence of intent on the part of all universities to discriminate against women. Many of these same commentors noted an absence of concern in the proposed Policy Interpretation for those universities that have in good faith attempted to meet what they felt to be a vague compliance standard in the regulation.

Response: The description of the current status and development of intercollegiate athletics for men and women was designed to be a factual, historical overview. There was no intent to imply the universal presence of discrimination. The Department recognizes that there are many colleges and universities that have been and are making good faith efforts, in the midst of increasing financial pressures, to provide equal athletic opportunities to their male and female athletes.

Comment B: Commentors stated that the statistics used were outdated in some areas, incomplete in some areas, and inaccurate in some areas.

Response: Comment accepted. The statistics have been updated and corrected where necessary.

Question No. 2: Is the proposed two-stage approach to compliance practical? Should it be modified? Are there other approaches to be considered?

Comment: Some commentors stated that Part II of the proposed Policy Interpretation "Equally Accommodating the Interests and Abilities of Women" represented an extension of the July 1978, compliance deadline established in '86.41(d) of the Title IX regulation.

Response: Part II of the proposed Policy Interpretation was not intended to extend the compliance deadline. The format of the two stage approach, however, seems to have encouraged that perception; therefore, the elements of both stages have been unified in this Policy Interpretation.

Question No. 3: Is the equal average per capita standard based on participation rates practical? Are there alternatives or modifications that should be considered?

Comment A: Some commentors stated it was unfair or illegal to find noncompliance solely on the basis of a financial test when more valid indicators of equality of opportunity exist.

Response: The equal average per capita standard was not a standard by which noncompliance could be found. It was offered as a standard of presumptive compliance. In order to prove noncompliance, HEW would have been required to show that the unexplained disparities in expenditures were discriminatory in effect. The standard, in part, was offered as a means of simplifying proof of compliance for universities. The widespread confusion concerning the significance of failure to satisfy the equal average per capita expenditure standard, however, is one of the reasons it was withdrawn.

Comment B: Many commentors stated that the equal average per capita standard penalizes those institutions that have increased participation opportunities for women and rewards institutions that have limited women's participation.

Response: Since equality of average per capita expenditures has been dropped as a standard of presumptive compliance, the question of its effect is no longer relevant. However, the Department agrees that universities that had increased participation opportunities for women and wished to take advantage of the presumptive compliance standard, would have had a bigger financial burden than universities that had done little to increase participation opportunities for women.

Question No. 4: Is there a basis for treating part of the expenses of a particular revenue producing sport differently because the sport produces income used by the university for non-athletic operating expenses on a non-discriminatory basis? If, so, how should such funds be identified and treated?

Comment: Commentors stated that this question was largely irrelevant because there were so few universities at which revenue from the athletic program was used in the university operating budget.

Response: Since equality of average per capita expenditures has been dropped as a standard of presumed compliance, a decision is no longer necessary on this issue.

Question No. 5: Is the grouping of financially measurable benefits into three categories practical? Are there alternatives that should be considered? Specifically, should recruiting expenses be considered together with all other financially measurable benefits?

Comment A: Most commentors stated that, if measured solely on a financial standard, recruiting should be grouped with the other financially measurable items. Some of these commentors held that at the current stage of development of women's intercollegiate athletics, the amount of money that would flow into the women's recruitment budget as a result of separate application of the equal average per capita standard to recruiting expenses, would make recruitment a disproportionately large percentage of the entire women's budget. Women's athletic directors, particularly, wanted the flexibility to have the money available for other uses, and they generally agreed on including recruitment expenses with the other financially measurable items.

Comment B: Some commentors stated that it was particularly inappropriate to base any measure of compliance in recruitment solely on financial expenditures. They stated that even if proportionate amounts of money were allocated to recruitment, major inequities could remain in the benefits to athletes. For instance, universities could maintain a policy of subsidizing visits to their campuses of prospective students of one sex but not the other. Commentors suggested that including an examination of differences in benefits to prospective athletes that result from recruiting methods would be appropriate.

Response: In the final Policy Interpretation, recruitment has been moved to the group of program areas to be examined under '86.41(c) to determine whether overall equal athletic opportunity exists. The Department accepts the comment that a financial measure is not sufficient to determine whether equal opportunity is being provided. Therefore, in examining athletic recruitment, the Department will primarily review the opportunity to recruit, the resources provided for recruiting, and methods of recruiting.

Question No. 6: Are the factors used to justify differences in equal average per capita expenditures for financially measurable benefits and opportunities fair? Are there other factors that should be considered?

Comment: Most commentors indicated that the factors named in the proposed Policy Interpretation (the "scope of competition" and the "nature of the sport") as justifications for differences in equal average per capita expenditures were so vague and ambiguous as to be meaningless. Some stated that it would be impossible to define the phrase "scope of competition," given the greatly differing competitive structure of men's and women's programs. Other commentors were concerned that the "scope of competition" factor that may currently be designated as "nondiscriminatory" was, in reality, the result of many years of inequitable treatment of women's athletic programs.

Response: The Department agrees that it would have been difficult to define clearly and then to quantify the "scope of competition" factor. Since equal average per capita expenditures has been dropped as a standard of presumed compliance, such financial justifications are no longer necessary. Under the equivalency standard, however, the "nature of the sport" remains an important concept. As explained within the Policy Interpretation, the unique nature of a sport may account for perceived inequities in some program areas.

Question No 7: Is the comparability standard for benefits and opportunities that are not financially measurably fair and realistic? Should other factors controlling comparability be included? Should the comparability standard be revised? Is there a different standard which should be considered?

Comment: Many commentors stated that the comparability standard was fair and realistic. Some commentors were concerned, however, that the standard was vague and subjective and could lead to uneven enforcement.

Response: The concept of comparing the non-financially measurable benefits and opportunities provided to male and female athletes has been preserved and expanded in the final Policy Interpretation to include all areas of examination except scholarships and accommodation of the interests and abilities of both sexes. The standard is that equivalent benefits and opportunities must be provided. To avoid vagueness and subjectivity, further guidance is given about what elements will be considered in each program area to determine the equivalency of benefits and opportunities.

Question No. 8: Is the proposal for increasing the opportunity for women to participate in competitive athletics appropriate and effective? Are there other procedures that should be considered? Is there a more effective way to ensure that the interest and abilities of both men and women are equally accommodated?

Comment: Several commentors indicated that the proposal to allow a university to gain the status of presumed compliance by having policies and procedures to encourage the growth of women's athletics was appropriate and effective for future students, but ignored students presently enrolled. They indicated that nowhere in the proposed Policy Interpretation was concern shown that the current selection of sports and levels of competition effectively accommodate the interests and abilities of women as well as men.

Response: Comment accepted. The requirement that universities equally accommodate the interests and abilities of their male and female athletes (Part II of the proposed Policy Interpretation) has been directly addressed and is now a part of the unified final Policy Interpretation.

Additional Comments

The following comments were not responses to questions raised in the proposed Policy Interpretation. They represent additional concerns expressed by a large number of commentors.

(1) *Comment*: Football and other "revenue producing" sports should be totally exempted or should receive special treatment under Title IX.

Response: The April 18, 1978, opinion of the General Counsel, HEW, concludes that "an institution of higher education must comply with the prohibition against sex discrimination imposed by that title and its implementing regulation in the administration of any revenue producing activity." Therefore, football or other "revenue producing" sports cannot be exempted from coverage of Title IX.

In developing the proposed Policy Interpretation the Department concluded that although the fact of revenue production could not justify disparity in average per capita expenditure between men and women, there were characteristics common to most revenue producing sports that could result in legitimate nondiscriminatory differences in per capita expenditures. For instance, some "revenue producing" sports require expensive protective equipment and most require high expenditures for the management of events attended by large numbers of people. These characteristics and others described in the proposed Policy Interpretation were considered acceptable, nondiscriminatory reasons for differences in per capita average expenditures.

In the final Policy Interpretation, under the equivalent benefits and opportunities standard of compliance, some of these non-discriminatory factors are still relevant and applicable.

(2) *Comment*: Commentors stated that since the equal average per capita standard of presumed compliance was based on participation rates, the word should be explicitly defined.

Response: Although the final Policy Interpretation does not use the equal average per capita standard of presumed compliance, a clear understanding of the word "participant" is still necessary, particularly in the determination of compliance where scholarships are involved. The word "participant" is defined in the final Policy Interpretation.

(3) *Comment*: Many commentors were concerned that the proposed Policy Interpretation neglected the rights of individuals.

Response: The proposed Policy Interpretation was intended to further clarify what colleges and universities must do within their intercollegiate athletic programs to avoid discrimination against individuals on the basis of sex. The Interpretation, therefore, spoke to institutions in terms of their male and female athletes. It spoke specifically in terms of equal, average per capita expenditures and in terms of comparability of other opportunities and benefits for male and female participating athletes.

The Department believes that under this approach the rights of individuals were protected. If women athletes, as a class, are receiving opportunities and benefits equal to those of male athletes, individuals within the class should be protected thereby. Under the proposed Policy Interpretation, for example, if female athletes as a whole were receiving their proportional share of athletic financial assistance, a university would have been presumed in compliance with that section of the regulation. The Department does not want and does not have the authority to force universities to offer identical programs to men and women. Therefore, to allow flexibility within women's programs and within men's programs, the proposed Policy Interpretation stated that an institution would be presumed in compliance if the average per capita expenditures on athletic scholarships for men and women, were equal. This same flexibility (in scholarships and in other areas) remains in the final Policy Interpretation.

(4) *Comment*: Several commentors stated that the provision of a separate dormitory to athletes of only one sex, even where no other special benefits were involved, is inherently discriminatory. They felt such separation indicated the different degrees of importance attached to athletes on the basis of sex.

Response: Comment accepted. The provision of a separate dormitory to athletes of one sex but not the other will be considered a failure to provide equivalent benefits as required by the regulation.

(5) *Comment*: Commentors, particularly colleges and universities, expressed concern that the differences in the rules of intercollegiate athletic associations could result in unequal distribution of benefits and opportunities to men's and women's athletic programs, thus placing the institutions in a posture of non-compliance with Title IX.

Response: Commentors made this point with regard to '86.6(c) of the Title IX regulation, which reads in part:

"The obligation to comply with (Title IX) is not obviated or alleviated by any rule or regulation of any * * * athletic or other * * * association * * *"

Since the penalties for violation of intercollegiate athletic association rules an have a severe effect on the athletic opportunities within an affected program, the Department has reexamined this regulatory requirement to determine whether it should be modified. Our conclusion is that modification would not have a beneficial effect, and that the present requirement will stand.

Several factors enter into this decision. First, the differences between rules affecting men's and women's programs are numerous and change constantly. Despite this, the Department has been unable to discover a single case in which those differences require members to act in a discriminatory manner. Second, some rule differences may permit decisions resulting in discriminatory distribution of benefits and opportunities to men's and women's programs. The fact that institutions respond to differences in rules by choosing to deny equal opportunities, however, does not mean that the rules themselves are at fault; the rules do not prohibit choices that would result in compliance with Title IX. Finally, the rules in question are all established and subject to change by the membership of the association. Since all (or virtually all) association member institutions are subject to Title IX, the opportunity exists for these institutions to resolve collectively any wide-spread Title IX compliance problems resulting from association rules. To the extent that this has not taken place, Federal intervention on behalf of statutory beneficiaries is both warranted and required by the law. Consequently, the Department can follow no course other than to continue to disallow any defenses against findings of noncompliance with Title IX that are based on intercollegiate athletic association rules.

(6) *Comment*: Some commentors suggested that the equal average per capita test was unfairly skewed by the high cost of some "major" men's sports, particularly

football, that have no equivalently expensive counterpart among women's sports. They suggested that a certain percentage of those costs (e.g., 50% of football scholarships) should be excluded from the expenditures on male athletes prior to application of the equal average per capita test.

Response: Since equality of average per capita expenditures has been eliminated as a standard of presumed compliance, the suggestion is no longer relevant. However, it was possible under that standard to exclude expenditures that were due to the nature of the sport, or the scope of competition and thus were not discriminatory in effect. Given the diversity of intercollegiate athletic programs, determinations as to whether disparities in expenditures were nondiscriminatory would have been made on a case-by-case basis. There was no legal support for the proposition that an arbitrary percentage of expenditures should be excluded from the calculations.

(7) *Comment*: Some commentors urged the Department to adopt various forms of team-based comparisons in assessing equality of opportunity between men's and women's athletic programs. They stated that well-developed men's programs are frequently characterized by a few "major" teams that have the greatest spectator appeal, earn the greatest income, cost the most to operate, and dominate the program in other ways. They suggested that women's programs should be similarly constructed and that comparability should then be required only between "men's major" and "women's major" teams, and between "men's minor" and "women's minor" teams. The men's teams most often cited as appropriate for "major" designation have been football and basketball, with women's basketball and volleyball being frequently selected as the counterparts.

Response: I here are two problems with this approach to assessing equal opportunity. First, neither the statute nor the regulation calls for identical programs for male and female athletes. Absent such a requirement, the Department cannot base noncompliance upon a failure to provide arbitrarily identical programs, either in whole or in part.

Second, no subgrouping of male or female students (such as a team) mat be used in such a way as to diminish the protection of the larger class of males and females in their rights to equal participation in educational benefits or opportunities. Use of the "major/minor" classification does not meet this test where large participation sports (e.g., football) are compared to smaller ones (e.g., women's volleyball) in such a manner as to have the effect of disproportionately providing benefits or opportunities to the members of one sex.

(8) *Comment*: Some commentors suggest that equality of opportunity should be measured by a "sport-specific" comparison. Under this approach, institutions offering the same sports to men and women would have an obligation to provide equal opportunity within each of those sports. For example, the men's basketball team and the women's basketball team would have to receive equal opportunities and benefits.

Response: As noted above, there is no provision for the requirement of identical programs for men and women, and no such requirement will be made by the Department. Moreover, a sport-specific comparison could actually create unequal opportunity. For example, the sports available for men at an institution might include most or all of those available for women; but the men's program might concentrate resources on sports not available to women (e.g., football, ice hockey). In addition, the sport-specific concept overlooks two key elements of the Title IX regulation.

First, the regulation states that the selection of sports is to be representative of student interests and abilities (86.41(c)(1)). A requirement that sports for the members of one sex be available or developed solely or the basis of their existence or development in the program for members of the other sex could conflict with the regulation where the interests and abilities of male and female students diverge.

Second, the regulation frames the general compliance obligations of recipients in terms of program-wide benefits and opportunities (86.41(c)). As implied above, Title IX protects the individual as a student-athlete, not all a basketball player, or swimmer.

(9) *Comment*: A coalition of many colleges and universities urged that there are no objective standards against which compliance with Title IX in intercollegiate athletics could be measured. They felt that diversity is so great among colleges and universities that no single standard or set of standards could practicably apply to all affected institutions. They concluded that it would be best for individual institutions to determine the policies and procedures by which to ensure nondiscrimination in intercollegiate athletic programs.

Specifically, this coalition suggested that each institution should create a group representative of all affected parties on campus.

This group would then assess existing athletic opportunities for men and women, and, on the basis of the assessment, develop a plan to ensure nondiscrimination. This plan would then be recommended to the Board of Trustees or other appropriate governing body.

The role foreseen for the Department under this concept is:

(a) The Department would use the plan as a framework for evaluating complaints and assessing compliance;

(b) The Department would determine whether the plan satisfies the interests of the involved parties; and

(c) The Department would determine whether the institution is adhering to the plan.

These commentors felt that this approach to Title IX enforcement would ensure an environment of equal opportunity.

Response: Title IX is an antidiscrimination law. It prohibits discrimination based on sex in educational institutions that are recipients of Federal assistance. The legislative history of Title IX clearly shows that it was enacted because of discrimination that currently was being practiced against women in educational institutions. The Department accepts that colleges and universities are sincere in their intention to ensure equal opportunity in intercollegiate athletics to their male and female students. It cannot, however, turn over its responsibility for interpreting and enforcing the law. In this case, its responsibility includes articulating the standards by which compliance with the Title IX statute will be evaluated.

The Department agrees with this group of commentors that the proposed self-assessment and institutional plan is an excellent idea. Any institution that engages in the assessment/planning process, particularly with the full participation of interested parties as envisioned in the proposal, would clearly reach or move well toward compliance. In addition, as explained in Section VIII of this Policy Interpretation, any college or university that has compliance problems but is implementing a plan that the Department determines will correct those problems within a reasonable period of time, will be found in compliance.

Source: http://www.ed.gov/about/offices/list/ocr/docs/t9interp.html.

Appendix C: Clarification of Intercollegiate Athletics Policy Guidance: The Three-Part Test, 1996

The Office for Civil Rights (OCR) enforces Title IX of the Education Amendments of 1972, 20 U.S.C. § 1681 *et seq.* (Title IX), which prohibits discrimination on the basis of sex in education programs and activities by recipients of federal funds. The regulation implementing Title IX, at 34 C.F.R. Part 106, effective July 21, 1975, contains specific provisions governing athletic programs, at 34 C.F.R. § 106.41, and the awarding of athletic scholarships, at 34 C.F.R. § 106.37(c). Further clarification of the Title IX regulatory requirements is provided by the Intercollegiate Athletics Policy Interpretation, issued December 11, 1979 (44 *Fed. Reg.* 71413 *et seq.* (1979)).

The Title IX regulation provides that if an institution sponsors an athletic program it must provide equal athletic opportunities for members of both sexes. Among other factors, the regulation requires that an institution must effectively accommodate the athletic interests and abilities of students of both sexes to the extent necessary to provide equal athletic opportunity.

The 1979 Policy Interpretation provides that as part of this determination OCR will apply the following three-part test to assess whether an institution is providing nondiscriminatory participation opportunities for individuals of both sexes:

1. Whether intercollegiate level participation opportunities for male and female students are provided in numbers substantially proportionate to their respective enrollments; or

2. Where the members of one sex have been and are underrepresented among intercollegiate athletes, whether the institution can show a history and continuing practice of program expansion which is demonstrably responsive to the developing interests and abilities of the members of that sex; or

3. Where the members of one sex are underrepresented among intercollegiate athletes, and the institution cannot show a history and continuing practice of

program expansion, as described above, whether it can be demonstrated that the interests and abilities of the members of that sex have been fully and effectively accommodated by the present program.

44 *Fed. Reg.* at 71418.

Thus, the three-part test furnishes an institution with three individual avenues to choose from when determining how it will provide individuals of each sex with nondiscriminatory opportunities to participate in intercollegiate athletics. If an institution has met any part of the three-part test, OCR will determine that the institution is meeting this requirement.

It is important to note that under the Policy Interpretation the requirement to provide nondiscriminatory participation opportunities is only one of many factors that OCR examines to determine if an institution is in compliance with the athletics provision of Title IX. OCR also considers the quality of competition offered to members of both sexes in order to determine whether an institution effectively accommodates the interests and abilities of its students.

In addition, when an "overall determination of compliance" is made by OCR, 44 *Fed. Reg.* 71417, 71418, OCR examines the institution's program as a whole. Thus OCR considers the effective accommodation of interests and abilities in conjunction with equivalence in the availability, quality and kinds of other athletic benefits and opportunities provided male and female athletes to determine whether an institution provides equal athletic opportunity as required by Title IX. These other benefits include coaching, equipment, practice and competitive facilities, recruitment, scheduling of games, and publicity, among others. An institution's failure to provide nondiscriminatory participation opportunities usually amounts to a denial of equal athletic opportunity because these opportunities provide access to all other athletic benefits, treatment, and services.

This Clarification provides specific factors that guide an analysis of each part of the three-part test. In addition, it provides examples to demonstrate, in concrete terms, how these factors will be considered. These examples are intended to be illustrative, and the conclusions drawn in each example are based solely on the facts included in the example.

THREE-PART TEST—Part One: Are Participation Opportunities Substantially Proportionate to Enrollment?

Under part one of the three-part test (part one), where an institution provides intercollegiate level athletic participation opportunities for male and female students in numbers substantially proportionate to their respective full-time undergraduate enrollments, OCR will find that the institution is providing nondiscriminatory participation opportunities for individuals of both sexes.

OCR's analysis begins with a determination of the number of participation opportunities afforded to male and female athletes in the intercollegiate athletic program. The Policy Interpretation defines participants as those athletes:

a. Who are receiving the institutionally-sponsored support normally provided to athletes competing at the institution involved, e.g., coaching, equipment, medical and training room services, on a regular basis during a sport's season; and

b. Who are participating in organized practice sessions and other team meetings and activities on a regular basis during a sport's season; and

c. Who are listed on the eligibility or squad lists maintained for each sport, or

d. Who, because of injury, cannot meet a, b, or c above but continue to receive financial aid on the basis of athletic ability.

44 *Fed. Reg.* at 71415.

OCR uses this definition of participant to determine the number of participation opportunities provided by an institution for purposes of the three-part test.

Under this definition, OCR considers a sport's season to commence on the date of a team's first intercollegiate competitive event and to conclude on the date of the team's final intercollegiate competitive event. As a general rule, all athletes who are listed on a team's squad or eligibility list and are on the team as of the team's first competitive event are counted as participants by OCR. In determining the number of participation opportunities for the purposes of the interests and abilities analysis, an athlete who participates in more than one sport will be counted as a participant in each sport in which he or she participates.

In determining participation opportunities, OCR includes, among others, those athletes who do not receive scholarships (e.g., walk-ons), those athletes who compete on teams sponsored by the institution even though the team may be required to raise some or all of its operating funds, and those athletes who practice but may not compete. OCR's investigations reveal that these athletes receive numerous benefits and services, such as training and practice time, coaching, tutoring services, locker room facilities, and equipment, as well as important non-tangible benefits derived from being a member of an intercollegiate athletic team. Because these are significant benefits, and because receipt of these benefits does not depend on their cost to the institution or whether the athlete competes, it is necessary to count all athletes who receive such benefits when determining the number of athletic opportunities provided to men and women.

OCR's analysis next determines whether athletic opportunities are substantially proportionate. The Title IX regulation allows institutions to operate separate athletic programs for men and women. Accordingly, the regulation allows an institution to control the respective number of participation opportunities offered to men and women. Thus, it could be argued that to satisfy part one there should be no difference between the participation rate in an institution's intercollegiate athletic program and its full-time undergraduate student enrollment.

However, because in some circumstances it may be unreasonable to expect an institution to achieve exact proportionality—for instance, because of natural fluctuations in enrollment and participation rates or because it would be unreasonable to expect an institution to add athletic opportunities in light of the small number of students that would have to be accommodated to achieve exact proportionality—the Policy Interpretation examines whether participation opportunities are "substantially" proportionate to enrollment rates. Because this determination depends on the institution's specific circumstances and the size of its athletic program, OCR makes this determination on a case-by-case basis, rather than through use of a statistical test.

As an example of a determination under part one: If an institution's enrollment is 52 percent male and 48 percent female and 52 percent of the participants in the athletic program are male and 48 percent female, then the institution would clearly satisfy part one. However, OCR recognizes that natural fluctuations in an institution's enrollment and/or participation rates may affect the percentages in a subsequent year. For instance, if the institution's admissions the following year resulted in an enrollment rate of 51 percent males and 49 percent females, while the participation rates of males and females in the athletic program remained constant, the institution would continue to satisfy part one because it would be unreasonable to expect the institution to fine tune its program in response to this change in enrollment.

As another example, over the past five years an institution has had a consistent enrollment rate for women of 50 percent. During this time period, it has been expanding its program for women in order to reach proportionality. In the year that the institution reaches its goal—i.e., 50 percent of the participants in its athletic program are female—its enrollment rate for women increases to 52 percent. Under these circumstances, the institution would satisfy part one.

OCR would also consider opportunities to be substantially proportionate when the number of opportunities that would be required to achieve proportionality would not be sufficient to sustain a viable team, i.e., a team for which there is a sufficient number of interested and able students and enough available competition to sustain an intercollegiate team. As a frame of reference in assessing this situation, OCR may consider the average size of teams offered for the underrepresented sex, a number which would vary by institution.

For instance, Institution A is a university with a total of 600 athletes. While women make up 52 percent of the university's enrollment, they only represent 47 percent of its athletes. If the university provided women with 52 percent of athletic opportunities, approximately 62 additional women would be able to participate. Because this is a significant number of unaccommodated women, it is likely that a viable sport could be added. If so, Institution A has not met part one.

As another example, at Institution B women also make up 52 percent of the university's enrollment and represent 47 percent of Institution B's athletes. Institution B's athletic program consists of only 60 participants. If the University provided women with 52 percent of athletic opportunities, approximately 6 additional women would be able to participate. Since 6 participants are unlikely to support a viable team, Institution B would meet part one.

THREE-PART TEST—Part Two: Is there a History and Continuing Practice of Program Expansion for the Underrepresented Sex?

Under part two of the three-part test (part two), an institution can show that it has a history and continuing practice of program expansion which is demonstrably responsive to the developing interests and abilities of the underrepresented sex. In effect, part two looks at an institution's past and continuing remedial efforts to provide nondiscriminatory participation opportunities through program expansion.

OCR will review the entire history of the athletic program, focusing on the participation opportunities provided for the underrepresented sex. First, OCR will assess whether past actions of the institution have expanded participation opportunities for the underrepresented sex in a manner that was demonstrably responsive to their developing interests and abilities. Developing interests include interests that already exist at the institution. There are no fixed intervals of time within which an institution must have added participation opportunities. Neither is a particular number of sports dispositive. Rather, the focus is on whether the program expansion was responsive to developing interests and abilities of the underrepresented sex. In addition, the institution must demonstrate a continuing (i.e., present) practice of program expansion as warranted by developing interests and abilities.

OCR will consider the following factors, among others, as evidence that may indicate a history of program expansion that is demonstrably responsive to the developing interests and abilities of the underrepresented sex:

- an institution's record of adding intercollegiate teams, or upgrading teams to intercollegiate status, for the underrepresented sex;
- an institution's record of increasing the numbers of participants in intercollegiate athletics who are members of the underrepresented sex; and
- an institution's affirmative responses to requests by students or others for addition or elevation of sports.

OCR will consider the following factors, among others, as evidence that may indicate a continuing practice of program expansion that is demonstrably responsive to the developing interests and abilities of the underrepresented sex:

- an institution's current implementation of a nondiscriminatory policy or procedure for requesting the addition of sports (including the elevation of club or intramural teams) and the effective communication of the policy or procedure to students; and
- an institution's current implementation of a plan of program expansion that is responsive to developing interests and abilities.

OCR would also find persuasive an institution's efforts to monitor developing interests and abilities of the underrepresented sex, for example, by conducting periodic nondiscriminatory assessments of developing interests and abilities and taking timely actions in response to the results.

In the event that an institution eliminated any team for the underrepresented sex, OCR would evaluate the circumstances surrounding this action in assessing whether the institution could satisfy part two of the test. However, OCR will not find a history and continuing practice of program expansion where an institution increases the proportional participation opportunities for the underrepresented sex by reducing opportunities for the overrepresented sex alone or by reducing participation opportunities for the overrepresented sex to a proportionately greater degree than for the underrepresented sex. This is because part two considers an institution's good faith remedial efforts through actual program expansion. It is only necessary to examine part two if one sex is overrepresented in the athletic program. Cuts in the program for the underrepresented sex, even when coupled with cuts in the program for the overrepresented sex, cannot be considered remedial because they burden members of the sex already disadvantaged by the present program. However, an institution that has eliminated some participation opportunities for the underrepresented sex can still meet part two if, overall, it can show a history and continuing practice of program expansion for that sex.

In addition, OCR will not find that an institution satisfies part two where it established teams for the underrepresented sex only at the initiation of its program for the underrepresented sex or where it merely promises to expand its program for the underrepresented sex at some time in the future.

The following examples are intended to illustrate the principles discussed above.

At the inception of its women's program in the mid-1970s, Institution C established seven teams for women. In 1984 it added a women's varsity team at the request of students and coaches. In 1990 it upgraded a women's club sport to varsity team status based on a request by the club members and an NCAA survey that showed a significant increase in girls high school participation in that sport. Institution C is currently implementing a plan to add a varsity women's team in the spring of 1996 that has been identified by a regional study as an emerging women's sport in the region. The addition of these teams resulted in an increased percentage of women participating in varsity athletics at the institution. Based on these facts, OCR would find Institution C in compliance with part two because it has a history of program expansion and is continuing to expand its program for women to meet their developing interests and abilities.

By 1980, Institution D established seven teams for women. Institution D added a women's varsity team in 1983 based on the requests of students and coaches. In 1991 it added a women's varsity team after an NCAA survey showed a significant increase in girls' high school participation in that sport. In 1993 Institution D eliminated a viable women's team and a viable men's team in an effort to reduce its athletic budget. It has taken no action relating to the underrepresented sex since 1993. Based on these facts, OCR would not find Institution D in compliance with part two. Institution D cannot show a continuing practice of program expansion that is responsive to the developing interests and abilities of the underrepresented sex where its only action since 1991 with regard to the underrepresented sex was to eliminate a team for which there was interest, ability and available competition.

In the mid-1970s, Institution E established five teams for women. In 1979 it added a women's varsity team. In 1984 it upgraded a women's club sport with twenty-five participants to varsity team status. At that time it eliminated a women's varsity team that had eight members. In 1987 and 1989 Institution E added women's varsity teams that were identified by a significant number of its enrolled and incoming female students when surveyed regarding their athletic interests and abilities. During this time it also increased the size of an existing women's team to provide opportunities for women who expressed interest in playing that sport. Within the past year, it added a women's varsity team based on a nationwide survey of the most popular girls high school teams. Based on the addition of these teams, the percentage of women participating in varsity athletics at the institution has increased. Based on these facts, OCR would find Institution E in compliance with part two because it has a history of program expansion and the elimination of the team in 1984 took place within the context of continuing program expansion for the underrepresented sex that is responsive to their developing interests.

Institution F started its women's program in the early 1970s with four teams. It did not add to its women's program until 1987 when, based on requests of students and coaches, it upgraded a women's club sport to varsity team status and expanded the size of several existing women's teams to accommodate significant expressed interest by students. In 1990 it surveyed its enrolled and incoming female students; based on that survey and a survey of the most popular sports played by women in the region, Institution F agreed to add three new women's teams by 1997. It added a women's team in 1991 and 1994. Institution F is implementing a plan to add a women's team by the spring of 1997. Based on these facts, OCR would find Institution F in compliance with part two. Institution F's program history since 1987 shows that it is committed to program expansion for the underrepresented sex and it is continuing to expand its women's program in light of women's developing interests and abilities.

THREE-PART TEST—Part Three: Is the Institution Fully and Effectively Accommodating the Interests and Abilities of the Underrepresented Sex?

Under part three of the three-part test (part three) OCR determines whether an institution is fully and effectively accommodating the interests and abilities of its students who are members of the underrepresented sex—including students who are admitted to the institution though not yet enrolled. Title IX provides that at recipient must provide equal athletic opportunity to its students. Accordingly, the Policy Interpretation does not require an institution to accommodate the interests and abilities of potential students.

While disproportionately high athletic participation rates by an institution's students of the overrepresented sex (as compared to their enrollment rates) may indicate that an institution is not providing equal athletic opportunities to its students of the underrepresented sex, an institution can satisfy part three where there is evidence that the imbalance does not reflect discrimination, i.e., where it can be demonstrated that, notwithstanding disproportionately low participation rates by the institution's students of the underrepresented sex, the interests and abilities of these students are, in fact, being fully and effectively accommodated.

In making this determination, OCR will consider whether there is (a) unmet interest in a particular sport; (b) sufficient ability to sustain a team in the sport; and (c) a reasonable expectation of competition for the team. If all three conditions are present OCR will find that an institution has not fully and effectively accommodated the interests and abilities of the underrepresented sex.

If an institution has recently eliminated a viable team from the intercollegiate program, OCR will find that there is sufficient interest, ability, and available competition to sustain an intercollegiate team in that sport unless an institution can provide strong evidence that interest, ability, or available competition no longer exists.

a) Is there sufficient unmet interest to support an intercollegiate team?

OCR will determine whether there is sufficient unmet interest among the institution's students who are members of the underrepresented sex to sustain an intercollegiate team. OCR will look for interest by the underrepresented sex as expressed through the following indicators, among others:

- requests by students and admitted students that a particular sport be added;
- requests that an existing club sport be elevated to intercollegiate team status;
- participation in particular club or intramural sports;
- interviews with students, admitted students, coaches, administrators and others regarding interest in particular sports;
- results of questionnaires of students and admitted students regarding interests in particular sports; and
- participation in particular in interscholastic sports by admitted students.

In addition, OCR will look at participation rates in sports in high schools, amateur athletic associations, and community sports leagues that operate in areas from which the institution draws its students in order to ascertain likely interest and ability of its students and admitted students in particular sport(s). For example, where OCR's investigation finds that a substantial number of high schools from the relevant region offer a particular sport which the institution does not offer for the underrepresented sex, OCR will ask the institution to provide a basis for any assertion that its students and admitted students are not interested in playing that sport. OCR may also interview students, admitted students, coaches, and others regarding interest in that sport.

An institution may evaluate its athletic program to assess the athletic interest of its students of the underrepresented sex using nondiscriminatory methods of its choosing. Accordingly, institutions have flexibility in choosing a nondiscriminatory method of determining athletic interests and abilities provided they meet certain requirements. See 44 Fed. Reg. at 71417. These assessments may use straightforward and inexpensive techniques, such as a student questionnaire or an open forum, to identify students' interests and abilities. Thus, while OCR expects that an institution's assessment should reach a wide audience of students and should be open-ended regarding the sports students can express interest in, OCR does not require elaborate scientific validation of assessments.

An institution's evaluation of interest should be done periodically so that the institution can identify in a timely and responsive manner any developing interests and abilities of the underrepresented sex. The evaluation should also take into account sports played in the high schools and communities from which the institution draws its students both as an indication of possible interest on campus and to permit the institution to plan to meet the interests of admitted students of the underrepresented sex.

b) Is there sufficient ability to sustain an intercollegiate team?

Second, OCR will determine whether there is sufficient ability among interested students of the underrepresented sex to sustain an intercollegiate team. OCR will examine indications of ability such as:

- the athletic experience and accomplishments—in interscholastic, club or intramural competition—of students and admitted students interested in playing the sport;
- opinions of coaches, administrators, and athletes at the institution regarding whether interested students and admitted students have the potential to sustain a varsity team; and
- if the team has previously competed at the club or intramural level, whether the competitive experience of the team indicates that it has the potential to sustain an intercollegiate team.

Neither a poor competitive record nor the inability of interested students or admitted students to play at the same level of competition engaged in by the institution's other athletes is conclusive evidence of lack of ability. It is sufficient that interested students and admitted students have the potential to sustain an intercollegiate team.

c) Is there a reasonable expectation of competition for the team?

Finally, OCR determines whether there is a reasonable expectation of intercollegiate competition for a particular sport in the institution's normal competitive region. In evaluating available competition, OCR will look at available competitive opportunities in the geographic area in which the institution's athletes primarily compete, including:

- competitive opportunities offered by other schools against which the institution competes; and

- competitive opportunities offered by other schools in the institution's geographic area, including those offered by schools against which the institution does not now compete.

Under the Policy Interpretation, the institution may also be required to actively encourage the development of intercollegiate competition for a sport for members of the underrepresented sex when overall athletic opportunities within its competitive region have been historically limited for members of that sex.

Conclusion

This discussion clarifies that institutions have three distinct ways to provide individuals of each sex with nondiscriminatory participation opportunities. The three-part test gives institutions flexibility and control over their athletics programs. For instance, the test allows institutions to respond to different levels of interest by its male and female students. Moreover, nothing in the three-part test requires an institution to eliminate participation opportunities for men.

At the same time, this flexibility must be used by institutions consistent with Title IX's requirement that they not discriminate on the basis of sex. OCR recognizes that institutions face challenges in providing nondiscriminatory participation opportunities for their students and will continue to assist institutions in finding ways to meet these challenges.

Source: http://www.ed.gov/about/offices/list/ocr/docs/clarific.html.

Appendix D: Further Clarification of Intercollegiate Athletics Policy Guidance Regarding Title IX Compliance, 2003

July 11, 2003

Dear Colleague:

It is my pleasure to provide you with this Further Clarification of Intercollegiate Athletics Policy Guidance Regarding Title IX Compliance.

Since its enactment in 1972, Title IX has produced significant advancement in athletic opportunities for women and girls across the nation. Recognizing that more remains to be done, the Bush Administration is firmly committed to building on this legacy and continuing the progress that Title IX has brought toward true equality of opportunity for male and female student-athletes in America.

In response to numerous requests for additional guidance on the Department of Education's (Department) enforcement standards since its last written guidance on Title IX in 1996, the Department' s Office for Civil Rights (OCR) began looking into whether additional guidance on Title IX requirements regarding intercollegiate athletics was needed. On June 27, 2002, Secretary of Education Rod Paige created the Secretary's Commission on Opportunities in Athletics to investigate this matter further, and to report back with recommendations on how to improve the application of the current standards for measuring equal opportunity to participate in athletics under Title IX. On February 26, 2003, the Commission presented Secretary Paige with its final report, "Open to All: Title IX at Thirty," and in addition, individual members expressed their views.

After eight months of discussion and an extensive and inclusive fact-finding process, the Commission found very broad support throughout the country for the goals and spirit of Title IX. With that in mind, OCR today issues this Further Clarification in order to strengthen Title IX's promise of non-discrimination in the athletic programs of our nation's schools.

Title IX establishes that: "No person in the United States shall, on the basis of sex, be excluded from participation in, be denied the benefits of, or be subjected to discrimination under any education program or activity receiving Federal financial assistance."

In its 1979 Policy Interpretation, the Department established a three-part test for compliance with Title IX, which it later amplified and clarified in its 1996 Clarification. The test provides that an institution is in compliance if 1) the inter-collegiate- level participation opportunities for male and female students at the institution are "substantially proportionate" to their respective full-time undergraduate enrollments, 2) the institution has a "history and continuing practice of program expansion" for the underrepresented sex, or 3) the institution is "fully and effectively" accommodating the interests and abilities of the underrepresented sex.

First, with respect to the three-part test, which has worked well, OCR encourages schools to take advantage of its flexibility, and to consider which of the three-parts best suits their individual situations. All three-parts have been used successfully by schools to comply with Title IX, and the test offers three separate ways of assessing whether schools are providing equal opportunities to their male and female students to participate in athletics. If a school does not satisfy the "substantial proportionality" part, it would still satisfy the three-part test if it maintains a history and continuing practice of program expansion for the underrepresented sex, or if "the interests and abilities of the members of [the underrepresented] sex have been fully and effectively accommodated by the present program." Each of the three-parts is thus a valid, alternative way for schools to comply with Title IX.

The transmittal letter accompanying the 1996 Clarification issued by the Department described only one of these three separate parts—substantial proportionality—as a "safe harbor" for Title IX compliance. This led many schools to believe, erroneously, that they must take measures to ensure strict proportionality between the sexes. In fact, each of the three-parts of the test is an equally sufficient means of complying with Title IX, and no one part is favored. The Department will continue to make clear, as it did in its 1996 Clarification, that "[i]nstitutions have flexibility in providing nondiscriminatory participation opportunities to their students, and OCR does not require quotas."

In order to ensure that schools have a clear understanding of their options for compliance with Title IX, OCR will undertake an education campaign to help educational institutions appreciate the flexibility of the law, to explain that each part of the test is a viable and separate means of compliance, to give practical examples of the ways in which schools can comply, and to provide schools with technical assistance as they try to comply with Title IX.

In the 1996 Clarification, the Department provided schools with a broad range of specific factors, as well as illustrative examples, to help schools understand the flexibility of the three-part test. OCR reincorporates those factors, as well as those illustrative examples, into this Further Clarification, and OCR will continue to assist schools on a case-by-case basis and address any questions they have about Title IX compliance. Indeed, OCR encourages schools to request individualized assistance from OCR as they consider ways to meet the requirements of Title IX. As OCR works with schools on Title IX compliance, OCR will share information on successful approaches with the broader scholastic community.

Second, OCR hereby clarifies that nothing in Title IX requires the cutting or reduction of teams in order to demonstrate compliance with Title IX, and that the elimination of teams is a disfavored practice. Because the elimination of teams diminishes opportunities for students who are interested in participating in athletics instead of enhancing opportunities for students who have suffered from discrimination, it is contrary to the spirit of Title IX for the government to require or encourage an institution to eliminate athletic teams.

Therefore, in negotiating compliance agreements, OCR's policy will be to seek remedies that do not involve the elimination of teams.

Third, OCR hereby advises schools that it will aggressively enforce Title IX standards, including implementing sanctions for institutions that do not comply. At the same time, OCR will also work with schools to assist them in avoiding such sanctions by achieving Title IX compliance.

Fourth, private sponsorship of athletic teams will continue to be allowed. Of course, private sponsorship does not in any way change or diminish a school's obligations under Title IX.

Finally, OCR recognizes that schools will benefit from clear and consistent implementation of Title IX. Accordingly, OCR will ensure that its enforcement practices do not vary from region to region.

OCR recognizes that the question of how to comply with Title IX and to provide equal athletic opportunities for all students is a challenge for many academic institutions. But OCR believes that the three-part test has provided, and will continue to provide, schools with the flexibility to provide greater athletic opportunities for students of both sexes.

OCR is strongly reaffirming today its commitment to equal opportunity for girls and boys, women and men. To that end, OCR is committed to continuing to work in partnership with educational institutions to ensure that the promise of Title IX becomes a reality for all students.

Thank you for your continuing interest in this subject.

Sincerely,
Gerald Reynolds
Assistant Secretary for Civil Rights
Source: http://www.ed.gov/about/offices/list/ocr/title9guidanceFinal.html.

Appendix E: Additional Clarification of Intercollegiate Athletics Policy: Three-Part Test—Part Three

March 17, 2005

Dear Colleague:

On behalf of the Office for Civil Rights (OCR) of the U.S. Department of Education (Department), and as a follow-up to OCR's commitment to providing schools with technical assistance on Title IX of the Education Amendments of 1972 (Title IX), I am sending you this "Additional Clarification of Intercollegiate Athletics Policy: Three-Part Test—Part Three" (Additional Clarification). Accompanying the Additional Clarification is a "User's Guide to Student Interest Surveys Under Title IX" (User's Guide) and a related technical report. The Additional Clarification outlines specific factors that guide OCR's analysis of the third option for compliance with the "three-part test," a test used to assess whether institutions are effectively accommodating the interests and abilities of male and female student athletes under Title IX of the Education Amendments of 1972. The User's Guide contains a model survey instrument to measure student interest in participating in intercollegiate varsity athletics.

As you know, OCR enforces Title IX, an anti-discrimination statute, which prohibits discrimination on the basis of sex in education programs or activities by recipients of federal financial assistance. Specifically, OCR investigates complaints of such discrimination and may, at its discretion, conduct compliance reviews. The Department's regulation implementing Title IX, published in 1975, in part, requires recipients to provide equal athletic opportunity for members of both sexes and to effectively accommodate the interests and abilities of their male and female students to participate in intercollegiate athletics. In the Intercollegiate Athletics Policy Interpretation published in 1979 (Policy Interpretation), the Department established a three-part test that OCR will apply to determine whether an institution is effectively accommodating student athletic interests and abilities. An institution is in compliance with the three-part test if it has met any one of the following three-parts of the test: (1) the percent of male and female athletes is substantially proportionate to the percent of male and female students enrolled at the school; or (2) the school has a history and continuing practice of expanding participation opportunities for the underrepresented sex; or (3) the school is fully and effectively accommodating the interests and abilities of the underrepresented sex.

OCR has pledged to provide further guidance on recipients' obligations under the three-part test, which was described only in very general terms in the Policy Interpretation, and to further help institutions appreciate the flexibility of the test. Based on OCR's experience investigating complaints and conducting compliance reviews involving the three-part test, OCR believes that institutions may benefit from further specific guidance on part three.

Today, in response, OCR issues this Additional Clarification to explain some of the factors OCR will consider when investigating a recipient's program in order to make a Title IX compliance determination under the third compliance option of

175

the three-part test. The Additional Clarification reflects OCR's many years of experience and expertise in administering the three-part test, which is grounded in the Department's long-standing legal authority under Title IX and its implementing regulation to eliminate discrimination on the basis of sex in education programs and activities receiving federal financial assistance.

Under the third compliance option, an educational institution is in compliance with Title IX's mandate to provide equal athletic participation opportunities if, despite the under representation of one sex in the intercollegiate athletics program, the institution is fully and effectively accommodating the athletic interests and abilities of its students who are underrepresented in its current varsity athletic program offerings. An institution will be found in compliance with part three unless there exists a sport(s) for the underrepresented sex for which all three of the following conditions are met: (1) unmet interest sufficient to sustain a varsity team in the sport(s); (2) sufficient ability to sustain an intercollegiate team in the sport(s); and (3) reasonable expectation of intercollegiate competition for a team in the sport(s) within the school's normal competitive region. Thus, schools are not required to accommodate the interests and abilities of all their students or fulfill every request for the addition or elevation of particular sports, unless all three conditions are present. In this analysis, the burden of proof is on OCR (in the case of an OCR investigation or compliance review), or on students (in the case of a complaint filed with the institution under its Title IX grievance procedures), to show by a preponderance of the evidence that the institution is not in compliance with part three.

Many institutions have used questionnaires or surveys to measure student athletic interest as part of their assessment under part three. To assist institutions, this Additional Clarification is being issued with a User's Guide prepared by the National Center for Education Statistics (NCES), as well as a detailed technical report prepared by the National Institute of Statistical Sciences (NISS). These documents were prepared after careful analysis of 132 of OCR's cases involving 130 colleges and universities from 1992 to 2002. They evaluate both the effective and problematic aspects of survey instruments. OCR intends this combined document to serve as a guide to facilitate compliance with part three of the three-part test.

Based on the analysis of the OCR cases and other information, the User's Guide provides a web-based prototype survey (the "Model Survey") that, if administered consistent with the recommendations in the User's Guide, institutions can rely on as an acceptable method to measure students' interests in participating in sports. When the Model Survey is properly administered to all full-time undergraduate students, or to all such students of the underrepresented sex, results that show insufficient interest to support an additional varsity team for the underrepresented sex will create a presumption of compliance with part three of the three-part test and the Title IX regulatory requirement to provide nondiscriminatory athletic participation opportunities. The presumption of compliance can only be overcome if OCR finds direct and very persuasive evidence of unmet interest sufficient to sustain a varsity team, such as the recent elimination of a viable team for the underrepresented sex or a recent, broad-based petition from an existing club team for elevation to varsity status. Where the Model Survey shows insufficient interest to field a varsity team, OCR will not exercise its discretion to conduct a compliance review of that institution's implementation of the three-part test.

Although more than two-thirds of the institutions involved in the 132 cases complied with the three-part test using part three, OCR believes that some institutions may be uncertain about the factors OCR considers under part three, and they may mistakenly believe that part three offers less than a completely safe harbor. Therefore, for colleges and universities seeking to achieve Title IX compliance using part three, OCR intends that the Additional Clarification and User's Guide serve to facilitate an institution's determination of whether it is in compliance with part three of the three-part test. A recipient may choose to use this information to assess its own athletic programs and then take appropriate steps to ensure that its athletic programs will be operated in compliance with the Title IX regulatory requirements.

Despite the focus on part three, OCR strongly reiterates that each part of the three-part test is an equally sufficient and separate method of complying with the Title IX regulatory requirement to provide nondiscriminatory athletic participation opportunities. In essence, each part of the three-part test is a safe harbor. OCR will continue to determine that a school has met its obligations to provide nondiscriminatory participation opportunities in athletics so long as OCR finds that the school has satisfied any one of the three options for compliance under the three-part test. Schools are also reminded that nothing in Title IX or the three-part test requires the cutting or reduction of opportunities for the overrepresented sex, and OCR has pledged to seek remedies that do not involve the elimination of opportunities.

OCR hopes the Additional Clarification and User's Guide will help reinforce the flexibility of the three-part test and will facilitate application of part three for those schools that choose to use it to ensure Title IX compliance. OCR welcomes requests for individualized technical assistance and is prepared to join with institutions in assisting them to address their particular situations.

Thank you for your continuing interest in this subject.

Sincerely,
James F. Manning
Delegated the Authority of the
Assistant Secretary for Civil Rights

Source: http://www.ed.gov/about/offices/list/ocr/docs/title9guidanceadditional.html.

Resource Guide

Selected Bibliography

Acosta, R. Vivian, and Linda Jean Carpenter. "As the Years Go By: Coaching Opportunities in the 1990s." *Journal of Physical Education, Recreation and Dance* 63.3 (March 1992): 36–41.

———. "Women in Intercollegiate Sport: A Longitudinal Study. Twenty Nine Year Update, 1977–2006," http://webpages.charter.net/womeninsport/AC_29Year Study.pdf.

Agthe, Donald E., and R. Bruce Billings. "The Role of Football Profits in Meeting Title IX Gender Equity Regulations and Policy." *Journal of Sport Management* 14.1 (Jan. 2000): 28–40.

Blais, Madeleine. *In These Girls, Hope Is a Muscle.* New York: Warner Books, 1996.

Blumenthal, Karen. *Let Me Play: The Story of Title IX: The Law that Changed the Future of Girls in America.* New York: Antheneum, 2005.

Bonnette, Valerie McMurtrie, and Mary Von Euler. *Title IX and Intercollegiate Athletics: How It All Works—In Plain English.* San Diego, CA: Good Sports, Inc., 2004.

Brake, Deborah, and Elizabeth Catlin. "The Path of Most Resistance: The Long Road Toward Gender Equity in Intercollegiate Athletics." *Duke Journal of Gender Law & Policy* 51 (Spring 1996): 71–72.

Bunker, Linda K. *Check It Out: Is the Playing Field Level for Women and Girls at Your School?: An Athletics Equity Checklist for Students, Athletes, Coaches, Parents, Administrators, and Advocates.* Washington, DC: National Women's Law Center, 2000.

Byers, Walter. *Unsportsmanlike Conduct: Exploiting College Athletes.* Ann Arbor: University of Michigan Press, 1995.

Cahn, Susan K. *Coming on Strong: Gender and Sexuality in Twentieth-century Women's Sport.* New York: Free Press, 1994.

Carpenter, Linda Jean, and R. Vivian Acosta. "Playing by the Rules: Equity in Sports." *CUPA Journal* 44.2 (Summer 1993): 55–60.

———. *Title IX*. Champaign, IL: Human Kinetics, 2005.

Chronicle of Higher Education. *Chronicle Facts and Figures 2000*. Available from http://chronicle.com.

Chu, Donald. *The Character of American Higher Education and Intercollegiate Sport*. Albany: State University of New York Press, 1989.

Clark, Patricia. *Sports Firsts*. New York: Facts on File, 1981.

Cohen, Greta, ed. *Women in Sport: Issues and Controversies*. Newberry Park, CA: Sage Publications, 1993.

Cohen, Leah Hager. *Without Apology: Girls, Women, and the Desire to Fight*. New York: Random House, 2005.

Colton, Larry. *Counting Coup: A True Story of Basketball and Honor on the Little Big Horn*. New York: Warner Books, 2000.

Condon, Robert J. *Great Women Athletes of the 20th Century*. Jefferson, NC: McFarland & Co., 1991.

Congressional Research Service. Library of Congress. *Title IX and Sex Discrimination in Education: Overview of Title IX*. CRS Report for Congress RS20710 (available at http://www.house.gov/htbin/crsprodget?/rs/RS20710).

———. *Title IX, Sex Discrimination and Intercollegiate Athletics: A Legal Overview*. CRS Report for Congress RL31709 (available at http://wwwc.house.gov/case/crs_reports/TitleIX.pdf).

———. *Title IX and Gender Bias in Sports: Frequently Asked Questions*. CRS Report for Congress RS20460 (available at http://holt.house.gov/pdf/CRSonTitleIXMar2003.pdf).

Corbett, Sara. *Venus to the Hoop: A Gold Medal Year in Women's Basketball*. New York: Doubleday, 1997.

Creedon, Pamela J. *Women, Media and Sport: Challenging Gender Values*. Thousand Oaks, CA: Sage Publications, 1994.

Delano, Linda C. "Understanding Barriers that Women Face in Pursuing High School Athletic Administrative Positions: A Feminist Perspective." PhD diss., University of Iowa, 1988.

Duffy, Tony, and Paul Wade. *Winning Women: Changing Image of Women in Sports*. New York: Times Books, 1983.

Dunkle, Margaret. *Competitive Athletics: In Search of Equal Opportunity*. Washington, DC: Department of Health, Education, and Welfare, Office of Education, 1977.

Dunkle, Margaret, and Bernice Sandler. *Sex Discrimination Against Students: Implication of Title IX of the Education Amendments of 1972*. Washington, DC: Project on the Status and Education of Women, Association of American Colleges, 1975.

Edelson, Paula. *A to Z of American Women in Sports*. New York: Facts on File, 2002.

Festle, Mary Jo. *Playing Nice: Politics and Apologies in Women's Sports*. New York: Columbia University Press, 1996.

Fidler, Merrie A. *The Origins and History of the All-American Girls Professional Baseball League*. Jefferson, NC: McFarland & Co., 2006.

Fields, Sarah. *Female Gladiators: Gender, Law, and Contact Sport in America*. Urbana: University of Illinois Press, 2004.

Flansburg, Sundra, and Katherine Hanson. *Legislation for Change: A Case Study of Title IX and the Women's Educational Equity Act Program*. Newton, MA: Center for Equity and Cultural Diversity, 1993.

Ford, Linda. *Lady Hoopsters: A History of Women's Basketball in America.* Northampton, MA: Half Moon Books, 1999.

Francis, Leslie P. "Title IX: Equality for Women's Sports?" in *Ethics in Sport*, eds. William John Morgan, Klaus V. Meier, and Angela Jo-Anne Schneider, Champaign, IL: Human Kinetics Publishers, 2001, pp. 247–266.

Gaines, Ann Graham. *Female Firsts in their Fields: Sports and Athletics.* Philadelphia: Chelsea House Publishers, 1999.

Gavora, Jessica. *Tilting the Playing Field: Schools, Sports, Sex, and Title IX.* San Francisco: Encounter Books, 2002.

George, B. Glenn. "Who Plays and Who Pays: Defining Equality in Intercollegiate Athletics." *Wisconsin Law Review* 1081 (1995).

Gogol, Sara. *Hard Fought Victories: Women Coaches Making a Difference.* Terre Haute, IN: Wish Publishers, 2002.

———. *Playing in a New League: The Women of the American Basketball League's First Season.* Indianapolis, IN: Masters Press, 1998.

Gottesman, Jane. *Game Face: What Does a Female Athlete Look Like?* New York: Random House, 2001.

Greenberg, Judith E. *Getting into the Game: Women and Sports.* New York: Franklin Watts, 1997.

Gregorich, Barbara. *Women at Play: The Story of Women in Baseball.* San Diego: Harcourt Brace & Co., 1993.

Grundman, Adolph H. *The Golden Age of Amateur Basketball: The AAU Tournament, 1921–1968.* Lincoln: University of Nebraska Press, 2004.

Grundy, Pamela, and Susan Shackelford. *Shattering the Glass: The Remarkable History of Women's Basketball.* New York: New Press, 2005.

Guttmann, Allen. *Women's Sports: A History.* New York: Columbia University Press, 1991.

Hargreaves, Jennifer. *Sporting Females: Critical Issues in the History and Sociology of Women's Sports.* New York: Routledge, 1994.

Hawkes, Nena Rey, and John F. Seggar. *Celebrating Women Coaches: A Biographical Dictionary.* Westport, CT: Greenwood Press, 2000.

Heckman, Diane. "Women & Athletics: A Twenty Year Retrospective on Title IX." *University of Miami Entertainment & Sport Law Review* 9.1 (1992): 1–64.

———. *The Women's Sports Foundation Report on Title IX, Athletics, and the Office for Civil Rights: An Executive Summary.* East Meadow, NY: Women's Sports Foundation, 1997.

Heywood, Leslie. *Pretty Good for a Girl.* New York: Free Press, 1998.

Heywood, Leslie, and Shari L. Dworkin. *Built to Win: The Female Athlete as Cultural Icon.* Minneapolis: University of Minnesota Press, 2003.

Howell, Reet. *Her Story in Sport: A Historical Anthology of Women in Sports.* Westpoint, NY: Leisure Press, 1982.

Ikard, Robert W. *Just for Fun: The Story of AAU Women's Basketball.* Fayetteville: University of Arkansas Press, 2005.

Isaac, T. A. "Sports—The Final Frontier: Sex Discrimination in Sports Leadership." *Women Lawyers Journal* 73 (1987): 15–19.

Jordan, Pat. *Broken Patterns.* New York: Dodd, Mead, and Co., 1977.

Kiernan, Denise. "The Little Law That Could." *Ms. Magazine* 11.2 (Feb./March 2001): 18–25.

Korsgaard, Robert. "A History of the Amateur Athletic Union of the United States." DEd diss., Teachers College, Columbia University, 1952.

Kovach, John M. *Women's Baseball*. Charleston, SC: Arcadia Publishing, 2005.

Kuersten, Ashlyn K. *Women and the Law: Leaders, Cases, and Documents*. Santa Barbara: ABC-CLIO, 2003.

Lamber, Julia. "Gender and Intercollegiate Athletics: Data and Myths." *University of Michigan Journal of Law Reform* 34.1–2 (Fall 2001/Winter 2002): 151.

Layden, Joseph. *Women in Sports: The Complete Book on the World's Greatest Women Athletes*. Los Angeles: General Publishing Group, 1997.

Lenskyj, Helen Jefferson. *Out on the Field: Gender, Sport & Sexuality*. Toronto: Women's Press, 2003.

Lite Beer from Miller and Women's Sports Foundation. *Miller Lite Report on Sports and Fitness in the Lives of Working Women*. Milwaukee, WI: Miller Brewing Company, 1993.

———. *Miller Lite Report on Women in Sports*. Milwaukee, WI: Miller Brewing Company, 1985.

Long, Amanda K. "The Rise and Fall of the First Professional Women's Basketball League." MA thesis, Springfield College, 1999.

Lopiano, Donna A. "Equity in Women's Sports: A Health and Fairness Perspective." *Clinics in Sports Medicine* 13.2 (April 1994): 281–296.

———. "Modern History of Women in Sports: Twenty-five Years of Title IX." *Clinics in Sports Medicine* 19.2 (April 2000): 163–173.

Lutter, J.M. "History of Women in Sports: Societal Issues." *Clinics in Sports Medicine* 13.2 (April 1994): 263–279.

Macy, Sue. *Girls Got Game: Sports Stories and Poems*. New York: Henry Holt, 2001.

———. *Winning Ways: A Photohistory of American Women in Sports*. New York: Henry Holt, 1996.

Macy, Sue, and Jane Gottesman. *Play Like a Girl: A Celebration of Women in Sports*. New York: Henry Holt and Co., 1999.

Markel, Robert, and Nancy Brooks. *For the Record: Women in Sports*. New York: World Almanac Publications, 1985.

Matthews, Bonnie, ed. *More Hurdles to Clear: Women and Girls in Competitive Athletics*. Washington, DC: United States Commission on Civil Rights, 1980.

Miller, Ernestine Gichner. *Making Her Mark: Firsts and Milestones in Women's Sports*. Chicago: Contemporary Books, 2002.

Nagasankara Rao, Dittakavi. *Sex Discrimination and Law: A Selected Bibliography*. Monticello, IL: Vance Bibliographies, 1985.

National Association for Girls & Women in Sport. *NAGWS Title IX Toolbox*. Reston, VA: American Alliance for Health, Physical Education, Recreation, and Dance, 1992.

National Coalition for Women and Girls in Education. *Title IX Athletics Policies: Issues and Data for Education Decision Makers*. Washington, DC: National Coalition for Women and Girls in Education, 2002.

———. *Title IX: A Practical Guide to Achieving Sex Equity in Education*. Washington, DC: National Coalition for Women and Girls in Education, 1988.

———. *Title IX at 30: Report Card on Gender Equity*. Washington, DC: National Coalition for Women and Girls in Education, 2002.

National Collegiate Athletic Association. *2003–2004 NCAA Gender-Equity Report.* Available from http://www.ncaa.org/library/research/gender_equity_study/2003-04/2003-04_gender_equity_report.pdf.

National Women's Law Center. *The Battle for Gender Equity in Athletics: Title IX at Thirty.* Washington, DC: National Women's Law Center, 2002.

Nelson, Mariah Burton. *Are We Winning Yet? How Women Are Changing Sports and Sports Are Changing Women.* New York: Random House, 1991.

Oglesby, Carole A. *Women and Sport: From Myth to Reality.* Philadelphia: Lea & Febiger, 1978.

Oglesby, Carole A., and Doreen L. Greenberg, eds. *Encyclopedia of Women and Sports in America.* Phoenix: Oryx Press, 1998.

Olson, Wendy M. "Beyond Title IX: Toward an Agenda for Women and Sports in the 1990s." *Yale Journal of Law and Feminism* 3.1 (Fall 1990): 105–151.

O'Reilly, Jean, and Susan K. Hahn. *Women and Sport in the United States: A Documentary Reader.* Boston: Northeastern University Press, 2007.

Orleans, Jeffrey H. "An End to the Odyssey: Equal Athletic Opportunities for Women." *Duke Journal of Gender Law & Policy* 3.1 (Spring 1996): 131–141.

Pemberton, Cynthia Lee A. *More Than a Game: One Woman's Fight for Gender Equity in Sport.* Boston: Northeastern University Press, 2002.

Picket, Lynn Snowden. *Looking for a Fight: A Memoir.* New York: Dial Press, 2000.

Pieronek, Catherine. "Title IX and Intercollegiate Athletics in the Federal Appellate Courts: Myth vs. Reality." *Journal of College & University Law* 27.2 (Fall 2000): 447–518.

Porter, Karra. *Mad Seasons: The Story of the First Women's Professional Basketball League, 1978–1981.* Lincoln: University of Nebraska Press, 2006.

Porto, Brian L. *A New Season: Using Title IX to Reform College Sports.* Westport, CT: Praeger, 2003.

President's Council on Physical Fitness and Sports. *Physical Activity and Sport in the Lives of Girls: Physical and Mental Health Dimensions from an Interdisciplinary Approach.* Washington, DC: The Council, 1997.

Rapoport, Ron. *A Kind of Grace: A Treasury of Sportswriting by Women.* Berkley, CA: Zenobia Press, 1994.

Rappoport, Ken. *Ladies First: Women Athletes Who Made a Difference.* Atlanta: Peachtree, 2003.

Rappoport, Ken, and Barry Wilner. *Girls Rule: The Glory and Spirit of Women in Sports.* Kansas City, MO: Andrews McMeel Publishers, 2000.

Reith, Kathryn M. *Playing Fair: A Guide to Title IX in High School and College Sports.* New York: Women's Sports Foundation, 1994.

Roberts, Kristi. *My Thirteenth Season.* New York: Henry Holt and Co., 2005.

Sabo, Donald F. *Women's Sports Foundation Gender Equity Report Card: A Survey of Athletic Opportunity in Higher Education.* East Meadow, NY: Women's Sports Foundation, 1997.

Sadker, Myra. *A Student Guide to Title IX.* Washington, DC: U.S. Department of Health, Education, and Welfare, Office of Education, 1976.

Salter, David E. *Crashing the Old Boys' Network: The Tragedies and Triumphs of Girls and Women in Sports.* Westport, CT: Praeger, 1996.

Selected Bibliography

Sandler, Bernice R. "'Too Strong for a Woman': The Five Words That Created Title IX." *Equity & Excellence in Education* 33.1 (April 2000): 9–13.

Sandoz, Joli, and Joby Winans, eds. *Whatever It Takes: Women on Women's Sport.* New York: Farrar, Straus, and Giroux, 1999.

Savage, Jeff. *Julie Krone: Unstoppable Jockey.* Minneapolis, MN: Lerner Publications, 1996.

Simon, Rita. *Sporting Equality: Title IX Thirty Years Later.* New Brunswick, NJ: Transaction Publishers, 2005.

Skaine, Rosemarie. *Women College Basketball Coaches.* Jefferson, NC: McFarland & Co., 2001.

Smith, Lissa. *Nike Is a Goddess: The History of Women in Sports.* New York: Atlantic Monthly Press, 1998.

Sparhawk, Ruth M. *American Women in Sport, 1887–1987: A 100-Year Chronology.* Metuchen, NJ: Scarecrow Press, 1989.

Stanek, Carolyn. *The Complete Guide to Women's College Athletics.* Chicago: Contemporary Books, 1981.

Steiner, Andy. *Girl Power on the Playing Field.* Minneapolis, MN: Lerner Publications, 2000.

Suggs, Welch. *A Place on the Team: The Triumph and Tragedy of Title IX.* Princeton, NJ: Princeton University Press, 2005.

———. "Will Female Kicker's Legal Victory Reshape Gender Roles in Athletics?" *Chronicle of Higher Education* 47.8 (Oct. 20, 2000): A53–A54.

Thelin, John R. "Good Sports? Historical Perspective on the Political Economy of Intercollegiate Athletics in the Era of Title IX, 1972–1997." *The Journal of Higher Education* 71.4 (July/Aug. 2000): 391–410.

Twin, Stephanie L. *Out of the Bleachers: Writings on Women and Sport.* New York: McGraw-Hill, 1979.

United States Department of Education. Office for Civil Rights. *Title IX: 25 Years of Progress.* Washington, DC: U.S. Government Printing Office, 1997.

United States Department of Education. Secretary of Education's Commission on Opportunity in Athletics. *Open to All: Title IX at Thirty.* Jessup, MD: Education Publications Center, 2003.

United States General Accounting Office. *Intercollegiate Athletics: Status of Efforts to Promote Gender Equity.* Washington, DC: The Office, 1996.

Valentin, Iram. *Title IX: A Brief History.* Newton, MA: Women's Educational Equity Act Resource Center, 1997.

Vargyas, Ellen J. *Breaking Down Barriers: A Legal Guide to Title IX.* Washington, DC: National Women's Law Center, 1994.

Weatherspoon, Teresa, Tara Sullivan, and Kelly Whiteside. *Teresa Weatherspoon's Basketball for Girls.* New York: John Wiley & Sons, 1999.

Wilner, Barry. *Superstars of Women's Golf.* Philadelphia: Chelsea House Publishers, 1997.

Wilson Sporting Goods, Co. *The Wilson Report: Moms, Dads, Daughters, and Sports.* River Grove, IL: 1988.

Women's Sports Foundation. *Title IX at 30: Athletics Receive C+.* East Meadow, NY: Women's Sports Foundation, 2002.

———. *Title IX: An Educational Resource Kit.* East Meadow, NY: Women's Sports Foundation, 1996.

———. *Women's Sports Foundation Education Guide: Special Issues for Coaches of Women's Sports*. East Meadow, NY: Women's Sports Foundation, 2001.

Woolum, Janet. *Outstanding Women Athletes: Who They Are and How They Influenced Sports in America*. Phoenix, AZ: Oryx Press, 1998.

Wu, Ying. "Early NCAA Attempts at the Governance of Women's Intercollegiate Athletics, 1968–1973." *Journal of Sport History* 26.3 (Fall 1999): 585–601.

Wushanley, Ying. *Playing Nice and Losing: The Struggle for Control of Women's Intercollegiate Athletics, 1960–2000*. Syracuse, NY: Syracuse University Press, 2004.

Zirkel, Perry A., Sharon Nalbone Richardson, and Steven S. Goldberg. *A Digest of Supreme Court Decisions Affecting Education*. Bloomington, IN: Phi Delta Kappa Educational Foundation, 2001.

Web Sites

BAM! Body and Mind, www.bam.gov. BAM! was developed by the Centers for Disease Control and Prevention as a way for adolescents to obtain information on physical fitness, safety, nutrition, etc.

Center for Sports Parenting, www.sportsparenting.org. The Center for Sports Parenting, under revision, is designed as a companion resource to *The Encyclopedia of Sports Parenting*. The Web site will also include advice from experts.

Commission on Equal Opportunities in Athletics, www.ed.gov/about/bdscomm/list/athletics/index.html. This Web site contains all the reports, transcripts, speeches, etc. from the Commission on Equal Opportunity in Athletics, which was charged with collecting information, analyzing issues, and obtaining public opinions concerning current application of federal standards for measuring participation for men and women under Title IX.

Equity in Athletics Data Analysis Cutting Tool, http://ope.ed.gov/athletics. The Equity in Athletics Data Analysis Cutting Tool Web site provides data that give customized reports dealing with equity in athletics. The data is submitted annually by all coeducational postsecondary schools that receive Title IX funding.

Game Face: What Does a Female Athlete Look Like?, www.gamefaceonline.org. The Game Face Web site is a companion resource to both the traveling exhibition and book that includes numerous pictures of women athletes. Its goal is to "convey that athletics is a catalyst for girls' and women's self creation, self knowledge, and self expression."

Gender Equity in Sports, http://bailiwick.lib.uiowa.edu/ge/. Maintained by Drs. Mary Curtis and Christine H. B. Grant, the Gender Equity Web site contains a host of information on Title IX, including a timeline and information on federal and state legislation.

Girls Inc., www.girlsinc.org. Girls, Inc. is a national nonprofit organization that develops programs that encourage girls to take athletic and intellectual challenges. Programs range from math and science to athletics to drug abuse prevention and pregnancy.

Girls Learn To Ride, www.girlslearntoride.com. Girls' Lean to Ride (GLTR) is a series of clinics and camps for female-only action sports, including skateboarding, surfing, snowboarding, mountain biking, and motorcross. The Web site includes a magazine as well as personal success stories.

GoGirlGo!, www.gogirlgo.com. GoGirlGo is designed for girls to learn about more than 100 sports. The site also includes a teen area with a message board, surveys, and tips on getting involved.

Her Sports Magazine, www.hersports.com. Hersport.com is the companion resource for *Her Sports* magazine. The magazine and Web site are geared toward women interested in health and fitness.

Melpomene Institute for Women's Health Research, www.melpomene.org. Melpomene's mission is to help females learn about nutrition, fitness, and safety. Established in 1992, Melpomene is dedicated to answering questions that are not addressed through conventional means.

Mid-Atlantic Equity Consortium, www.maec.org. Dedicated to creating learning environments free of gender, race, class, ethnic, and other biases, the Mid-Atlantic Equity Consortium is a not-for-profit corporation that provides technical assistance to educators and parents.

New Moon Publishing, www.newmoon.org. *New Moon Magazine* is a magazine for girls from age eight to fourteen. Girl athletes contribute all sorts of materials for the magazine, including poetry, artwork, letters, and articles.

President's Council on Physical Fitness and Sports, www.fitness.gov. The official Web site of the President's Council on Physical Fitness and Sports.

Pretty Tough Sports, www.prettytough.com. A new brand for female athletes, Pretty Tough provides a forum for female athletes to share stories, including MySpace and blogs in addition to selling merchandise.

Save Title IX, www.savetitleix.com. Sponsored by titleix.info, this Web site advocates for the continued enforcement of Title IX.

She Got Game: A Celebration of Women's Sports, www.shegotgame.com. Created by Tandaleya Wilder, *She Got Game* is a women's sport radio show. The companion Web site features profiles, interviews, and stories highlighting all aspects of sport.

She Loves Sports, www.shelovessports.com. This Web site for girls and women provides information on products and services that help women achieve an active, athletic, and healthy life.

Title IX: I Exercise My Rights, www.titleix.info. This public service site seeks to educate everyone about Title IX.

Organizations

Amateur Athletic Union (AAU)
AAU National Headquarters
P.O. Box 22409
Lake Buena Vista, FL 32830
Phone: 407-934-7200
Fax: 407-934-7242
District Info: 1-800-AAU-4USA
Web site: www.aausports.org

American Association of University Women (AAUW)
1111 Sixteenth St. NW
Washington, DC 20036
Phone: 1-800-326-AAUW
Fax: 202-872-1425
E-mail: helpline@aauw.org
Web site: www.aauw.org

Association for Gender Equity Leadership in Education (AGELE)
317 S. Division, PMB 54
Ann Arbor, MI 48104
Phone: 734-769-2456
Web site: http://agele.org

Association for Women in Sports Media (AWSM)
P.O. Box F
Bayville, NJ 08721
Web site: www.awsmonline.org

Black Women in Sport Foundation (BWSF)
4300 Monument Avenue
Philadelphia, PA 19121
Phone: 215-8777-1925 ext. 320
Fax: 215-877-1942
Web site: www.blackwomeninsport.org

Feminist Majority Foundation
1600 Wilson Boulevard, Suite 801
Arlington, VA 22209
Phone: 703-522-2214
Fax: 703-522-2219
Web site: www.feminist.org

Good Sports Inc., Title IX and Gender Equity Specialists
P. O. Box 500505
San Diego, CA 92150
Phone: 858-695-9995
Fax: 858-695-9909
Email: goodsports@earthlink.net
Web site: www.titleixspecialists.com

Ms. Foundation for Women
120 Wall Street, 33rd Floor
New York, NY 10005
Phone: 212-742-2300
Fax: 212-742-1653
Email: info@ms.foundation.org
Web site: www.ms.foundation.org

Myra Sadker Advocates
8608 Carlynn Drive
Bethesda, MD 20817
Phone: 301-229-8483
Fax: 301-229-5823
Email: dsadker@american.edu
Web site: www.sadker.org

National Association for Girls and Women in Sport (NAGWS)
1900 Association Dr.
Reston, VA 20191-1598
Phone: 703-476-3400
Web site: www.aahperd.org/nagws

National Association of Collegiate Women Athletic Administrators (NACWAA)
5018 Randall Parkway, Suite 3
Wilmington, NC 28403
Phone: 910-793-8244
Fax: 910-793-8246
Web site: www.nacwaa.org

National Coalition for Women and Girls in Education (NCWGE)
Web site: www.ncwge.org

National Collegiate Athletics Association (NCAA)
700 W. Washington Street
P.O. Box 6222
Indianapolis, IN 46206-6222
Phone: 317-917-6222
Fax: 317-917-6888
Web site: www.ncaa.org

National Organization of Women
P.O. Box 1848
Merrifield, VA 22116-8048
Phone: 202-628-8669
Fax: 202-785-8576
Web site: www.now.org

National Women's Law Center (NWLC)
11 Dupont Circle NW, Suite 800
Washington, DC 20036
Phone: 202-588-5180
Fax: 202-588-5185
Web site: www.nwlc.org

Office for Civil Rights, U.S. Department of Education
400 Maryland Avenue, SW
Washington, DC 20202-1100

Phone: 1-800-421-3481
Fax: 202-245-6840
Email: ocr@ed.gov
Web site: www.ed.gov/about/offices/list/ocr/index.html

Tucker Center for Research on Girls and Women in Sport
University of Minnesota
203 Cooke Hall
1900 University Ave. SE
Minneapolis, MN 55455
Phone: 612-625-7327
Email: info@tuckercenter.org
Web site: www.tuckercenter.org

Women in Sports and Events (WISE)
244 Fifth Avenue
Suite 2087
New York, NY 10001
Phone: 202-726-8282
Web site: www.wiseworks.org or www.womeninsportsandevents.com

Women in Sports Careers Network (WISC)
P.O. Box 11
Huntington Beach, CA 92648
Phone: 714-848-1201
Fax: 714-848-5111
Web site: www.wiscnetwork.com

Women's Basketball Coaches Association (WBCA)
646 Lawrenceville Highway
Lilburn, GA 30047
Phone: 770-279-8027
Fax: 770-279-8473
Email: wbca@wbca.org
Web site: www.wbca.org

Women's National Basketball Association
Web site: www.wnba.com

Women's Professional Football League
2620 Cullen Blvd, Ste 202
Pearland, TX. 77581
Phone: 281-997-2323
Fax: 281-412-7178
Web site: www.womensprofootball.com

Women's Sports Foundation
Eisenhower Park
East Meadow, NY 11554

Phone: 1-800-227-3988
Fax: 516-542-4716
Email: info@womenssportsfoundation.org
Web site: www.womenssportsfoundation.org

Women's Sports Services
Phone: 714-848-1201
Fax: 714-848-5111
Email: info@wsservices.com
Web site: www.wsservices.com

Films and Videos

Battle of the Sexes. VHS tape (60 min.). Atlanta, GA; Turner Mulimedia, 1994.

A Cinderella Season: The Lady Vols Fight Back. VHS tape (77 min.). New York: Downtown Community TV Center, 1998.

An Equal Chance through Title IX. 1 film reel (25 min.). Washington, DC: AAHPER, 1977.

Evening the Odds: Is Title IX Working? VHS tape (12 min.). Princeton, NJ: Films for the Humanities and Sciences, 1999.

For the Sport of It: Female Athletics & Title IX. VHS tape (30 min.). Indianapolis, IN: DL Images, produced by the Indiana Women's History Association with the assistance of the NCAA, 2003.

Gender and the Law: Title IX. VHS tape (23 min.). New York: Ambrose Video, 1998.

Girl Wrestler: A Documentary. VHS tape (54 min.). New York: Women Make Movies, 2004.

A Hero for Daisy. VHS tape (40 min.). 50 Eggs Inc., 1999, www.aherofordaisy.com.

In the Game. VHS tape (55 min.). Coos Bay, OR: Smith Productions, 1994.

In the Spirit of Title IX. VHS tape (24 min.). New York: PTV Productions under contract with the Dept. of Health, Education and Welfare, U.S. Office of Education, Women's Educational Equity Act Program, 1981.

A Level Playing Field: The Athletic Administrator's Guide to Title IX, Gender Equity in Sports, & Office of Civil Rights Investigations. VHS tape (60 min.), with teaching guide. Baldwin, KS: Sports Law Publishing, 1997.

NCAA Title IX/Gender Equity. Online videos, available at http://www.ncaa.org/gender_equity/video/.

Sports and Equal Opportunity: Title IX and Gender Equality. VHS tape (28 min.). St. Petersburg, FL: Philosophy Lab Corp., 1999.

Playing Unfair: The Media Image of the Female Athlete. VHS tape or DVD (30 min.), with a teaching guide. Northampton, MA: Media Education Foundation, 2002.

This Is a Game Ladies. VHS tape (120 min.). Partisan Pictures, 2004, www.pbs.org/thisisagame.

Throw like a Girl: A Revolution in Women's Sports. VHS tape (24 min.), with a teaching guide. Minneapolis: KARE-TV, Tucker Center for Research on Girls and Women in Sport, University of Minnesota, 1999.

Title IX and the Supreme Court. DVD (44 min.). West Lafayette, IN: C-SPAN Archives, 2004.

Title IX and Women in Sports: What's Wrong with This Picture? VHS tape (60 min.). Whidbey Films and PBS Home Video, 1999.

Title IX: Don't Let Our Daughters Grow Up Without It. VHS tape (140 min.). Washington, DC: National Women's Law Center.

Title IX: On Equal Ground, On the Basis of Sex, ESPN Town Meeting. VHS tape (138 min.). East Meadow, NY: Women's Sports Foundation and ESPN, 2002.

True-Hearted Vixens. VHS tape (58 min.). Berkeley, CA: University of California, Center for Media and Independent Learning, 2000. Web site: www.pbs.org/pov/trueheartedvixens/.

The WNBA and the Changing Role of Women's Sports. VHS tape (21 min.). New Hudson, MI: ABC News Productions, 1997.

Women and Sports. VHS tape (26 min.), with a teaching guide. Bethesda, MD: Discovery Communications, 2001.

Women in Sports. VHS tape (60 min.). Washington, DC: PBS Video, 1997.

Selected Related Court Cases

Association for Intercollegiate Athletics for Women v. NCAA, 558 F. Supp. 487, 494–495 (DC 1983). The AIAW claimed that the NCAA was monopolizing women's college sports and therefore violated the Sherman Antitrust Act.

Attorney General v. Massachusetts Interscholastic Athletic Association, Inc., 393 N.E.2d 284 (Mass. 1979). Massachusetts Supreme Court determined that MIAA's policy of prohibiting boys from high school girls' sports was against the state's Equal Rights Amendment.

Beasley v. Alabama State University, 3 F. Supp.2d 1325 (M.D. Ala. 1998). Beasley and other African American students claimed that ASU violated the Equal Rights Amendment because the university (a historically black institution) did not allow them to apply for diversity (white) scholarships.

Boulahanis v. Board of Regents, Illinois State University, 198 F.3d 633 (7th Cir. 1999), *cert. denied* 530 U.S. 1284 (2000). Boulahanis claimed that the university discriminated against them on the basis of gender by eliminating the men's wrestling and soccer teams and adding a women's soccer team as a way to comply with Title IX.

Bowers v. Baylor University, 11 F. Supp.2d 895 (S.D. Tex. 1998). Bowers, head women's basketball coach, sued Baylor for back salary and benefits, claiming that she did not receive an equitable salary relative to the men's head basketball coach. She also claimed that the university retaliated against her for reporting discriminatory actions.

Brentwood Academy v. Tennessee Secondary School Athletic Association, 531 U.S. 288, 305 (2001). Brentwood Academy sued the TSSAA after being suspended for recruiting athletes. The Supreme Court found that the TSSAA is a state actor since 84 percent of its members are public schools.

Brzonkala v. Virginia Polytechnic Institute and State University, 935 F. Supp. 772 (WD Va. 1996); 132 F.3d 949 (CA4 1997); 169 F.3d 820 (CA4 1999). Brzonkala sued the university for violating Title IX by creating a sexually hostile environment when her rapists were given only a nominal punishment.

California National Organization for Women v. The Board of Trustees of The California State University, Civil No. 949207 (Cal. Sup. Ct. Oct. 20, 1993). California NOW claimed that the university discriminated against female student athletes. The university system agreed to provide participation opportunities and financial aid in proportionate percentages.

Clark v. Arizona Interscholastic Association, 695 F.2d 1126 (1982). High school students sued the AIA, claming that the organization's rule prohibiting male students from playing on female interscholastic volleyball teams violated Title IX.

Cureton v. NCAA, 198 F.3d 107 (3d Cir. 1999). Cureton and four other African American athletes sued the NCAA under Title IX and Title VI claiming that the NCAA discriminates against African Americans by utilizing the Proposition 16 component of its freshman eligibility test.

Davis v. Monroe County Board of Education, 526 U.S. 629 (1999); 120 F.3d 1390, *reversed and remanded*. Davis sued the Monroe County Board of Education, maintaining that her daughter had been sexually harassed by other students.

Deli v. University of Minnesota, 863 F. Supp. 958 (D. Minn. 1994). Deli, the women's gymnastics coach, sued the university claiming that she had been discriminated against because she was paid a lower salary than male coaches.

Gebser v. Lago Vista Independent School District, 96-1866, U.S. Supreme Court, 524 U.S. 274 (1998). Gebser sued Lago Vista under Title IX after her high school teacher sexually harassed her. The courts ruled in favor of the school district, maintaining that the school district was not liable for the individual actions of an employee since Title IX was aimed at ending discriminatory policies.

Harper v. Board of Regents of Illinois State University, 35 F. Supp.2d 1118 (C.D. Ill. 1999). Harper and other students filed suit after the university eliminated the men's soccer and wrestling programs.

Kiechel v. Auburn University, Civil No. 93-V-474-E (M.D. Ala. July 19, 1993). Female students sued the university in order to gain varsity status for the women's soccer team.

Kleczek v. Rhode Island Interscholastic League, 612 A.2d 734, 1992; 768 F. Supp. 951 (D. R.I. 1991). Kleczek sued the RIIL for violations of Title IX because the organization did not allow boys to play field hockey.

Klinger v. Department of Corrections, 887 F. Supp. 1281, 1282 n.2 (D. Neb. 1995); 31 F.3d 727, 731 (8th Cir. 1994), *cert. denied*; 513 U.S. 1185 (1995). Klinger and other female prisoners at the Nebraska Center for Women sued the Nebraska Department of Corrections Services claiming that the latter violated Title IX by not providing female prisoners equal educational opportunities.

Kurth v. University of California Regents, Civil No. SC 029577 (Cal. Sup. Ct. May 17, 1994). Kurth and others sued after the University of California, Los Angeles eliminated the men's swimming and gymnastics programs.

Lakoski v. James, 66 F.3d 751 (5th Cir. 1995). Lakoski brought a Title IX claim that she had not received tenure because of her gender. The court, however, ruled that Title VII was the proper avenue to pursue a workplace sex discrimination claim.

Miami University Wrestling Club v. Miami University, 302 F. 3d 608 (6th Cir. 2002); No. C-1-99-972 (S.D. Ohio, 1999). Miami University students brought a Title IX complaint against the university for eliminating men's wrestling, tennis, and soccer teams in an effort to meet the proportionality prong of the Three-Part Test.

National Wrestling Coaches Association et al. v. U.S. Department of Education, Civ. No. 02-0072 (EGS) (2003). A number of wrestling clubs sued the Department of Education for creating the regulations that allowed men's teams to be cut in attempts to meet the proportionality prong of the Three-Part Test.

Paddio v. Board of Trustees for State Colleges & Universities, 61 Fair Empl. Rac. Cas. (BNA) 86 (E.D. La.), *aff'd*; 12 F.3d 207 (5th Cir. 1993), *cert. denied*, 114 S. Ct. 1838 (1994). Paddio filed a Title IX suit claiming that she was fired from her position as head volleyball and softball coach because of her race and gender.

Pitts v. Oklahoma State University, Civil No. 93-1341-A (W.D. Okla. Apr. 21, 1994). Pitts, the women's golf coach, sued the university under Title IX because her salary was $20,000 less than the coach of the men's golf team.

Sanders v. University of Texas at Austin, Civil No. A-92-CA-405 (W.D. Tex. Oct. 24, 1993). Sanders and other female students, who wanted the university to add four varsity women's sports, claimed that the institution did not accommodate the interests of female students.

Schuck v. Cornell University, Civil No. A-93-CV-756 FJs-GJD (N.D.N.Y. Dec. 8, 1993). Schuck sued Cornell after the university eliminated the women's gymnastics and fencing programs.

Smith v. NCAA, 139 F.3d 180 (3d Cir.), *cert. granted*, 119 S. Ct. 31 (1998) (argued Jan. 20, 1999). Smith, a female athlete, sued the NCAA after being denied a waiver of eligibility. Smith claimed that the NCAA violated Title IX by granting a disproportionate number of waivers of eligibility to males.

Stanley v. University of Southern California, 13 F.3d 1313 (9th Cir. 1994); 178 F.3d 1069 (9th Cir. 1999). Stanley, head women's basketball coach, claimed that she was discriminated against because she did not receive the same salary as the men's basketball coach.

Tyler v. Howard University, Civil No. 91-CA11239 (D.C. Sup. Ct. June 24, 1993). Tyler, women's basketball coach at Howard, sued the university claiming that she was discriminated against because her salary was half the amount of the men's basketball coach, she had less support staff, and the women's basketball facilities were not equal to the men's facilities.

Williams v. School District of Bethlehem, 998 F.2d 168 (3rd Cir. 1993); *cert. denied*, 510 U.S. 1043 (1994). Williams sued the school district for violating Title IX because boys were not allowed to try out for girls' field hockey unless there was a history of discrimination against male athletes.

Index

Index

Index

About the Authors

LISA ENNIS, MS, MA, is the systems librarian and assistant professor at the University of Alabama at Birmingham's Lister Hill Library of the Health Sciences. She holds an MA in history from Georgia College (1994) and an MS in information sciences from the University of Tennessee (1997). Lisa is the author of numerous encyclopedia entries, articles, and book chapters on a variety of topics, including "Crashing the Boards: Evolution of an Image in the WNBA" in *Basketball in America: From the Playgrounds to Jordan's Game* (2005) and entries in *Basketball: A Biographical Dictionary* (Greenwood 2005), *Native Americans in Sport* (2004), *Affirmative Action: An Encyclopedia* (2004), and *Scribner's Encyclopedia of American Lives: Sports Figures* (2002).

NICOLE MITCHELL, MLIS, MA, is a reference librarian and instructor at the University of Alabama at Birmingham's Lister Hill Library of the Health Sciences. She received her MA in history from Georgia College and State University (2003) and was assistant archivist for the Ina Dillard Russell Library Special Collections. In fall 2005, Nicole accepted one of ten Institute of Museum and Library Services (IMLS) fellowships from the University of Alabama. Receiving her MLIS in December 2006, Nicole also serves as a technology column editor for *The Journal of Hospital Librarianship* and is the author of several book chapters in both *The Industrial Revolution in America Series* (2006) and *The Uniting States: The Story of Statehood for the 50 United States of America* (Greenwood, 2004) as well as a number of encyclopedia entries in *Home Front Heroes: A Biographical Dictionary of Americans During Wartime* (Greenwood, 2006).